Questions & Answers

COMPANY LAW

Questions & Answers

COMPANY LAW

Fourth edition

Stephen Judge

Specialist in company and commercial law

Imogen Moore

Senior Lecturer in Law,
University of Exeter

2014 and 2015

OXFORD
UNIVERSITY PRESS

OXFORD
UNIVERSITY PRESS

Great Clarendon Street, Oxford, OX2 6DP,
United Kingdom

Oxford University Press is a department of the University of Oxford.
It furthers the University's objective of excellence in research, scholarship,
and education by publishing worldwide. Oxford is a registered trade mark of
Oxford University Press in the UK and in certain other countries

First edition 2008
Second edition 2010
Third edition 2012

Impression: 1

Published in the United States of America by Oxford University Press
198 Madison Avenue, New York, NY 10016, United States of America

British Library Cataloguing in Publication Data
Data available

Library of Congress Control Number: 2013949548

ISBN 978-0-19-968922-4

Printed in Great Britain by
Ashford Colour Press Ltd, Gosport, Hampshire

CONTENTS

Key features

The Q&A series provides full coverage of key subjects in a clear and logical way. This book contains the following features:

- Questions
- Commentaries
- Bullet-pointed answer plans and answer plan diagrams
- Examiner's tips
- Suggested answers
- Further reading suggestions

online resource centre

www.oxfordtextbooks.co.uk/orc/qanda/

Titles in the Q&A series are supported by additional online materials to aid study and revision.

Online resources for this title are hosted at the URL above, which is open access and free to use.

This book aims to assist you in learning, understanding, and revising company law. Company law is a potentially vast subject, reflecting the enormous range of companies and their differing interests and issues. While there are clearly some core topics (such as corporate personality, corporate contracts, directors' duties, and minority shareholder remedies), company law courses also often branch out into related areas such as business enterprise, corporate governance, corporate finance, securities law, and corporate insolvency. This book considers both the core topics and those related topics that are most commonly included in university courses.

While this text is designed to help your revision generally (reminding you of the various topics you have studied and how they interrelate), it is written in particular with a view to final examinations in the subject, showing you how issues might be explained and analysed in the context of exam questions. With exams in mind the answers are relatively short, generally not exceeding 1,500 words.

The best way to make use of the book is to attempt the questions yourself (having reminded yourself of the topic using your course materials, appropriate textbooks and further reading), and only then compare your answer with that provided, using the answer for guidance on appropriate areas, depth of coverage, and application. The answers are not designed to provide you with model answers that could simply be repeated in any exam—the questions you face will naturally be different from the ones here—instead the book aims to give you the understanding and skills you need to answer your own exam questions. Working through the questions and answers should also help you to develop your skills more generally in structuring answers and using the law to address questions.

Good exam answers require a good balance of information and application—or, if you prefer, evidence of knowledge, understanding, and analysis. Knowledge underpins everything—you will not do well without adequate knowledge—but it is not enough in itself. You also need to demonstrate understanding (providing relevant knowledge and using it, rather than simply presenting it) and analysis or application (applying the law appropriately to a particular problem or essay title, and questioning and critiquing issues). At all times you need to remember to address the question—even brilliant knowledge is no use in an exam if it is not relevant to the question and directed to it.

In answering your exam questions aim to show the examiner that you are really thinking about the question throughout your answer and not just as an afterthought in a conclusion. In using your material try not to simply regurgitate basic information, such as statutory provisions; think about how you can use the material to inform your discussion. Examiners like an interested student and an interesting answer so be prepared to have an opinion (preferably well supported) and try to engage with the topic and the material by bringing in relevant academic viewpoints or even topical news stories.

This new edition of *Questions & Answers Company Law* develops previous editions to reflect important judicial developments in a number of areas, notably corporate personality (including the Supreme Court decisions in **Prest v Petrodel Resources Ltd** [2013] UKSC 34 and **VTB Capital plc v Nutritek International Corp** [2013]

UKSC 5), shareholder remedies (including *Bamford v Harvey* [2012] EWHC 2858 (Ch), *Re Tobian Properties Ltd* [2012] EWCA Civ 998, and *Universal Project Management Ltd v Fort Gilkicker Ltd* [2013] EWHC 348 (Ch)) and corporate insolvency (including *BNY Corporate Trustee Services Ltd v Eurosail-UK 2007-3BL plc* [2013] UKSC 28 in the Supreme Court). It also includes recent statutory changes to registration of charges and relevant government consultations as well as reflecting continuing public interest in corporate governance issues. This edition also incorporates developments in the structure and presentation of the *Questions and Answers* series by the publisher, designed to provide the reader with further tips and guidance.

Finally, I would like to offer some thanks and acknowledgements. First to Stephen Judge, my co-author and sole author of the previous editions of this text—I can only hope that this edition does justice to the breadth, depth, and clarity of coverage that he has brought to this text over many years. Secondly to all at OUP, and in particular the ever-cheerful and efficient Kirsten Shankland and Hannah Marsden. Thirdly thanks are due to my family, who allowed me (apparently all too willingly) to spend the best summer for many years in the company of my laptop. And finally I am indebted to my students—intelligent, hard-working, enthusiastic, and occasionally willing to laugh at my jokes—who help to make company law so enjoyable.

I hope that you will find the book useful in your studies and wish you every success. This edition states the law as known to the authors on 20 August 2013.

Imogen Moore
August 2013

TABLE OF CASES

1

Business organizations and company formation

Introduction

Company law is obviously all about the law of companies. But companies are simply one type of business organization—albeit one of the most important and interesting kinds. While it is not uncommon for non-lawyers to use the term 'company' to mean 'business', a business may, or may not, be run through the medium of a company. In order to understand the key features of companies, and how they operate, it is helpful to appreciate the other main legal forms used for businesses in the UK and to recognize how companies come into existence. One important distinction between business forms is whether the business is incorporated (given a legal existence) or not—of the main types of trading vehicle, companies and limited liability partnerships are incorporated forms, while sole traders and general partnerships are not.

The simplest form of business is a sole trader (or sole proprietor/practitioner). It requires no formalities to create (although there will be tax and other legal responsibilities depending on the nature of the business). Sole traders have unlimited (personal) liability for all business losses. If a sole trader carries on business under a name other than the trader's own name it must comply with **Part 41 of the Companies Act 2006 (CA 2006), ss. 1192–208.**

A general partnership is 'the relation which subsists between persons carrying on a business in common with a view of profit' (**Partnership Act 1890 (PA 1890), s. 1(1)**) and is known as a 'firm' (**PA 1890, s. 4(1)**). Accordingly a partnership can only exist if there are at least two persons, carrying on a business (any 'trade, profession or occupation' (**PA 1890, s. 45**) and intending to make a profit (even if, in fact, the business is unsuccessful). The partnership is not a legal entity in its own right and the partners have unlimited joint liability for all the debts of the firm. There are no formalities required to create a partnership, but if the firm uses a name other than the partners' names it must comply with **CA 2006, Part 41.**

Another type of partnership is the limited liability partnership (LLP) created by registration under the **Limited Liability Partnership Act 2000.** An LLP is a legal entity in its own right, separate from the partners (called 'members' in an LLP). The members have limited liability; they are not liable for the debts of the firm. An LLP is a hybrid form—in some ways like a partnership (particularly in structure and internal relations) but in many other ways much more like a limited company.

Company law courses focus on registered companies limited by shares. A registered company is created by registration under the **CA 2006**. In a registered company limited by shares, members (also known as shareholders) are not liable for the debts of the company. There are other types of company (companies can be incorporated by royal charter or by statute, as well as by registration, and companies may be limited by guarantee or unlimited instead of limited by shares) but these other types are unusual and would not be used for a normal trading business.

Formation of a registered company limited by shares is through one or more persons subscribing their names to a memorandum of association and complying with the requirements of the **CA 2006** as to registration (**CA 2006, s. 7**). This entails the delivery of various documents to the registrar of companies (at Companies House) and the payment of a fee. There are various topics that can be considered when looking at company formation, in particular the pre-formation stage (including company promotion and pre-incorporation contracts); the process and effect of registration itself; and then issues such as the choice of company name.

The vast majority of registered companies are private companies (whose names end in 'Ltd'), but the economy is dominated by public companies ('plc'). Public companies, unlike private companies, can offer their shares to the public (**CA 2006, s. 755**) and are generally subject to higher levels of regulation. Listed (or quoted) companies are a small sub-set of public companies whose shares are listed on a stock exchange and are subject to additional regulations, both through statute and the Stock Exchange Listing Rules. A group of companies may be made up of public or private companies (or a mix) and comes into existence when a company (the parent, or holding, company) owns shares in another company (the subsidiary company); see **CA 2006, s. 1159** for the statutory definition of 'subsidiary'.

 Question 1

Edna, Fred, and Gabor run a business buying and selling antiques as a partnership. They have been advised by their solicitor to form a private company to run the business. They have contacted you for a second opinion. They are particularly concerned to know:

(a) To what extent their liability for the company's debts will be limited

(b) Whether they will be able to exercise the same control over the membership as with a partnership

(c) The extent to which they will have the same right to be involved in the management of the company

(d) The public disclosure to which the business would be subject as a limited company

Having discussed these aspects, advise them of what choice they should make between the two alternatives, or of any other options available to them.

Commentary

This question requires you to be able to identify ways in which the relationship between partners of a general partnership differs from that of members of a limited liability company. These differences are important in determining the vehicle to be selected for the carrying on of a business, depending on the priorities of the entrepreneurs. While it may appear that the question crosses individual topic boundaries, it is important to recognize that they are all factors in the essential choice of trading vehicle.

 Answer plan

- Limited liability as opposed to unlimited liability but subject to potential liability beyond their capital contribution in certain circumstances
- Restrictions on membership in a partnership as opposed to a limited company
- Right to be involved in management of a partnership as opposed to management delegated to board of directors in a limited company
- Extent to which right to involvement can be ensured or enforced in a limited company
- Public disclosure of affairs of a limited company as opposed to a partnership by annual return and audit
- Relaxation of disclosure and audit for small private companies

 Suggested answer

This question raises topics for discussion under four headings: limited liability, control over membership, involvement in management, and public disclosure. These points will be dealt with separately and advice will be given in a conclusion.

In respect of the liability of the members, a limited liability company would offer distinct advantages to Edna, Fred, and Gabor in the sense that, as members of a limited liability company, their liability would be limited to the extent of their capital contribution to the company (most companies are companies limited by shares, so their liability would be limited to the amount (if any) unpaid on their shares, **Companies Act 2006 (CA 2006), s. 3(2)**) as opposed to their being exposed to unlimited personal liability up to the full extent of their private fortunes.

One problem that they would face is that, if the newly established company were to be under-capitalized, one or more of them would be required to stand as guarantor/surety for the debts of the company in order to operate with an overdraft from the company's bank or in respect of securing supplies of goods and services on credit. In effect, in respect of securing the bank loan, this might not be greatly different from the current situation, since many banks will encourage partners of firms who have accounts with them to move their personal accounts to the bank. In the event of the business account being overdrawn and the firm becoming insolvent, the bank will be able to exercise a lien on the accounts of the individual partners and offset any credit balances on these accounts against the overdraft on the business account.

Another problem could be that if, in the event of the insolvency of the newly formed company, it was discovered that the members/directors of the company had acted in breach of their duties towards the company or its creditors, they could be held liable to contribute to the assets of the company as the court determines in powers under CA 2006 and the **Insolvency Act 1986 (IA 1986)**, or disqualified from acting as directors under the **Company Directors Disqualification Act 1986**.

The issue in respect of control over the future membership of the business is that, as regards a partnership, in the absence of any agreement to the contrary, new partners can only be introduced by the unanimous consent of the existing partners: **Partnership Act 1890 (PA 1890), s. 24(7)**. In a company, membership is through the acquisition of shares which are, unless special provision is made, freely transferable. This would mean that there would appear to be no control over the membership of the company. In practice, most private companies will, in their articles of association (the main constitutional document of the company), impose restrictions on the free transfer of their shares by giving first priority to existing members before they can be offered to outsiders. In addition, most private companies will insert in their articles a provision to the effect that the directors can, without giving reasons, refuse to register any transfer of shares. If these restrictions on the transferability of the company's shares were inserted into the articles, there would be no difference in effect from the current partnership.

As regards participation in management, all partners in a general partnership have a right to be involved in the management of the firm: **PA 1890, s. 24(5)**. In a company, however, management is delegated to the board of directors. It could be thought that this problem could be resolved by the appointment of all three 'partners' to the board of the new company. The problem is that, even if they are all made directors of their company initially, directors can be removed by ordinary resolution of the Annual General Meeting (AGM) with special notice under **CA 2006, s. 168**. Thus if, in the future, two of the current partners fell out with the third, that person could be voted off the board of the company by the votes of the other two.

This can be avoided, however, by drafting a clause in the new company's articles whereby, in the event of a resolution to remove a director from the board, the shares held by that director would give him, or her, three votes per share on a poll, so that a resolution to remove him, or her, could be defeated. The validity of this was established in *Bushell v Faith* [1970] AC 1099. In addition, in a small quasi-partnership company (as established in *Ebrahimi v Westbourne Galleries Ltd* [1973] AC 360) such as this, an attempt to remove a member from the board would enable that person to petition on the grounds of unfair prejudice under **CA 2006, s. 994**. If successful, the court is likely to order that the shares of the petitioner should be purchased by the company or by the other shareholders at a valuation fixed by the court: **CA 2006, s. 996**. Should the court find that the majority were justified in removing the member from the board because of his lack of attention to company affairs, etc the minority might be able to petition for the winding up of the company on just and equitable grounds under **IA 1986, s. 122(1)(g)**. Thus in *RA Noble & Sons (Clothing) Ltd* [1983] BCLC 273, although the court in respect of a petition for unfair prejudice under **CA 1985, s. 459** (now **CA 2006, s. 994**) held that the claimant's exclusion from the management was prejudicial but not unfair because of the lack of interest he had taken in the firm's affairs, he was nevertheless entitled to petition for the compulsory liquidation of the company on the grounds that his exclusion from the management of a small quasi-partnership company was not just and equitable. *Hawkes v Cuddy* [2009] EWCA Civ 291 has confirmed that **IA 1986, s. 122(1)(g)** continues to operate notwithstanding the development of the **CA 2006, s. 994** jurisdiction.

The disclosure of certain information about a company is regarded as 'the price of incorporation' and so Edna, Fred, and Gabor should be aware that some company information will be available for public inspection. However, as long as the company qualifies as a 'small' company under **CA 2006, ss. 382–3**, the extent of the disclosure of its affairs would be greatly reduced, and it will be exempt from the audit requirement of **CA 2006, s. 477** (the audit exemption criteria having been aligned with the small company criteria from 1 October 2012). The criteria are: two out of three (tested every other year) of: turnover—not more than £6.5m; balance sheet total—not more than £3.26m; number of employees—not more than 50 (**CA 2006, ss. 382–3**). The proposed company is unlikely to exceed any of these limitations. To this extent, the threat of disclosure is greatly diminished and the company can enjoy almost the same degree of privacy in respect of its affairs as a partnership. While companies are subject to more regulation, and thus a higher administrative burden than partnerships, some of this administrative burden has been reduced for small companies by the **CA 2006** (the reform following a 'Think Small First' agenda), eg by removing the need for a company secretary and AGMs.

In conclusion, for most businesses the manifest advantages of incorporation vastly outweigh the problems associated with it, including the cost involved in setting up the company. In any event the direct costs of registering a company are low (currently registration can be obtained for as little as £13), while some legal and accounting costs are likely to be incurred whatever the form of business organization selected. The partners would, therefore, be advised that—subject to having taken the right precautions in fixing the constitution of the company—they would benefit from the change. However, it should be pointed out that the formation of a registered company is not the only avenue open to them. They could instead decide to form a limited liability partnership (LLP) under the **Limited Liability Partnership Act 2000** which, as a hybrid form between a general partnership and a limited liability company, enjoys the benefits of each. Thus, it is regulated as a private company in all respects except in relation to the management structure of the partnership.

This would enable the partners to retain their current veto over new members and to decide on the operation of the firm's management as they wished. As members of an LLP, they would also still be regarded as self-employed for taxation purposes as at present. LLPs are increasingly popular with over half a million now registered in the UK, although there is still a long way to go before they match the popularity of the limited company (nearly 3 million registered in the UK).

Question 2

It is said that the two advantages for a business of forming a company are the concepts of legal personality and limited liability. In practice, however, for small companies these concepts may prove to be as much of a handicap as a blessing, and in some respects may prove irrelevant.

Discuss.

 Commentary

This question requires you to look into the supposed advantages associated with trading as a limited liability company limited by shares and to consider the potential pitfalls. Problems arise through the under-capitalization of small private companies, as this means that lenders will insist on some form of personal guarantee from those behind the company—thus losing at least some of the protection of limited liability. Problems also arise because people forming companies as a trading vehicle are often not completely aware of the legal ramifications of such a step. A final aspect to consider is the remote possibility of directors being personally liable for negligent mis-statement or misrepresentation, or the greater danger of falling foul of provisions of the **CA 2006**, **IA 1986**, or **CDDA 1986** should the company run into difficulty.

 Answer plan

- Potential advantages of the corporate structure
- Practical realities of under-capitalization
- Ramifications of incorporation to which attention should be paid
- Potential for personal liability

 Examiner's tip

Combine your knowledge of the legal position with some awareness of relevant research in order to give a fully thought-out response to the question.

 Suggested answer

It is generally assumed that most traders choosing the vehicle of the company limited by shares, do so largely to benefit from the protection afforded by the rule in *Salomon v A. Salomon & Co Ltd* [1897] AC 22. This rule creates 'the veil of incorporation'—that is, the separation of the company from the members—and protects traders' personal wealth in the event of the company's insolvency. Interestingly, however, research has indicated that this protection is only one of many factors influencing a trader—other factors as diverse as tax and prestige/credibility can also be highly influential (see, eg Freedman, J., 'Small businesses and the corporate form: burden or privilege?' (1994) 57 MLR 555 and Hicks, A., 'Corporate form: questioning the unsung hero' [1997] JBL 306).

Clearly limited liability is an important element in selecting the corporate form, yet many people commencing trading may not realize that the benefits of limited liability may be compromised by the scale of their operation so as to render the protection illusory. In addition, since most of these entrepreneurs will not have the benefit of expert legal advice in the creation of their corporate vehicle and its operation, they may not be aware of the full impact of the legal consequences on other aspects of their life.

As regards the scale of the operation, it should be remembered that there is no minimum capital requirement for private companies, which often have a nominal capital (a public company by way of contrast must have a minimum capital of £50,000 (**Companies Act 2006, s. 763**)). The inadequate capital of many small companies may mean that the company cannot borrow sums of money or buy in goods and services against the security of its own assets, making it impossible for the company to secure credit lines from banks and suppliers without external support. Banks will generally require some form of security in consideration for any loans (Freedman's research revealed that over 50 per cent of respondents had personal guarantees to the bank), and suppliers may also seek some form of protection through a third party guarantee. This means that the company's proprietors—those seeking protection in the form of limited liability—are likely to be liable as guarantors for any corporate loans or lines of credit, and credit facilities offered by the company's bank will often be secured by a mortgage to the bank of the family home. If the company fails the lender may take possession of, and sell, the home to recover the loans (subject of course to the requirement for the lender to ensure that both spouses/civil partners have fully understood and consented to the mortgage). In such situations, limited liability is illusory.

Entrepreneurs often commence trading using the company form without the benefit of legal advice and may fail to appreciate fully the consequences of forming a limited liability company. Both Freedman and Hicks point out that the majority of entrepreneurs are not particularly aware of, or interested in, the precise legal form their business will take. That is regrettable as the veil of incorporation may have negative as well as positive effects. For example, in *Macaura v Northern Assurance Company* [1925] AC 619, Macaura was unaware that his transfer of property previously belonging to himself to a limited liability company, in which he was virtually the sole shareholder, meant that he no longer had legal or equitable title to the property. As a result, a policy taken out in his name, but covering property that now belonged to the company, was not covered by the insurance since he no longer had an insurable interest in the property.

A further example is in *Tunstall v Steigman* [1962] 1 QB 593 where Steigman, the landlord of a pair of shops, gave notice to the lessee of one on the ground (**Landlord and Tenant Act 1954, s. 30(1)(g)**) that she intended to occupy the premises for the purpose of her business. However, Steigman actually intended to conduct the business through a company in which she held all the shares except two which were held by nominees. The court held that she had failed to establish her intention 'to occupy ... for the purposes ... of a business to be carried on by her' since the business was to be carried on by a company which was a separate legal entity. Obviously Steigman had failed to appreciate the full impact of transferring her business to a limited liability company. Similarly in *Re Lewis's Will Trusts* [1985] 1 WLR 102 a farmer's bequest of 'my freehold farm and premises' to his son failed because the farm had been transferred to a company. Although Lewis owned three-quarters of the shares in the company (his son owned the other shares) the bequest was not effective as the farm was owned by the company, not Lewis. Clearly here Lewis had not been sufficiently aware of the separation between the company and its members.

Other cases concern shareholder/directors who fail to recognize that the company is a separate legal person and who treat their company's assets and bank accounts as mere extensions of their private assets. In *Attorney-General's Reference (No. 2 of 1982)* [1984] QB 624 it was established that a sole shareholder of a company could nevertheless be guilty of stealing from the company and the controlling shareholder could not fall back on the identification theory in their defence claiming that, as the directing mind and will of the company, the company consented to the alleged offence.

There is also the possibility of statutory removal of the protection of the veil of incorporation under the **Insolvency Act 1986** (**IA 1986**). Thus, in *Re Purpoint Ltd* [1991] BCC 121 the proprietor of a company was ordered under **IA 1986, s. 212** to contribute towards the assets of the company, now in insolvent liquidation, in respect of money of the company used to purchase a car on hire purchase where the evidence showed that the car was for the proprietor's new business venture rather than the company's business. Directors may also find themselves liable to contribute to the assets of the company in insolvent liquidation where they have engaged in fraudulent trading (**IA 1986, s. 213**), wrongful trading (**IA 1986, s. 214**), or where they have misused the name of a company that had previously gone into insolvent liquidation (**IA 1986, s. 217**). Of these, wrongful trading is the most important in practice, as shown in cases such as *Re DKG Contractors Ltd* [1990] BCC 903 and *Re Produce Marketing Consortium Ltd (No. 2)* [1989] 2 BCLC 520 where directors were ordered to contribute £400,000 and £75,000 respectively. In these cases then the benefits of limited liability were significantly reduced.

Directors can also be personally liable for negligent misstatements made by the company. In *Fairline Shipping Co v Adamson* [1974] 2 All ER 967, a cold-store company failed to keep its store at the correct temperature and Fairline's meat perished. The company went into liquidation and Fairline sued Adamson, the ex-managing director, in person. All correspondence was on Adamson's personal notepaper, and he had indicated that the business was his own. The court held that he was liable since the contract had become his personal contract. It is not common to establish liability in this way however. In *Williams v Natural Life Health Food Ltd* [1998] 1 WLR 830, the House of Lords stated that liability depended on whether: 'the director, or anybody on his behalf, conveyed directly or indirectly ... that the director assumed personal responsibility'. Directors have no reason to fear personal liability for negligent misstatements or advice unless they do something leading to a reasonably held belief that they accepted personal responsibility.

Directors have been held personally liable for other torts, eg in *Standard Chartered Bank v Pakistan National Shipping Corpn (Nos. 2 and 4)* [2002] 3 WLR 1547 the court held the managing director liable in deceit and in *Lindsay v O'Loughnane* [2010] EWHC 529 (QB) the managing director of a company was held personally liable for fraudulent misrepresentations inducing the claimant into entering transactions causing a substantial loss. The veil of incorporation will, thus, not protect all those behind it in respect of all actions they may take.

It can be seen that the principle of the separate legal personality of the company may result in unplanned and undesired outcomes. While limited liability is an attractive proposition for many entrepreneurs, its benefits are often illusory and it will not always guarantee total protection from personal liability. Furthermore, the 'privilege' of limited liability is balanced by the need to comply with formalities and disclose information at Companies House. Entrepreneurs using the corporate form, therefore, have increased administrative burdens in filing documentation such as annual returns. Although disclosure obligations are reduced for small companies, even small additional burdens with the attendant cost of compliance and potential loss of privacy may be too much if the benefits of limited liability are not fully available. Furthermore, entrepreneurs need to remain aware of the potential for personal liability under provisions such as **IA 1986, ss. 212–4** or even disqualification under the **Company Directors Disqualification Act 1986**.

 Question 3

Gerhard and Angeline are friends who recently graduated from the University of Exford and decided to set up a fashion design business. Having considered their options, they have decided to set up a company to conduct the business. They are considering calling their business either 'F U Fashion' or 'Great University Trends'.

Advise Gerhard and Angeline on the steps they will need to take, and any issues or restrictions they should bear in mind, in creating and naming their company.

 Commentary

This problem question requires you to consider in some depth the issues arising on forming a company. You will need to have a good understanding of the registration process and requirements, and should reflect upon the differences between registering a company and buying an 'off-the-shelf' company. You also need to be able to explain and apply the provisions on company and business names. The question doesn't specifically raise the often related issues of promoters, pre-incorporation contracts, or the features of companies more generally so while you can indicate that you realize these are important issues you should not spend a lot of time on these.

Examiner's tip

Make sure you don't simply recite or copy out statutory material—remember to link your advice to the particular facts of the question.

Answer plan

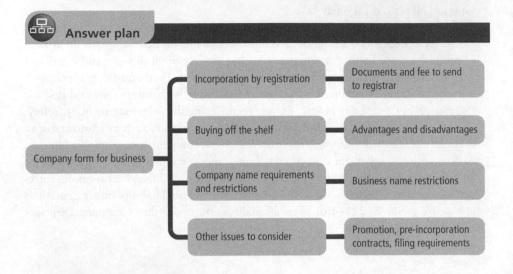

Suggested answer

Gerhard and Angeline should be aware that the company will (unlike a partnership) have its own separate legal personality and they will not be liable for the company's debts or other liabilities (*Salomon v A. Salomon & Co Ltd* [1897] AC 22). From the facts of the question it appears that they intend to be the sole directors and shareholders of the company, but the flexibility of the company form means they could easily involve others if they wanted—whether by appointing someone as director to share management of the business, or by providing shares to people, eg family members who wish to invest without running the business. However, unlike a partnership (which can arise under the **Partnership Act 1890, s. 1(1)** without any need for formality), Gerhard and Angeline will need to observe various formalities in order to create a company.

Creating the company

Gerhard and Angeline can choose between creating the company by registering it themselves, or purchasing a company 'off the shelf'. A shelf company is one that has already been created by a company formation agent and is available for immediate purchase. If Gerhard and Angeline choose to register their own company (see **Companies Act 2006 (CA 2006), ss. 7–13**) they will need to complete various documents and send these off to the registrar of companies at Companies House (based in Cardiff for companies registered in England and Wales) either in paper form or electronically:

- Memorandum of association (**s. 8**)
  - Gerhard and Angeline must subscribe their names to the memorandum—the document that forms the company. It is no longer part of the company's constitution.
- Application for registration (**s. 9(2)**)
  - This states the company's basic details including its proposed name, the address of its registered office, and that it is (in this case) a private company.
- Articles of association (**s. 9(5)(b)**)
  - Articles of association (the company's constitution) need not be filed if Gerhard and Angeline wish to use model (standard form) articles. The current model articles are found in the **Companies (Model Articles) Regulations 2008**. If Gerhard and Angeline want to have some bespoke articles, they could register these and the model articles would then fill any gaps by virtue of **s. 20**.
- Statement of capital and initial shareholdings (**ss. 9(4)(a) and 10**)
  - This states the company's share capital and shareholdings. Most small private companies (as this will be) have minimal share capital, eg Gerhard and Angeline could have a share capital of £2 with each taking a single £1 share.
- Statement of proposed officers (**ss. 9(4)(c) and 12**)
  - It is assumed that Gerhard and Angeline will be the company's first directors so their names, addresses, and consent to act should go in here. As it will be a private company they do not need a company secretary (**s. 270(1)**).
- Statement of compliance (**s. 13**)
  - Gerhard and Angeline must state that all the registration requirements have been complied with and the registrar can take this statement as evidence of compliance.

Gerhard and Angeline must also pay a registration fee, which is currently £40 for paper registration (less for electronic registration). Same-day registration can be obtained for a higher fee. If all documents are in order the registrar registers them under **CA 2006, s. 14** and issues a Certificate of Incorporation (**CA 2006, s. 15**) which is conclusive evidence that the registration requirements have been complied with. The company comes into existence at the point of registration (**CA 2006, s. 16**).

If Gerhard and Angeline did not want the trouble of preparing and sending the incorporation documentation they could buy a shelf company, which is ready to use straight away. It costs more to buy a shelf company than register a company yourself, but it is still not expensive (£50 is a fairly standard price but cheaper options are available). There are potential disadvantages to buying a company off the shelf as it will not be in exactly the form that Gerhard and Angeline might have chosen, so they should make changes to the articles to avoid problems later on. A shelf company will not have the desired name but they can change the name if they want to by means of a special resolution (or other procedure specified in the articles) under **CA 2006, s. 77(1)**, or they could leave the company's name unchanged and trade under a different business name. As a company comes into existence on registration (not on purchase from the company formation agent or change of name) they should bear in mind that their company exists prior to their purchase. This is not normally a problem but can lead to complications, eg the pre-incorporation contract provisions (**CA 2006, s. 51**) do not apply where a company is already in existence at the time of the contract but under a different name (see *Oshkosh B'Gosh Inc v Dan Marbel Inc Ltd* [1989] BCLC 507).

Naming the company

There are some important requirements and restrictions in the choice of name for the company (see **CA 2006, Part 5**), and the restrictions also apply to business (or trading) names under **CA 2006, Part 41**. First, as a private company the company's name must end with 'limited' or 'Ltd' (or the Welsh equivalent if the company were to be registered in Wales, rather than England and Wales) (**CA 2006, s. 59**). Further, a company must not be registered if, in the opinion of the Secretary of State, use of its name would constitute an offence or be offensive (**CA 2006, s. 53**). It is possible that 'F U Fashions' would be perceived as offensive: eg *R v Registrar of Companies ex parte Attorney-General* [1991] BCLC 476 revealed that the registrar had rejected 'Prostitutes Ltd' and 'Hookers Ltd' as possible names for a new company (although he accepted 'Lindi St Claire (Personal Services) Ltd').

Approval of the Secretary of State is required if a company's proposed name would be likely to give the impression that the company is associated with the government, local authority, or specified public authorities (**CA 2006, s. 54**). This does not seem to be a problem in this case. The Secretary of State's approval must also be obtained if the name contains any word or expression specified in regulations under **CA 2006, s. 55**— currently the **Company, Limited Liability Partnerships and Business Names (Sensitive Words and Expressions) Regulations 2009**. These include words as diverse as 'abortion' and 'Windsor' and do include 'University' so if Gerhard and Angeline wanted to use this name they would have to go through the process of obtaining approval of the Secretary of State. The Department of Business, Innovation, and Skills consulted in 2013 ('Company and Business Names Consultation' BIS/13/648 (2013)) on removal of some restrictions on company and business names (as part of its 'Red Tape Challenge' to remove unnecessary regulation) so Gerhard and Angeline might soon have more freedom in choice of company name.

The company name must not be the same as, or too similar to, any other company name on the register (**CA 2006, s. 66**). To avoid this problem Gerhard and Angeline can check the register of company names via the Companies House website. If the company was registered with a name that is the same as, or too similar to, another company's name then it could be directed to change it under **CA 2006, s. 67**. Furthermore, if someone were to complain that the company name is sufficiently similar to a name associated with them so as to be likely to mislead by suggesting a connection between them, there is an adjudication process under **CA 2006, ss. 69–74** which could also lead to a direction to change the company's name.

The company's name (whether or not a business name is used) must be disclosed at the registered office, any business premises, on all business communications, and on websites (**CA 2006, s. 82** and the **Companies (Trading Disclosures) Regulations 2008**).

Other issues

Gerhard and Angeline should keep in mind that during the pre-formation process they can be regarded as company promoters: 'one who undertakes to form a company with reference to a given project, and to set it going, and who takes the necessary steps to accomplish that purpose' (*Twycross v Grant* (1877) 2 CPD 469). As promoters they owe fiduciary duties to the company (see, eg *Erlanger v New Sombrero Phosphate Co* (1878) 3 App Cas 1218) and they must ensure that all material facts are disclosed and any profits they make personally must be accounted for to the company. They should also be aware that any contracts entered into prior to incorporation will operate as contracts with them personally under **CA 2006, s. 51** (*Phonogram Ltd v Lane* [1982] QB 938). Once the company is incorporated, it will only be bound by such contracts if the parties novate the contract and so Gerhard and Angeline should ensure this is done following incorporation to avoid any potential personal liability.

Once the company is registered, there are ongoing responsibilities. Annual accounts and annual reports must be filed at Companies House (**CA 2006, s. 441**) unless the company is exempt and any changes to the company's constitution, directorships, membership, etc must also be notified to Companies House. Filing fees are due each time.

Further reading

Freedman, J., 'Small businesses and the corporate form: burden or privilege?' (1994) 57 MLR 555

Freedman, J., and Finch, V., 'The limited liability partnership: pick and mix or mix-up?' [2002] JBL 475

Henning, J. J., 'Limited partnerships reform: Parts 1 and 2' (2011) 32 Co Law 178 and 208

Hicks, A., 'Reforming the law of private companies' (1995) 16 Co Law 171

Hicks, A., 'Corporate form: questioning the unsung hero' [1997] JBL 306

Lower, M., 'What's on offer? A consideration of the legal forms available for use by small- and medium-sized enterprises in the United Kingdom' (2003) 24 Co Law 166

Randell, C., 'Joint ventures: an overview' (2005) 16 PLC 29

2

Corporate personality and the veil of incorporation

Introduction

A registered company is a body corporate (**Companies Act 2006 (CA 2006), s. 16**) and is a legal person separate from the shareholders. A company is therefore said to have 'separate legal personality' or 'corporate personality'. This was recognized most famously in *Salomon v A. Salomon & Co Ltd* [1897] AC 22 (*Salomon*): 'The company is at law a different person altogether from the subscribers to the memorandum: and ... the company is not in law the agent of the subscribers or trustee for them' (Lord Macnaghten).

The effect of corporate personality is to create a 'veil of incorporation' between the shareholders (and directors) and the company, preventing recourse to the shareholders for the debts of the company. This applies whether the shareholders are natural persons or corporate persons, so the veil is effective even in a corporate group, as recognized in *The Albazero* [1977] AC 774: '... each company in a group of companies ... is a separate legal entity possessed of separate legal rights and liabilities' (Roskill LJ). Accordingly parent companies are not liable for the debts of their subsidiaries (or vice versa).

The circumstances in which this veil of incorporation can be 'lifted' or 'pierced' (in other words, when corporate personality can be ignored for some purpose), whether by statute or by common law, are a matter of some discussion. For many years the key case was the decision of the Court of Appeal in *Adams v Cape Industries plc* [1990] Ch 433. That case is still important but it is now essential also to be aware of the recent Supreme Court decisions of *VTB Capital plc v Nutritek International Corp* [2013] UKSC 5 and *Prest v Petrodel Resources Ltd* [2013] UKSC 34. The latter, in particular, provided a detailed analysis of veil-piercing cases and policy.

Corporate personality and piercing (or lifting) the veil of incorporation tends to be a popular topic for exam questions, and can also connect with most other topics in company law.

Question 1

In January 1999, Ben set up in business as a sole trader supplying cakes and desserts to local restaurants from leased premises. In January 2000, he formed Just Desserts Ltd and, in consideration of the transfer of the business and its assets, including the leased premises, to the company, he was issued with 10,000 £1 shares in Just Desserts Ltd. Ben was the sole shareholder and director. He signed a contract of employment with the company and drew a salary. In December 2004, Ben made a loan to the company of £25,000 to buy new equipment. The loan was secured by a floating charge over the company's assets. In July 2006, Ben was injured in a gas explosion while at work and the building was badly damaged. Ben's insurance policy on the building and contents was taken out in his name in January 1999.

In 2007, although the business was trading profitably, Ben decided that, in view of his injuries, he would retire and dissolve the company.

Advise Ben on the following:

(a) The validity of the one-man company

(b) His right to claim under his insurance policy for the fire damage to the property

(c) His claim against the company for compensation for his injuries

(d) His right to claim as a secured creditor in respect of his floating charge and for arrears of salary

Commentary

This problem question requires you to apply a number of decisions made after *Salomon*, that follow the general principle established in that case, and extend this to other aspects of the shareholder's relationship with the company.

Answer plan

- Principle of separate legal personality
- Possibility of a one-man company post-1897
- Members' lack of legal or equitable interest in company property
- Possibility of controlling shareholder being employee of company
- Controlling shareholder's rights as creditor

Suggested answer

This problem requires the application of the consequences of *Salomon v A. Salomon & Co Ltd* [1897] AC 22 (*Salomon*) and subsequent decisions applying the principle of separate legal personality. This principle underpins the whole of company law and recognizes that the company is a legal person separate from its members and directors.

In respect of (a), one of the major aspects of importance of the *Salomon* decision was the implied recognition of the 'one-man company'. At that time, company law required a minimum of seven subscribers to the memorandum of association in order to incorporate a company. The subscribers in this case were Mr and Mrs Salomon and their five children, but Mr Salomon's wife and children held only a single share each and held their shares as nominees for Mr Salomon. Although the Court of Appeal (*Broderip v Salomon* [1895] 2 Ch 323) had taken the view that such an arrangement was an abuse of the companies legislation, the House of Lords did not accept that the status of the shareholders was relevant to the legality of the company. Since the statute 'enacts nothing as to the extent or degree of interest which may be held by each of the seven or as to the proportion of interest or influence possessed by one or the majority over the others' (Lord Halsbury), the court would not impose any such requirement and Mr Salomon's company was valid. Accordingly the 'one-man company' was established *de facto* in English law long before the position was recognized in the **Companies (Single Member Private Limited Companies) Regulations 1992** which allowed the registration of the one-man private company (in **Companies Act 1985, s. 1(3A)**). Under the **CA 2006**, both private and public companies can be registered with one member (although a public company must have at least two directors: **Companies Act 2006 (CA 2006), s. 154(2)**).

In this case, the company was registered after the coming into effect of the 1992 Regulations and the company is perfectly legally established. The only problem would be if Ben had formed his company to escape some existing legal liability or as part of a scheme to evade the rules of company law. In this case, the company could be regarded as a 'mere façade' and the veil of incorporation could be pierced: *Gilford Motor Co Ltd v Horne* [1933] Ch 935. This ground for piercing the veil of incorporation, provided there is clear impropriety in the use of the corporate structure, appears to have survived the Supreme Court's recent analysis of piercing the veil in *Prest v Petrodel Resources Ltd* [2013] UKSC 34.

In respect of (b), in spite of the fact that Ben is the sole shareholder of the company, he has no legal or equitable title over the company's property. This was established in *Macaura v Northern Assurance Company* [1925] AC 619 where Macaura tried unsuccessfully to claim under an insurance policy taken out in his own name to cover the destruction of property that had previously been transferred to a company that he had incorporated and in respect of which he held all the shares except for some held by nominees. Since the policy was taken out in Ben's name prior to the incorporation of Just Desserts Ltd, any claim under the policy would fail on the grounds of the lack of Ben's insurable interest. The only thing that could change the position would be if Ben had assigned the policy to the company along with the rest of the property. This does not appear to have happened. This shows the risks of incorporation when an individual is not fully aware of the consequences of the *Salomon* principle; although the principle operates to protect a shareholder's assets from the company's creditors it can also, on occasion, work against the shareholder, as here.

In respect of (c), *Lee v Lee's Air Farming Ltd* [1961] AC 12 established that a person could be the controlling shareholder, managing director, and also an employee under a contract of employment with their own company: 'it is a logical consequence of the decision in *Salomon's case* that one person may function in dual capacities' (Lord Morris). The court in that case allowed Mr Lee's wife to recover compensation for Mr Lee's death as he had been an employee. However, in *Clark v Clark Construction Initiatives Ltd* **[2008] EWCA Civ 1446** the court held that an alleged contract of employment could be ignored (i) where the company itself was a sham; (ii) where it was entered into for an ulterior purpose; and (iii) where the parties did not conduct their relationship in accordance with the contract—although the mere fact that an individual had a controlling shareholding did not, of itself, prevent a contract of employment arising but might raise doubts as to whether he was an employee. The court, therefore, held that the employment tribunal had reached a reasonable decision in rejecting Clark's claim to be an employee. Subject to this, Ben should be able to claim as an employee for compensation.

In respect of (d), the separate personality of the company means that there is no reason why Ben cannot also be a creditor of the company and claim in the company's liquidation. In *Salomon*, Mr Salomon had taken security over the company's assets and this was held by the House of Lords to be valid, allowing him to recover in front of the unsecured creditors on the company's insolvent liquidation. Ben's potential claims could be (i) as an employee in respect of any arrears of salary and unpaid holiday remuneration; (ii) as a secured creditor in respect of his loan to the company secured on a floating charge over the company's assets; and (iii) as a shareholder for a return of capital once all the debts are paid off. In respect of the latter it is important to note that the shares in the company were allotted to him in respect of non-cash consideration. Since the company is a private company, there is no legal requirement for the business to be valued as would be the case for a public limited company under **CA 2006, s. 593**. The company is entitled to place whatever value it likes on the assets transferred to it in the absence of fraud: *Re Wragg Ltd* **[1897] 1 Ch 796**. In *Salomon*, the House of Lords was not concerned that the consideration paid by the company for Mr Salomon's business (£39,000) was 'extravagant' and 'represented the sanguine expectations of a fond owner rather than anything that can be called a businesslike or reasonable estimate value'. Accordingly, provided it was done honestly, there is no cause to question the consideration provided for the shares.

? Question 2

Paradise Ltd imports furniture from India. Adam is the managing director and there are three other directors. In 1999, the board decided to set up a retail business and created a wholly owned subsidiary, Indus Ltd, for the purpose. The registered office of Indus Ltd is the same as that of Paradise Ltd, and Adam is the sole director of Indus Ltd.

The retail business was successful until late 2006 when other suppliers continued to supply the company only on Adam's assurance that Paradise Ltd would give Indus Ltd financial support. By June 2006, Indus Ltd could not pay its debts as they fell due. It continued trading until February 2007 when it went into insolvent liquidation.

Advise the liquidator of Indus Ltd of any common law or statutory liability of Adam and Paradise Ltd and its directors for Indus Ltd's debts.

Commentary

This problem raises issues relating to the veil of incorporation and the judicial and statutory exceptions to the rule when the veil is lifted or pierced. Although the context of the question is the liquidation of a company within a small group, the question does not require a discussion of liquidation as such. The possibility of a business failing and going into insolvent liquidation is in many, if not most, cases the motivating factor for entrepreneurs to choose the form of a limited liability company limited by shares as a vehicle for their business. The context of the decision in *Salomon* was the failure of the company and whether the founder and principal shareholder was liable to indemnify the company's creditors. The question does, however, require you to apply sections of the **Insolvency Act 1986 (IA 1986)** relating to piercing the corporate veil.

 Answer plan

- The rule in *Salomon* and its application to a group of companies
- Judicial recognition of the separate identity of companies within a group
- Judicial exceptions to the rule
- Statutory piercing of the veil under the **IA 1986** to make directors and other persons liable to contribute to the assets of a company in liquidation
- *De facto* and shadow directors

 Suggested answer

The decision in *Salomon v A. Salomon & Co Ltd* [1897] AC 22 (*Salomon*) is always cited as having established that a company is a separate legal person from its shareholders, allowing persons to carry on trading without exposing them to the risk of personal insolvency in the event of the failure of the business. In effect, the separate nature of the corporation from that of its members had been recognized as early as the seventeenth century and the decision in *Foss v Harbottle (1843)* 2 Hare 461 is an earlier example. In the context of a group of companies, the rule also means that the companies of a group are all separate legal entities and that there is no liability on a company within a group if one of the other group companies collapses into insolvent liquidation. A frequently quoted statement which illustrates the general rule was provided by Templeman LJ in *Re Southard Ltd* [1979] 1 WLR 1198 at 1208:

> 'A parent company may spawn a number of subsidiary companies, all controlled directly or indirectly by the shareholders of the parent company. If one of the subsidiary companies, to change the metaphor, turns out to be the runt of the litter and

declines into insolvency to the dismay of its creditors, the parent company and other subsidiary companies may prosper to the joy of the shareholders without any liability for the debts of the insolvent subsidiary.'

There are, however, a number of judicial and statutory exceptions to this fundamental rule which operate to lift (or pierce) the corporate veil between the company and its shareholder and directors—although it should be noted that *Prest v Petrodel Resources Ltd* [2013] UKSC 34 casts serious doubt on whether all these cases should be considered to be true examples of piercing the veil. An early example of the company's separate personality being ignored is *Re Darby, ex p Brougham* [1911] 1 KB 95 where the High Court treated a company formed by two fraudsters as 'merely an alias for themselves'.

During the twentieth century, there was some enthusiasm for lifting the veil, particularly in relation to corporate groups. This culminated in decisions like *DHN Food Distributors Ltd v Tower Hamlets London Borough Council* [1976] 1 WLR 852 where the Court of Appeal treated the three companies in a group as a single economic entity. This much criticized decision marks the high point in judicial piercing of the veil of incorporation, and reinforced the demands for some principles to be established so that litigants could predict when the court would, or would not, lift the corporate veil.

The Court of Appeal decision in *Adams v Cape Industries plc* [1990] Ch 433 rationalized the judicial exceptions to the rule in *Salomon* and demonstrated that the veil would not be lifted easily even within a corporate group, rejecting claims that the companies were a 'single economic unit' or that the American subsidiary was a facade or that the subsidiary was the agent of the parent. In rejecting the submissions, Slade LJ stated: 'Neither in this class of case nor in any other class of case is it open to this court to disregard the principle of *Salomon* merely because it considers it just to do so.' Although the Court of Appeal accepted that the veil could be lifted if the subsidiary was a mere façade concealing the true facts, it did not accept that this applied to the company; the group was entitled to organize its affairs to take advantage of the *Salomon* principle. While this limited ground for lifting the veil seems to have survived the Supreme Court decisions of *VTB Capital plc v Nutritek International Corp* [2013] UKSC 5 and *Prest v Petrodel Resources Ltd* [2013] UKSC 34, it is clear that (in the absence of significant further evidence) the veil would not be lifted/pierced in the case of Indus Ltd—there is no relevant impropriety in the creation or operation of the company.

As regards the promise made by Adam on behalf of Paradise Ltd assuring Indus Ltd's creditors of Paradise Ltd's financial support to Indus Ltd, this would not create any legal liability on Paradise Ltd. This type of statement is sometimes made in writing and is called a comfort letter. Such statements have been held to be insufficient to make a parent liable for its subsidiary's debts: *Kleinwort Benson Ltd v Malaysia Mining Corporation Bhd* [1989] 1 WLR 379.

Applying these principles to the facts of the case, it would appear that neither Paradise Ltd nor its directors have any liability for Indus Ltd's debts at common law.

Relevant statutory exceptions to the veil of incorporation in the **Insolvency Act 1986** (**IA 1986**) must be examined to see whether they offer any solution. Under **IA 1986, s. 212** there is the possibility of a liquidator obtaining a summary remedy against delinquent directors. This applies where, in the course of the winding up of a company, an officer or a person who is or has been concerned, or has taken part, in the promotion, formation, or management of the company has been guilty of any misfeasance or breach of any fiduciary or other duty in relation to the company. If this is established, the court may compel him to contribute such sum as the court thinks just to the company's assets by way of compensation.

Section 213 of the IA 1986 creates the offence of fraudulent trading which provides that if, in the course of the winding up of a company, it appears that any business of the company has been carried on with intent to defraud creditors of the company or for any fraudulent purpose, the court may declare that persons who are knowingly parties to such conduct are liable to make such contribution to the company's assets as the court thinks proper.

Wrongful trading is dealt with by **IA 1986, s. 214**. This operates where, in the course of the insolvent liquidation of a company, a person who was a director of the company at a time prior to the commencement of the winding up knew, or ought to have concluded, that there was no reasonable prospect that the company would avoid insolvent liquidation and yet continued to trade. The court may order such a person to make a contribution to the company's assets as the court thinks proper: **IA 1986, s. 214**.

In respect of the summary remedy, when a company is insolvent or on the brink of insolvency, the interests of the creditors take over from the interests of the members in assessing a director's duty to the company (see *West Mercia Safetywear Ltd v Dodd* [1988] BCLC 250 and **CA 2006, s. 172(3)**). Accordingly directors should ensure that the company's property is not 'dissipated or exploited for the benefit of the directors to the prejudice of the creditors': *Winkworth v Edward Baron Development Co Ltd* [1987] 1 All ER 114. Continuing to trade and exposing the creditors to increased risk of loss could amount to a breach of directors' duties and trigger an order under **IA 1986, s. 212**.

In respect of fraudulent trading, if it could be established that Adam continued to trade with suppliers in the knowledge that the company would be unable to pay for the goods or services when they fell due, this could constitute fraudulent trading. Paradise Ltd could also be liable for fraudulent trading with the necessary intention attributed to the company through the intention of Adam, the managing director of Paradise Ltd, by way of the identification theory: *Tesco Supermarkets Ltd v Nattrass* [1971] 2 All ER 127. In order for Paradise Ltd to be liable, it is necessary to establish that Adam, the sole director, is guilty of fraudulent trading: *Re Augustus Barnett & Son Ltd* [1986] BCLC 170. The problem would be establishing intent.

It would be more straightforward to bring a claim against Adam under wrongful trading, where it is not necessary to establish any intention to defraud. The section catches 'honest but incompetent' directors. Since liability arises not only in respect of *de jure* directors but also *de facto* and shadow directors, the liquidator could potentially bring claims against Paradise Ltd and its other directors. However, this requires, for shadow directorship, evidence that Adam was accustomed to act in accordance with instructions or directions from Paradise Ltd or its directors (**IA 1986,**

s. 251; *Ultraframe (UK) Ltd v Fielding* [2005] EWHC 1638), or for *de facto* direct-orship that Paradise Ltd or its other directors conducted functions at the level of the board and was part of the corporate governing structure of the company (***Commissioners of HM Revenue and Customs v Holland*** [2010] UKSC 51). Although relating to directors of corporate directors rather than directors of parent companies, the latter case showed that it is not easy to establish a shadow or *de facto* directorship where the actions of the individual could be attributed to their principal (*de jure*) directorship.

Question 3

'*Salomon* is in the shadow. It is still alive but no longer occupies the centre of the corporate stage.' (Schmittoff, C.M., '*Salomon* in the shadow' [1976] JBL 305)

'The veil of incorporation is as opaque and impassable as an iron curtain.' (Samuels, A., 'Lifting the veil' [1964] JBL 218)

Which statement more accurately reflects the current law on lifting the veil of incorporation and why?

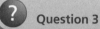

Commentary

This question requires you to consider the current approach of the law to lifting the veil of incorporation, and evaluate whether it is now generally permissive (as suggested by the Schmittoff quote) or strict (as Samuels suggests). This requires consideration of the different grounds on which the veil may be lifted, focusing on the 'mere facade concealing the true facts', but also looking at other ways in which the veil might be lifted. You should also consider the attitude of the law more generally, taking particular account of recent decisions. You will need to reflect upon the changing law but your focus should be on assessing the current law rather than simply describing the historical development of the law.

Examiner's tip

The quotes in this question are simply being used as a trigger for discussion so it is not necessary for you to have read the articles themselves before attempting the question. If you have read the articles don't be tempted simply to describe the articles as that is not what the question asks you to do.

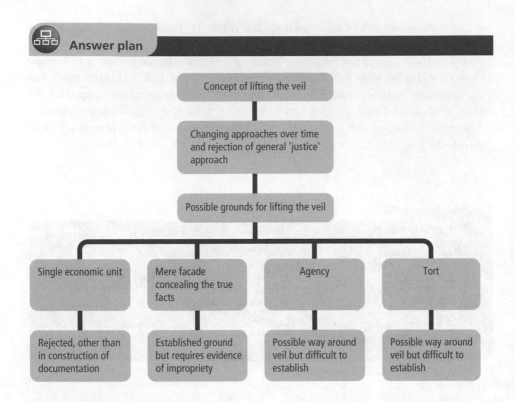

Answer plan

Concept of lifting the veil

Changing approaches over time and rejection of general 'justice' approach

Possible grounds for lifting the veil

| Single economic unit | Mere facade concealing the true facts | Agency | Tort |

| Rejected, other than in construction of documentation | Established ground but requires evidence of impropriety | Possible way around veil but difficult to establish | Possible way around veil but difficult to establish |

Suggested answer

The quotes reflect the changing approaches of the law to lifting the veil of incorporation over the years. This essay will show that, despite the attempts of some judges (notably Lord Denning) to move the principle of separate corporate personality into the shadow, the current law is much more in line with Samuels' quote than Schmittoff's. This restrictive approach has been emphasized recently with the Supreme Court decisions in *VTB Capital plc v Nutritek International Corp* [2013] UKSC 5 and *Prest v Petrodel Resources Ltd* [2013] UKSC 34. Although distinctions can be drawn between 'lifting' and 'piercing' the veil (see, eg *Prest v Petrodel Resources Ltd*) and some academics have advocated the use of a range of different expressions (eg Ottolenghi, S., 'From peeping behind the corporate veil, to ignoring it completely' (1990) 53 MLR 338), this essay will use the term 'lifting the veil' generally.

Lifting the veil by the courts

The veil of incorporation is a metaphor for the separation of a company and its members which ensures that the members are not responsible for the company's liabilities. Ever since the House of Lords in *Salomon v A. Salomon & Co Ltd* [1897] AC 22 (*Salomon*)

recognized the validity of Salomon's 'one-man company', attempts have been made to lift this veil, whether to impose liability on those behind the veil or for some other purpose (eg attributing 'enemy alien' status in *Daimler Co Ltd v Continental Tyre and Rubber Co Ltd* [1916] 2 AC 307). The veil can be lifted by statute (*Dimbleby v National Union of Journalists* [1984] 1 WLR 427), but such provisions are uncommon and tend to impose additional liability on individuals rather than ignoring the company's separate personality (eg liability for wrongful trading: **Insolvency Act 1986, s. 214**). Accordingly this essay will focus on when, if at all, the courts will lift the veil.

The trend of the courts is very much towards the Samuels statement. Suggestions that courts could lift the veil whenever justice required (eg *Re a Company* [1985] BCLC 333) were rejected in *Adams v Cape Industries plc* [1990] Ch 433 as was the argument that the veil could be lifted where a company and its members form a 'single economic unit' (*DHN Food Distributors v Tower Hamlets LBC* [1969] 1 WLR 852). *Woolfson v Strathclyde Regional Council,* 1978 SC (HL) 90 stated that the 'only' ground for lifting the veil is where the involvement of a company is a 'mere facade concealing the true facts' and this has been generally accepted (see *Adams v Cape Industries plc* and *Prest v Petrodel Resources Ltd*). This essay will first consider the 'single economic unit' and 'mere facade' grounds, and will then consider the use of agency or tort to avoid the veil by imposing liability directly on individual members or parent companies.

Single economic unit

The principle of separate corporate personality applies to corporate groups as it does to companies with human members (*The Albazero* [1977] AC 774; *Re Southard* [1979] 1 WLR 1198). However, in *Littlewoods Mail Order Stores Ltd v Inland Revenue Commissioners* [1969] 1 WLR 1241 and *DHN Food Distributors v Tower Hamlets LBC* [1976] 1 WLR 852 Lord Denning considered the economic reality of the situation—if a group was a 'single economic unit' in fact then it should be treated as such in law. Schmitthoff's quote dates from this period where courts were seen as more willing to lift the veil, pushing *Salomon* into the shadow. But in *Woolfson v Strathclyde Regional Council* the House of Lords doubted this approach and this was accepted in *Adams v Cape Industries plc* which held that the veil could be lifted on the basis of a 'single economic unit' only where this was the true construction of a statute, contract, or document. While this can allow veil-lifting on occasion (eg *Beckett Investment Management Group Ltd v Hall* [2007] ICR 1539), it is clearly very limited in scope. As far as this ground is concerned, the veil is indeed largely 'opaque and impassable'.

Mere facade concealing the true facts

Although the courts have stated that the veil can only be lifted if the company is a 'mere facade concealing the true facts' *Adams v Cape Industries plc* recognized there was sparse guidance on what that means. It seems there must be some impropriety on the part of those using the company (although not necessarily when forming the company: *Ben Hashem v Ali Shayif* [2009] 1 FLR 115) and this impropriety must be relevant—there must be a connection between the impropriety and the use of the corporate form: *Trustor AB v Smallbone (No. 2)* [2001] 1 WLR 1177. This was emphasized in *Prest v Petrodel Resources Ltd.*

Clearly the motivation of the individual is important. Where the corporate form has been used deliberately to evade an existing liability this has resulted in the veil being lifted (eg *Jones v Lipman* [1962] 1 WLR 832; *Gilford v Horne* [1933] Ch 935), as did the use of a company to hide misappropriated money (*Trustor AB v Smallbone (No. 2)* [2001] 1 WLR 1177) or abuse the companies legislation (*Re Bugle Press* [1961] Ch 270), although the Supreme Court decisions in *VTB Capital plc v Nutritek International Corp* and *Prest v Petrodel Resources Ltd* raise doubt as to whether all these are true examples of veil-lifting. What is clear is that merely using separate personality to push liability onto another member of a group is not impropriety ('the right to use a corporate structure in this manner is inherent in our corporate law': *Adams v Cape Industries plc*). *Ord v Belhaven Pubs Ltd* [1998] 2 BCLC 447, rejecting *Creasey v Breachwood Motors Ltd* [1993] BCLC 480, showed that even transferring assets from a company after a potential liability had arisen would not justify lifting the veil where this was not done with the purpose of evading that liability (the transfer was part of a group reorganization of assets). Similarly restrictively, *VTB Capital plc v Nutritek International Corp* denied that the veil could be lifted simply to impose liability on a person behind a 'dishonorable' transaction, and in *Prest v Petrodel Resources Ltd* an individual's impropriety in matrimonial proceedings was not considered relevant in lifting the veil.

It follows that while the courts remain willing to lift the veil on this ground, the principle is applied restrictively and so the current law is closer to the statement of Samuels than Schmittoff.

Agency

If a company is the agent of its shareholder(s) then liability for the company's debts will fall on the shareholder, by-passing the corporate veil (although not disturbing the separate personality of the company). The House of Lords in *Salomon* rejected the idea that the company was acting as Salomon's agent; the fact that a company has a single member or is a wholly-owned subsidiary is not enough to make it the agent of its member or parent company. In the past courts have found an agency relationship between a subsidiary company and its parent company (eg *Smith, Stone & Knight v Birmingham Corpn* [1939] 4 All ER 116) but *Adams v Cape Industries plc* made clear that agency cannot be presumed from the closeness of operations between a parent company and its subsidiary (see also *Yukong Line Ltd of Korea v Rendsburg Investments Corpn of Liberia (No. 2)* [1998] 1 WLR 294). The current law shows that it is very unlikely that an agency relationship will be found on the facts, leaving the veil intact.

Tort

If a member (or director) has personally committed a tort then personal (or joint) liability could follow. However, the courts have generally been reluctant to impose tortious liability on those behind the corporate veil, recognizing the potential for damage to the principle of separate personality (**Williams v Natural Life Health Foods Ltd** [1998] 1 **BCLC 689**). One area of tort liability of current interest is the responsibility of parent companies for activities of their subsidiaries. **Chandler v Cape Industries plc** [2012] 1 **WLR 3111** held that while responsibility does not arise by mere fact of the corporate relationship, on the facts the parent company had assumed a direct duty of care to the subsidiary's employees. While strictly outside the realms of lifting the veil, it shows there is some scope for avoiding the application of the **Salomon** principle.

Conclusion

To conclude it can be seen that the high-point of veil-lifting recognized in Schmittoff's quote is long gone. Despite occasional indications of more Denning-esque views (eg in **Ratiu v Conway and ors** [2005] **EWCA Civ 1302**) recent decisions show a clear reluctance to depart from the principle of separate corporate personality and lift the veil except where there is abuse of the corporate form. This is so regardless of the seriousness or moral force of the claimant's position. Largely in line with Samuels' quote, the current law starts from the assumption that the veil is indeed an 'iron curtain'; contrary to Schmittoff's statement **Salomon** is very much 'centre stage'.

Question 4

Write a case note on *Prest v Petrodel Resources Ltd* [2013] UKSC 34 focusing on the company law issues raised in the case.

Commentary

Writing a case note (or case comment) is a question technique that you might need to be able to deal with in exams, alongside more conventional essay and problem questions. It is a way of ensuring that you focus on a case—usually a particularly important case or an interesting recent decision on an important topic. Preparing your own case notes is also a useful revision and study technique to deepen your knowledge and develop your case analysis.

Prest v Petrodel Resources Ltd [2013] UKSC 34 is the most recent and authoritative judicial statement on the law of lifting (or piercing) the veil of incorporation, and is a case that will repay careful consideration. The case considers whether companies owned and controlled by Mr Prest could be ordered to transfer properties owned by the companies to Mrs Prest as part of a divorce settlement. In this case Mrs Prest's claim could not be met by the transfer of Mr Prest's shares in the company (as might seem an obvious solution) because both Mr Prest and the company were resident abroad, making enforcement impossible.

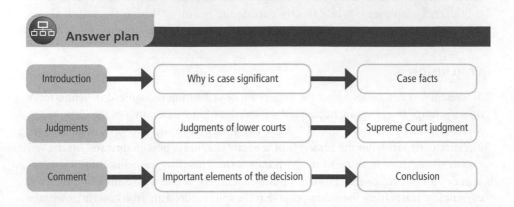

Examiner's tip

Focus on the case but don't look at it in isolation—link it to other cases and consider how a case has developed the law or might influence the law in the future.

Answer plan

Introduction	→	Why is case significant	→	Case facts
Judgments	→	Judgments of lower courts	→	Supreme Court judgment
Comment	→	Important elements of the decision	→	Conclusion

 Suggested answer

Prest v Petrodel Resources Ltd [2013] **UKSC 34** gave the Supreme Court a second chance in only a few months (the first being *VTB Capital plc v Nutritek International Corp* [2013] **UKSC 5**) to update and clarify the law on lifting the veil of incorporation. Prior to these cases the most recent authoritative guidance was that of *Adams v Cape Industries plc* [1990] **Ch 433** (Court of Appeal) and before that *Woolfson v Strathclyde Regional Council* 1978 SC (HL) 90. Since lifting (or, as the Supreme Court prefers, 'piercing') the veil means ignoring the separate personality of a company and its members (as established in *Salomon v A. Salomon & Co Ltd* [1897] AC 22) and thus potentially undermining the 'unyielding rock' of company law (Templeman, Lord, 'Forty years on' (1990) 11 Co Law 10), this issue is of great importance.

The case concerned proceedings for ancillary relief following the divorce of Yasmin Prest from her oil-tycoon husband, Michael Prest, in which Mr Prest was found to be the effective sole owner and controller of several companies holding properties in the UK. Mr Prest had not been co-operative—his conduct of the proceedings was 'characterised by persistent obstruction, obfuscation and deceit, and a contumelious refusal to comply with rules of court and specific orders' (Lord Sumption).

At first instance (*YP v MP and Petrodel Resources Ltd* [2011] **EWHC 2956**) Moylan J, in part satisfaction of a lump sum award to Mrs Prest, ordered Mr Prest to procure the transfer of properties held in the name of two companies and ordered the companies to execute documents as necessary. Although the judge concluded that he was not able to pierce the veil under general principles (as the impropriety of Mr Prest did not relate to the use of the companies), Moylan J interpreted the **Matrimonial Causes**

Act 1973 (MCA 1973), s. 24 widely by construing 'property' to include property over which an individual exercises control.

In the Court of Appeal (*Petrodel Resources Ltd v Prest* [2012] EWCA Civ 1395) the majority (Rimer and Patten LJJ) found in favour of the appellant companies, rejecting both any suggestion that the veil could be lifted and Moylan J's interpretation of the MCA 1973. The majority criticized the generous approach of the family courts to piercing the veil and decreed that this practice 'must now cease' (Patten LJ). However the minority (Thorpe LJ) favoured the looser approach to lifting the veil in family cases, describing the alternative as offering 'an open road and a fast car to the money maker'.

The Supreme Court judgment

The Supreme Court reversed the Court of Appeal decision, with the seven Justices unanimously finding in favour of Mrs Prest, but not by lifting the veil of incorporation, nor by restoring Moylan J's interpretation of the MCA 1973. Instead the court re-assessed the facts and concluded that Mr Prest had provided the purchase money for the properties, giving rise to a presumption (that was not rebutted) that the properties were held by the companies on resulting trust for Mr Prest. Nonetheless the Supreme Court offered some useful (albeit strictly obiter) discussion of veil-piercing.

The main judgment was given by Lord Sumption (whose reasons were expressly accepted, in the main, by Lords Neuberger, Mance, Clarke, and Walker). Lord Sumption recognized that the principle of separate corporate personality is in some sense a fiction, but is one that amounts to 'the whole foundation of English company and insolvency law'. Although a foundational principle should presumably not be easily disturbed, the Supreme Court accepted a limited jurisdiction to pierce the veil, allied to the broader principle that absolute legal principles can be overturned in the event of fraud. Lord Sumption indicated that 'piercing the veil' happens only where separate personality is disregarded. He separated authorities into 'evasion' cases—where the corporate form was being used improperly—and 'concealment' cases—where regard was simply had to facts behind the veil; only the first category were properly examples of veil-piercing.

The veil should, therefore, be pierced only where necessary 'to prevent the abuse of corporate legal personality', such abuse being using the company to evade the law or to frustrate its enforcement, and 'only for the purpose of depriving the company or its controller of the advantage they would otherwise have obtained' (Lord Sumption). This should be a remedy of 'last resort', following the approach taken by Munby J in *Ben Hashem v Al Shayif* [2009] 1 FLR 115, to be used only 'when all other more conventional remedies have proved to be of no assistance' (Lord Clarke).

Comment

The Supreme Court's judgment provides some welcome clarity. First, the explicit acknowledgement that a veil-piercing jurisdiction exists is helpful after doubts were sown by Lord Neuberger in *VTB Capital plc v Nutritek International Corp*. It is also now clear that family law cannot take an independent approach to this issue, contrary to dicta in cases such as *Nicholas v Nicholas* [1984] FLR 285.

Lord Sumption's distinction between 'concealment' and 'evasion' may help in assessing the different ways in which a court approaches the veil of incorporation and in reducing the cases where it is thought necessary to lift or pierce it. Nonetheless, as Lord Sumption recognized, many cases combine both elements, while Lady Hale doubted whether all cases could be classified in this way. There is obviously scope for confusion as Lords Sumption and Neuberger disagreed on whether to class some cases (eg *Gilford Motor Co Ltd v Horne* [1933] Ch 935) as evasion or concealment. This is an area that may need further consideration in later cases. Furthermore, not all judges fully accepted a strict limitation on the principle to 'evasion' cases, eg Lord Mance felt it would be 'dangerous' to foreclose all possible future situations in which the principle might arise.

The connecting of veil-piercing with the principle that statute should not be used as an engine of fraud shows clearly that veil-piercing relies on the corporate form being used for some deliberately dishonest purpose. This is in line with the approach of the Court of Appeal in *Adams v Cape Industries plc*. The impropriety must thus be relevant impropriety—bad behaviour in itself does not justify piercing the veil. What matters is an improper purpose in the use of the company, although there need not have been an improper purpose in creating the company (*Ben Hashem v Al Shayif*). Furthermore, although it was acknowledged that Mr Prest had himself ignored the corporate veil and misapplied corporate assets (the group was described as his 'money box which he uses at will' (Moylan J)), such behaviour does not allow a court to disregard the corporate veil in the same way.

Conclusion

Arguably *Prest v Petrodel Resources Ltd* made few changes to company law. After all, in essence it confirms the existence of a principle that was not generally in serious doubt and, to a significant extent, confirms earlier case law on when it should apply.

However, the case emphasizes the principle's status as a 'last resort'—where no other legal principle can aid the claimant. It also provides further guidance on the limited circumstances in which veil-piercing may be permitted. It might, therefore, be expected that the number of cases seeking to pierce the veil will reduce still further and claims evoking the principle will be more carefully formulated. Any future attempt to expand veil-piercing beyond 'evasion' cases will have little support; even Lord Mance (who, along with Lady Hale, declined to limit the principle) observed 'no-one should ... be encouraged to think that any further exception ... will be easy to establish, if any exists at all'.

Despite Mrs Prest's success on the facts, *Prest v Petrodel Resources Ltd* does not give a spouse in Mrs Prest's position much comfort from company law. Only if the company is being used in order to evade liability or frustrate enforcement will the veil be pierced, and only impropriety in that sense is relevant to the court's determination. This conclusion is undoubtedly positive from the sense of legal and commercial clarity but may be unappealing to a layperson who would, like Mr Prest himself, view the company and controller as one and the same. The use of trusts gives hope to the non-controlling spouse in these cases, but one must wonder if this re-opens uncertainty as to the ownership of 'corporate' assets that the case had otherwise sought to close.

Question 5

Analyse the way in which the law has evolved to enable corporate bodies to be held liable for tortious and criminal offences requiring the establishment of intent or privity with particular regard to corporate manslaughter.

Commentary

This question requires you to examine the development of the identification theory for the purpose of establishing tortious and criminal liability, recognizing the limitations of the common law approach as regards the successful prosecution of companies for manslaughter. The solution to this is the creation of a statutory offence of corporate manslaughter and the scope of the legislation in moving from the doctrine of attribution to the gross negligence test.

Answer plan

- Explanation of the 'identification theory' and its application to tort and criminal offences
- Limitations on the application of the theory to cases of corporate manslaughter, particularly in the case of large companies
- Explanation and analysis of the scope of the statutory offence of corporate manslaughter

Suggested answer

Very early on, English law solved the problem of making a company liable in tort and crime in cases where it is necessary to establish criminal or tortious intention. The courts developed the identification theory, or alter ego doctrine, which attributes the requisite intention or knowledge of a person, or persons, controlling the company to the company, making the company tortiously or criminally liable.

In respect of tortious liability, in *Lennard's Carrying Co Ltd v Asiatic Petroleum Co Ltd* [1915] AC 705, the appellant shipowners were sued for damages for the loss of cargo caused by a ship running aground due to its being unseaworthy because of defective boilers. The House of Lords ruled that the necessary fault or privity to establish liability could be identified in respect of the company where the fault or privity existed in the mind of a person who was 'the directing mind and will' of the company. Criminal liability of companies for crimes requiring a mental element was established in 1944 when companies were convicted of intent to deceive (*DPP v Kent and Sussex Contractors Ltd* [1944] KB 146) and conspiracy to defraud (*R v ICR Haulage Ltd* [1944] KB 551) with the court imputing the knowledge and intention of the company's 'human agents' to the company. In *HL Bolton (Engineering) Ltd v TJ Graham & Sons Ltd* [1957] 1 QB 159, Denning LJ stated, 'Some of the people in the company are ... nothing more than hands to do the work … Others are directors and managers who represent the directing mind and will of the company, and control what it does. The state of mind of these managers is the state of mind of the company and is treated by the law as such.' In *Stone & Rolls Ltd v Moore Stephens* [2009] UKHL 39 where a one-man company had been set up solely as a vehicle for defrauding banks, the House of Lords held that the company was primarily, rather than vicariously, liable for the frauds perpetrated by the sole member/director.

The limits of the identification theory were demonstrated in *Tesco Supermarkets Ltd v Nattrass* [1971] 2 All ER 127 where a branch manager was held not to be identified with the company, allowing the company to avoid liability for misleading pricing under the Trade Descriptions Act 1968, showing that the bigger and more complex the company, the easier it will be for liability to be avoided. In *Meridian Global Funds Management Asia Ltd v Securities Commission* [1995] 2 AC 500, Lord Hoffman considered the attribution of liability to companies in some detail. He emphasized that whose thoughts and/or acts should be attributed to the company will depend upon the rule of law that is being applied and so the 'directing mind and will' formulation is not the only test for attribution. Despite *Meridian Global Funds Management Asia Ltd v Securities Commission* it is clear that the 'directing mind and will' rule still applies in most cases (eg *A-G's Reference (No. 2 of 1999)* [2000] QB 796), as was apparent in *R v St Regis Paper Company Ltd* [2012] 1 Cr App R 14 where the Court of Appeal applied the principle and rejected any alternative special rule of attribution. The Law Commission has recently (July 2013) suggested that its next programme of law reform could include a full consideration of corporate liability (following consultation on liability in regulatory contexts in 2010) including consideration of whether liability should move away from the identification model.

Since there is a statutory penalty of life imprisonment, companies cannot be guilty of murder but *R v HM Coroners for East Kent, ex p Spooner* (1987) 3 BCC 636, DC established that a company could be guilty of manslaughter. Since this necessitated the identification of the company with an individual guilty of the crime, the prosecution of P&O Ferries failed when the guilt of the managers could not be established. The judge rejected prosecution arguments that the knowledge and intentions of the individual managers should be aggregated to establish the criminal intention of the company: *R v P&O Ferries (Dover) Ltd* (1991) 93 Cr App Rep 72.

The first conviction for corporate manslaughter arose from the deaths of four teenagers on a canoeing trip at sea against a one-man company operating an activity centre. The managing director's failure to heed previous warnings of potential danger by the company's instructors was attributed to the company and both were convicted of manslaughter: *R v Kite and OLL Ltd* [1996] 2 Cr App Rep (S) 295. The fact that it was easier to prosecute small companies was criticized in *Re Attorney-General's Reference (No. 2 of 1999)* [2000] QB 796.

Public pressure to reform the law on corporate manslaughter finally resulted in the **Corporate Manslaughter and Corporate Homicide Act 2007 (CMCHA 2007)** which came into force on 6 April 2008 and created a statutory offence of corporate manslaughter (corporate culpable homicide in Scotland).

The offence builds on gross negligence manslaughter and is concerned with the way in which an organization's activities were managed or organized and whether an adequate standard of care was applied to the fatal activity. The offence is committed where an organization owes a duty to take reasonable care for a person's safety and the way in which activities of the organization are managed or organized by senior management amounts to a gross breach of this duty causing death of a person or persons. A substantial part of the failing must have occurred at senior management level, ie those making significant decisions about the organization or substantial parts of it, including those carrying out HQ functions as well as those in senior operational management roles. The identification of senior management will depend on the nature and scale of the organization's activities. Apart from directors and similar senior management positions, roles likely to be considered include regional managers in national organizations and managers of different operational divisions.

The organization concerned must owe a 'relevant duty of care' to the victim in respect of systems of work and equipment used by employees; the condition of worksites and other premises occupied by an organization; and products or services supplied to customers. These duties are set out in **CMCHA 2007, s. 2** and include: employers' and occupiers' duties, duties connected to supplying goods and services, commercial activities, construction and maintenance work, using or keeping plant, vehicles, etc, and duties relating to holding a person in custody. The duty of care will apply to persons working or performing services for the organization and could include sub-contractors and persons supplying services other than employees. It is for the judge to decide whether a relevant duty of care is owed: **CMCHA 2007, s. 2(5)**. Common law rules preventing a duty of care being owed by one person to another through joint engagement in unlawful conduct or because of voluntarily acceptance of risks are to be disregarded: **CMCHA 2007, s. 2(6)**.

The **CMCHA 2007** sets out a number of exemptions covering deaths connected with certain public and government functions. The management of these functions involves wider questions of public policy and is already subject to other forms of accountability. Areas in which exemptions apply include military operations, policing, emergency response, child protection work, and probation.

Organizations convicted of the offence can receive: (a) an unlimited fine; (b) a publicity order requiring them to publicize the conviction and details of the offence; or (c) on the application of the prosecution after consultation with the appropriate regulatory authority or authorities, a remedial order requiring them to address the cause of the fatal injury. Failure to comply can lead to prosecution and an unlimited fine on conviction.

In England and Wales and in Northern Ireland the consent of the Director of Public Prosecutions is needed before a case can be taken to court. In Scotland all prosecutions are initiated by the Procurator Fiscal. Subject to this, in England and Wales and in Northern Ireland individuals can bring a private prosecution for the new offence, but it is no longer possible to bring proceedings for common law gross negligence manslaughter against an organization to which the 2007 Act applies: **CMCHA 2007, s. 20**. In Scotland, the common law continues in force and the Procurator Fiscal will determine the appropriate charge according to individual circumstances.

Instead of identifying the individual guilty of the breach of care, the **CMCHA 2007** identifies the senior management as those having a significant role in the decision making, management, or organization of the whole or a substantial part of the organization's activities (**CMCHA 2007, s. 1(4)(c)**) and avoids the problem with larger organizations where the complexity of the structure might otherwise lead to evasion of liability. In addition, the standard of gross negligence is an objective one whose breach falls below what can reasonably be expected of the organization in the circumstances: **CMCHA 2007, s. 1(4)(b)**.

In conclusion, the new offence should have far-reaching implications for a larger group of organizations, including government departments previously covered by Crown privilege and senior individuals within those organizations.

Further reading

Craig, R., 'Thou shall do no murder: a discussion paper on the Corporate Manslaughter and Corporate Homicide Act 2006' (2009) 30 Co Law 17

Ferran, E., 'Corporate attribution and the directing mind and will' (2011) 127 LQR 239

Field, S., and Jones, L., 'Death in the workplace: who pays the price?' (2011) 32 Co Law 166

Griffin, S., 'Holding companies and subsidiaries—the corporate veil' (1991) 12 Co Law 16

Griffin, S., 'Limited liability: a necessary revolution?' (2004) 24 Co Law 99

Hsaio, M. W. H., 'Abandonment of the doctrine of attribution in favour of gross negligence test in the Corporate Manslaughter and Corporate Homicide Act 2007' (2009) 30 Co Law 110

Kahn-Freund, O., 'Some reflections on company law reform' (1944) 7 MLR 54

Krishnaprasad, K. V., 'Agency, limited liability and the corporate veil' (2011) 32 Co Law 163

Law Commission, 'Legislating the Criminal Code: Involuntary Manslaughter' (1996) Law Com No. 237

Law Commission, 'Criminal liability in regulatory contexts' (2010) Consultation Paper No. 195

Linklater, L., '"Piercing the corporate veil"—the never ending story?' (2006) 27 Co Law 65

Moore, M., 'A temple built on faulty foundations' [2006] JBL 180

Ottolenghi, S., 'From peeping behind the corporate veil, to ignoring it completely' (1990) 53 MLR 338

Samuels, A., 'Lifting the veil' [1964] JBL 218

Schmitthoff, C. M., '*Salomon* in the shadow' [1976] JBL 305

Sullivan, G. R., 'The attribution of culpability to limited companies' [1996] CLR 515

Wickins, R., and Ong, C. A., 'Confusion worse confounded: the end of the directing mind theory?' [1997] JBL 524

3

Constitution of the registered company

Introduction

The company's constitution consists of the company's articles of association and any resolutions and agreements to which the **Companies Act 2006 (CA 2006), Ch 3** applies: **CA 2006, s. 17**.

The main constitutional document of a company is thus its articles. These are the internal rules of the company and cover everything from the authority of directors to the transfer of shares. A copy of a company's proposed articles should be sent to the registrar on initial registration (**CA 2006, s. 18**), but standard form (or 'model') articles will apply wherever articles are not registered or in so far as the registered articles do not exclude or modify the standard form articles (**CA 2006, s. 20**). The current versions of the model articles are found in the **Companies (Model Articles) Regulations 2008**; those for a private company limited by shares are in **Schedule 1** of the Regulations; those for a public company are in **Schedule 3**.

Prior to the **CA 2006**, the company's constitution also included the memorandum of association which contained the external aspects of a company's structure. However post-2006 the memorandum is now simply the document that forms the company and for companies formed prior to 2006 the provisions of the memorandum are deemed to be part of the articles (**CA 2006, s. 28**).

The company's constitution can be quite a popular area for examination questions—both problem and essay questions. The emphasis is often on one or more of: alteration of the articles; the legal effect of the articles; shareholder agreements.

Articles can generally be altered by special resolution (**CA 2006, s. 21(1)**), provided the alteration does not conflict with any provision of the **CA 2006** and is not illegal. The courts have also imposed restrictions on alterations of the articles that are not 'bona fide in the interests of the company' (*Allen v Gold Reefs of West Africa Ltd* [1900] 1 Ch 656). In addition the **CA 2006** introduced the option of 'entrenching' provisions in the articles—entrenched articles can only be amended or repealed using more stringent conditions than a special resolution (**CA 2006, s. 22**).

The legal effect of the company's constitution gives rise to many issues, and much judicial and academic discussion. Under **CA 2006, s. 33** (formerly **CA 1985, s. 14**) the company's articles bind the company and its members as if there were covenants on the part of the company and each member to observe those provisions—the articles have thus become known as 'the statutory contract'. Particular issues have arisen in determining quite who is bound and in what capacity.

Although the articles are the primary constitutional document, the articles can be supplemented by a formal contract on formation, or subsequently. Shareholder agreements operate outside the articles, binding only those who are party to them, but can be a very effective way to modify the constitution without having to alter the articles. Shareholder agreements may also have an important role in resolving shareholder disputes and avoiding having to make use of the statutory provisions for minority protection.

 Question 1

The **Companies Act 2006** provides that a company may alter its articles of association by special resolution: **s. 21(1)**.

What restrictions are there on this power? Illustrate your answer with reference to decided cases.

 Commentary

This is a fairly standard essay question on the company's power to alter its articles. You will need to be able to explain the statutory restrictions on alteration of the articles, including provisions of entrenchment and variation of class rights. However, the more complex aspect of this topic is the court's power to ensure that alterations are bona fide for the benefit of the company as a whole and not simply an abuse of majority power. Where members claim that an alteration is an abuse of majority power, you need to know how the court approaches the identification of an abuse of power and the available remedies for the victim. This requires detailed knowledge of the relevant cases.

 Answer plan

- Inalienable right of companies to alter their articles by special resolution under **CA 2006, s. 21(1)**
- Statutory restrictions in respect of provisions of entrenchment, alterations imposing obligations on members to increase their capital contribution, and where alteration constitutes a variation of class rights
- Court's authority to police alterations and strike out alterations that are not bona fide for the benefit of the company as a whole
- The tests by which the court reaches its decisions
- Remedies available to injured parties

Suggested answer

The company's articles contain the internal regulations of the company and, in general, registered companies have the statutory right to alter their articles at any time by special resolution under **Companies Act 2006 (CA 2006), s. 21** and cannot contractually restrict themselves from exercising this statutory right. This was decided in *Punt v Symons & Co Ltd* **[1903] 2 Ch 506** where the company's articles contained provisions restricting the appointment of directors to the company's founder and after his death provided that the power was limited to his executors. The company entered into a contractual agreement that it would not alter its articles to remove this restriction. The court held that the restriction was illegal. Where a company does enter into such an agreement and then alters its articles in breach of the agreement, the injured party cannot prevent the alteration from being made by way of injunction, but can sue for damages for breach of the contract: *Southern Foundries (1926) Ltd v Shirlaw* **[1940] AC 701**; *British Murac Syndicate Ltd v Alperton Rubber Co Ltd* **[1915] 2 Ch 186**.

The articles of a company bind the company and its members (**CA 2006, s. 33(1)**) but members are not bound by an alteration to its articles after the date on which they became a member if, and so far as, the alteration requires them to take or subscribe for shares other than those held at the date of the alteration, or in any way increases their liability to contribute to the company's share capital or otherwise pay money to the company: **CA 2006, s. 25**.

Prior to the **CA 2006**, the company's constitution was split between the memorandum of association and the articles of association. In addition to the clauses that were required to be in the memorandum, the company could include clauses in the memorandum and embed them against alteration. This was not possible for provisions contained in the articles which were always capable of alteration. The **CA 2006** now provides that a company's articles may contain provisions ('provision for entrenchment') to the effect that specified clauses of the articles may be amended or repealed only if conditions are met, or procedures are complied with, that are more restrictive than those applicable in the case of a special resolution: **CA 2006, s. 22(1)**. Provisions for entrenchment may only be made in the articles on formation, or by an amendment of the articles agreed to by all the members: **CA 2006, s. 22(2)** (not yet brought into force). Provision for entrenchment does not, however, prevent amendment of the articles by agreement of the members, or by order of the court or other authority having power to alter the company's articles: **CA 2006, s. 22(3)**. The registrar of companies must be notified of provisions for entrenchment and also of their removal: **CA 2006, s. 23**.

For companies in existence prior to the **CA 2006** coming into effect, **CA 2006, s. 28** provides that provisions contained in the company's memorandum are to be treated as provisions of the company's articles, including provision for entrenchment.

Where the alteration of the articles constitutes a variation of class rights, the alteration cannot be made under **CA 2006, s. 21(1)**, but only in accordance with **CA 2006, s. 630** which requires alteration in accordance with provision in the company's articles for the variation of those rights or, where the articles contain no such provision, if the holders of shares of that class consent to the variation either by (i) consent in writing of the holders of three-quarters of the issued shares, or (ii) a special resolution at a separate class meeting: *Cumbrian Newspapers Group Ltd v Cumberland & Westmorland Herald Newspaper & Printing Co Ltd* [1986] BCLC 286.

The most important restriction on companies' freedom to alter their articles is where the court decides that the alteration is not bona fide for the benefit of the company as a whole but is an abuse of majority power.

The power to police proposed alterations of the articles was established in *Allen v Gold Reefs of West Africa Ltd* [1900] 1 Ch 656. In this case, Zuccani held both fully paid up shares and not fully paid up shares in the company. Under its articles, the company had a lien for all debts and liabilities of any member 'upon all shares (not being fully paid) held by such member'. Zuccani was the only holder of fully paid shares in the company and, on his death, he owed the company arrears of calls on his unpaid shares but his assets were insufficient to pay this debt. By special resolution, the company then altered the article by omitting the words in parentheses and thus created a lien on Zuccani's fully paid shares. In an action brought by Zuccani's executor for a declaration that the alteration was void, the court held that the power of the company to alter its articles under what is now **CA 2006, s. 21(1)** had to be exercised, not only in the manner required by the law, but also bona fide for the benefit of the company as a whole. The fact that Zuccani was, at the time, the only holder of fully paid shares did not mean that it was an abuse of majority power and that it was not for the benefit of the company as a whole.

The principal issue in this respect is how the court should decide whether the alteration is bona fide in the interests of the company as a whole. Initially there were two possibilities: an objective and a subjective test. Under the objective test, the court itself determined whether or not the proposed alteration was in the interests of the company, whereas under the subjective test the court is merely concerned to establish whether the shareholders, in voting for the alteration, believed that they were acting in the best interests of the company as a whole. The clash between these approaches can best be seen in *Sidebottom v Kershaw, Leese & Co Ltd* [1920] 1 Ch 154, which followed the subjective test, and *Dafen Tinplate Co Ltd v Llanelly Steel Co* [1920] 2 Ch 124, which applied the objective test. Both of these cases concerned an alteration of the articles to give the company the power to acquire compulsorily the shares of minorities who were competing with the company. The conflict between these two approaches was resolved in favour of the subjective test in *Shuttleworth v Cox Brothers & Co Ltd* [1927] 2 KB 9, although this does not prevent the court questioning the shareholders' evidence—even with a subjective test, if an alteration is so oppressive as to cast doubt on the shareholders' honesty, or so extravagant that no reasonable man could really consider it for the company's benefit, the alteration will not be allowed.

A particular problem is how to determine what is in the interests of the company as a whole when the proposed alteration only concerns membership matters (as here the company has no separate interest). In *Greenhalgh v Arderne Cinemas Ltd* [1951]

Ch 286 the court stated that in these circumstances the court should ask whether the alteration was for the benefit of 'an individual hypothetical member', and whether the effect of the alteration was to discriminate between the majority and the minority shareholders. Although this test has met with criticism, the more recent case of *Citco Banking Corporation NV v Pusser's Ltd* [2007] BCC 205 declined to disturb it despite recognizing that it has not been found 'entirely illuminating'.

Where a minority shareholder alleges that there has been an alteration of the articles which constitutes an abuse by the majority of their power, the claim can now be brought as a claim of unfair prejudice under **CA 2006, s. 994**. If a claim is brought under this section and the court decides in favour of the claimant, the court has unlimited power to make orders under **CA 2006, s. 996(1)**. Without prejudice to the generality of its powers under that sub-section, the court may make specific orders under **s. 996(2)**. As regards the alteration of its articles, the court can require the company not to make any, or any specified, alterations in its articles without the leave of the court: **s. 996(2)(d)**.

? Question 2

The articles of Able Ltd contain the following clauses:

(a) Bertram should have the right to nominate a director for as long as he continues to hold a 10 per cent shareholding,

(b) Claude should be the company secretary for life, and

(c) the company's sales manager shall receive an annual bonus equal to 5 per cent of the company's profits.

David, the majority shareholder, has just sold his 75 per cent holding of shares to Edward. Edward proposes to alter the articles so that all the directors should be appointed by the general meeting, and that the annual bonus payable to the sales manager shall be reduced to 2 per cent. He also intends to appoint Frieda as company secretary. The sales manager has a contract with the company that makes no provision for the payment of any bonus. Bertram has a contract with the company stating that the company will not alter its articles so as to affect his rights without his consent.

Advise Edward.

Commentary

This problem question concerns the application of various judicial decisions concerning the nature of the contract contained in the articles of association between the company and its members. It involves explanation of **CA 2006, s. 33** and the application to the scenarios of judicial decisions on the section.

Answer plan

- Articles constitute a binding contract between the company and the members
- Relevant decisions concerning articles
- Recognition of issue of class rights and application of **CA 2006, s. 630**
- Relevant case law on outsider rights including directors' right to salary etc
- Indirect enforcement as implied term of service contract but still subject to variation on a prospective basis

Suggested answer

Section 33 of the Companies Act 2006 (CA 2006) provides that 'the provisions of a company's constitution bind the company and its members to the same extent as if there were covenants on the part of the company and of each member to observe those provisions'. The articles of association (the main element of the company's constitution) are thus said to amount to a statutory contract between the company and its members and amongst the members *inter se*. The contract is, however, an unusual one in that it can be unilaterally altered by a special resolution by the members of the company under **CA 2006, s. 21(1)** except where the proposed alteration relates to the variation of class rights, when **CA 2006, s. 630** applies. The scope of the contract is also restricted as a result of judicial decisions.

The legal positions of Bertram, Claude, and the sales manager are now considered in turn.

Bertram: The articles provide that Bertram has the right to nominate a director for as long as he continues to hold a 10 per cent stake in the company. In addition, the company has contracted with Bertram that the company will not alter its articles so as to affect his rights without his consent. The legal issue here is that the company has the statutory power under **CA 2006, s. 21(1)** to alter its articles and it has been held that this statutory power cannot be restricted contractually. This was established in *Punt v Symons & Co Ltd* [1903] 2 Ch 506. In this case, the defendant company was formed to carry on a business established by Symons. The articles provided that Symons was to be the governing director with full powers of management and the appointment of directors and that, after his death, these powers would be exercised by his trustees. The articles also provided that the company would not at any time alter, or attempt to alter, the articles in this respect. On Symons' death, the trustees appointed managing directors but, following a dispute between the managing directors and the trustees, the directors sought to alter the articles to deprive the trustees of their powers. The court held that the company could not contract out of its statutory right to alter its articles either by way of a separate contract or by a provision in the articles. Where the company has entered into a contract to that effect, the other party cannot, therefore, enforce his contract rights by way of an injunction, but can sue the company for damages where it proceeds to alter its articles in breach of the contract: *Southern Foundries* (1926) *Ltd v Shirlaw* [1940] AC 701.

The position in this case is further complicated by the fact that Bertram's right to appoint a director is conditional upon him continuing to hold a 10 per cent stake in the company. In *Cumbrian Newspaper Group Ltd v Cumberland & Westmorland Herald Newspaper & Printing Co Ltd* [1986] BCLC 286 the claimant was given various rights in respect of the defendant company contained in their articles. These included the right to nominate a director and pre-emption rights over new share issues conditional upon continuing to hold a 10 per cent stake in the defendant company. It was held that these rights constituted class rights, which could therefore not be varied under **CA 2006, s. 21(1)** but only in accordance with **s. 630(2)**. This requires any variation of the rights to be made under the terms of a variation of rights clause contained in the company's articles or, failing that, the variation must be sanctioned by the holders of three-quarters in nominal value of the issued shares of that class in writing or by a special resolution passed at a separate class meeting. Since Bertram, who opposes the variation, is the sole shareholder of the class, the variation cannot proceed without his approval.

Claude: One of the major restrictions applicable to contracts contained in the articles of association relates to enforcement of the contract by members against the company. Members are restricted in that they can only enforce against the company rights classified as membership rights (*Hickman v Kent or Romney Marsh Sheepbreeders' Association* [1915] 1 Ch 881). Rights in any other capacity are deemed outsider rights and cannot be enforced, as in *Beattie v E & F Beattie Ltd* [1938] Ch 708. A provision in the articles that Claude should be the company secretary for life is unenforceable through the articles by Claude, even though he is a member of the company, since the right to be the company secretary for life is not a membership right but an outsider right. The legal position that members can only enforce their rights as members was established in *Eley v Positive Govt Sec Life Assurance Co* (1876) 1 Ex D 88 in which Eley was named in the articles as the company's solicitor for life. The membership rights are defined as the personal rights enjoyed by the shareholders and include the right to attend meetings and to vote (*Pender v Lushington* (1877) 6 Ch D 70) and the right to receive payment of a dividend in cash where the articles so provide (*Wood v Odessa Waterworks Co* (1889) 42 Ch D 636).

In addition to these personal rights, they can also enforce their right for the company to be run in accordance with its constitution. Thus, in *Re HR Harmer Ltd* [1958] 3 All ER 689 the shareholders of the company were able to enforce their right as members for the company to be run in accordance with its constitution, namely through decisions of the board of directors. Since they were also directors of the company, it also meant that they could enforce their rights as directors. In *Quin and Axtens Ltd v Salmon* [1909] AC 442 the articles required the approval of both managing directors for certain transactions. When one refused to approve a particular transaction, the shareholders attempted to get round his refusal by passing an ordinary resolution authorizing the transaction. The court allowed the managing director's claim to enforce the company's compliance with its constitution.

Sales manager: This provision in the articles could not be enforced directly by the sales manager, even though he is a shareholder, for the same reasons as in the case of Claude.

The law provides that provisions in the company's articles relating to such things as the salary rights of the company's directors are still to be regarded as outsider rights. In *Re New British Iron Co, ex p Beckwith* **[1898] 1 Ch 324** the claimants had served the company as directors without any express agreement for remuneration, but the articles provided that the remuneration of the board of directors was to be the annual sum of £1,000 to be divided between them as they thought fit. On the company's liquidation, they claimed arrears of directors' fees. The court held that this provision did not constitute a contract between the company and the directors for the payment of fees to the directors. The court held, however, that, by accepting office on the understanding that the terms of the article applied, the article provision was impliedly incorporated in the contract of service between the company and the directors and they were entitled to payment. In the case of *Swabey v Port Darwin Gold Mining Co* **(1889) 1 Meg 385** the company's articles provided that the directors were to be remunerated at the rate of £200 per annum. Subsequently, the company by special resolution altered the articles to provide that the directors should henceforth receive £5 per month. Swabey, a director, immediately resigned his office and claimed for three months' fees at the old rate. The Court of Appeal held in his favour on the grounds that, even though article provisions incorporated into a contract of service must be on the understanding that the articles are alterable, the alteration can only be prospective and not retrospective.

If we apply the law established by these decisions to the case of the sales manager, it is clear that, although Edward can alter the articles to reduce the bonus to be awarded, it can only be altered prospectively. If the sales manager has therefore completed a period of service prior to the alteration on the basis of the incorporation of the article provision prior to its alteration, he can sue for the bonus for that period to be calculated at the old rate of 5 per cent.

Question 3

Fred and Ginger are directors and majority shareholders of Funtimes Ltd which organizes children's theme parties. They each hold 35 per cent of the issued share capital. Jerry, Lee, and Lewis each hold 10 per cent of the issued share capital. The articles contain *inter alia* the following provisions:

(a) Disputes between the company and members shall be referred to arbitration

(b) Fred and Ginger shall be directors for life

(c) If any member wishes to transfer his/her shares he/she shall offer them to the directors who will take them at a fair price

(d) The laundry service run by Jerry shall launder all table-linen, etc of the company.

Advise Jerry, Lee, and Lewis concerning the following situation:

(a) Jerry's laundry service has proved expensive and Fred and Ginger have signed a new, exclusive contract for laundering with Spin & Tonic Ltd

(b) Lee has become a shareholder/director of Sixes and Sevens Ltd which provides clowns and entertainers for private events including children's parties. Fred and Ginger have called a general meeting to propose the following, additional article: 'Any member must transfer his or her shares to the directors' nominee upon a request in writing by the holders of 75% of the issued shares.'

(c) Lewis, upset by the breakdown in relationships, decides to sell his shares and offers them to Fred and Ginger who refuse to buy them.

 Commentary

This problem question requires you to apply a number of principles of the law relating to the company's constitution. These include the enforceability of the contract contained in the articles, and binding the members and the company, and the restriction on the power to alter the articles where the alteration is an abuse of majority power.

 Answer plan

- Identification of the problems raised by the question
- Restriction on enforcement of outsider rights
- Alteration of the articles to compulsorily remove a shareholder
- Right of a member to enforce the articles against other members

 Suggested answer

The problem raises issues concerning the nature of the contract contained in the articles and the restriction on the alteration of those articles where the proposed alteration constitutes an abuse of majority control.

In respect of Jerry, he would clearly wish to enforce the terms of the contract under which his business is designated as the launderer for the company's linens, etc. While it would be unlikely for him to claim specific performance of such a contract, he would otherwise seek damages for the loss of the company's business.

In this situation, although Jerry is a member of the company holding 10 per cent of the issued share capital, the nature of the purported contract that he seeks to enforce against the company is a contract that is not in any way related to his membership rights in respect of the company since it is not concerned with his rights as a member. Neither is it concerned with the enforcement of a right that the constitution of the company be respected.

The relevant decision in this respect is *Eley v Positive Govt Sec Life Assurance Co* (1876) 1 Ex D 88 which decided that a person appointed as solicitor of a company for life could not, even as a member of the company, enforce this right against the company. The case established that members cannot enforce rights as outsiders contained in the articles (and see also *Hickman v Kent or Romney Marsh Sheepbreeders' Association* [1915] 1 Ch 881). The scope of who is defined as an outsider for this purpose is very wide and includes the directors of the company in their capacity as directors. Thus, in *Re New British Iron Co, ex p Beckwith* [1898] 1 Ch 324 the court held that directors could not claim enforceable contractual rights in respect of a statement of their right to remuneration contained in the articles, although they were indirectly allowed to enforce the right since it had become an implied term in the contract of service with the company.

In respect of Lee, the position is more complicated. He is faced with an alteration to the articles which will allow Fred and Ginger, the holders of 70 per cent of the issued shares of the company, to secure his enforced removal from the company if they gain the support of either Jerry or Lewis. Lee will try to contend that the proposed alteration of the articles is an abuse of majority power or, rather, not in 'good faith for the benefit of the company'. In *Allen v Gold Reefs of West Africa Ltd* [1900] 1 Ch 656 it was established that the court could set aside proposed alterations of the articles that were not bona fide for the benefit of the company as a whole.

The question then was how to assess whether the proposed alteration was bona fide for the benefit of the company as a whole. In respect of this, there were two approaches taken by the court: the objective test (where the court decided whether or not the proposal was for the company's benefit) which was favoured in *Dafen Tinplate Co Ltd v Llanelly Steel Co (1907) Ltd* [1920] 2 Ch 124 and the subjective test (where the court considered whether the members of the company, in voting for the proposed alteration, did so on the basis that it was for the benefit of the company) which was favoured in *Sidebottom v Kershaw, Leese & Co Ltd* [1920] 1 Ch 154. This issue was resolved in *Shuttleworth v Cox Bros & Co (Maidenhead) Ltd* [1927] 2 KB 9 where Atkin LJ stated:

> 'The only question is whether or not the shareholders, in considering whether they shall alter the articles, honestly intend to exercise their powers for the benefit of the company ... It is not a matter of law for the court [to decide] whether or not a particular alteration is for the benefit of the company; nor is it the business of a judge to review the decision of every company in the country on these questions.'

In *Greenhalgh v Arderne Cinemas Ltd* [1951] Ch 286 the court agreed with the correctness of the subjective test, but applied the 'benefit of the company' test in the form of whether the alteration was made bona fide for the benefit of 'an individual hypothetical member' as in this case the company had no separate interest in the alteration. The court concluded 'a special resolution of this kind would be liable to be impeached if the effect of it were to discriminate between the majority shareholders and the minority shareholders, so as to give to the former an advantage of which the latter were deprived'. In Lee's case it could be argued that the proposed new article, effectively allowing the expulsion of a member without cause, is not for the benefit of the company or 'an individual hypothetical member', although if the shareholders honestly believed it to be for the company's benefit then the alteration would not be challengeable.

In reality, rather than claiming under this ground, a shareholder in Lee's position would now petition under the **Companies Act 2006 (CA 2006), s. 994** on the grounds that the alteration is unfairly prejudicial to him and could ask the court to block the alteration of the articles under **CA 2006, s. 996(2)(d)**. Since it would appear that Lee is in competition with Funtimes Ltd because of his association with Sixes and Sevens Ltd, the court may find that Lee's exclusion from Funtimes Ltd is not unfair, even though prejudicial. Furthermore, the articles provide that all disputes between the company and members should be referred to arbitration. The company could seek a stay of proceedings in respect of any action by Lee: *Hickman v Romney Marsh Sheepbreeders' Association* [1915] 1 Ch 881. In *Fulham Football Club (1987) Ltd v Richards* [2010] EWHC 3111 (Ch) the court held that this would operate to stay a **CA 2006, s. 994** petition.

The issue for Lewis is the ability to enforce an apparent obligation in the articles to the effect that the directors, Fred and Ginger, must purchase his shares in the company. Relevant to this issue is the decision in *Rayfield v Hands* [1960] Ch 1. In this case, the articles of a private company provided that 'every member who intended to transfer shares shall inform the directors who will take the said shares equally between them at a fair value'. In this case, the directors claimed that the articles merely created an option but not an obligation to take the shares. The court held that the articles bound the directors, as members, to take the shares and that this obligation was a personal one which could be enforced against them by other members directly without joining the company as a party to the action. Accordingly, contrary to the statement in *Welton v Saffery* [1897] AC 299 that rights in the articles 'can only be enforced by or against a member through the company', such rights can be enforced directly against other members.

In conclusion, I would advise Jerry that he cannot enforce his right to provide laundry services to the company. I would advise Lee that he will have difficulty in preventing his removal from the company because it will be difficult to show the shareholders did not act in good faith in the interests of the company or that he was unfairly prejudiced where he is competing with the company. I would advise Lewis that, in accordance with the decision in *Rayfield v Hands*, the directors have an obligation to purchase his shares.

? Question 4

Unless the context otherwise requires, references in the Companies Acts to a company's constitution include—

(a) The company's articles, and

(b) Any resolutions and agreements to which **Chapter 3** applies (see **CA 2006, s. 29**). (**CA 2006, s. 17**)

Analyse the reference to resolutions and agreements in this context and any other agreements which impact on the constitution of the company.

Commentary

This question picks up the definition of the constitution of a registered company and considers the resolutions and agreements that have a bearing on the company's constitution. **Chapter 3 of Part 3 of the CA 2006** replaces the equivalent provisions in the **Companies Act 1985** on the registration of resolutions and agreements and on making these available to members.

The most important point to discuss in this respect is the courts' willingness to bypass the strict legal formalities of the Companies Acts for small, incorporated firms on the basis of unanimity, estoppel, or waiver.

A further important issue raised by the question is the possibility of a shareholder agreement as a supplement to the articles.

Answer plan

- Need for compliance with formal requirements of the Companies Acts to achieve constitutional changes
- Exceptions to compliance where unanimous, informal consent of members
- Criticism of these exceptions
- Shareholder agreements and their enforcement

Suggested answer

In this essay it is necessary to identify and explain the resolutions and agreements that also constitute the company's constitution, in addition to the articles.

The definition of the constitution comes in **Companies Act 2006 (CA 2006), s. 17** which refers to 'resolutions and agreements to which Part 3, Chapter 3 applies', with a forward reference to **CA 2006, s. 29** which sets out the resolutions and agreements affecting a company's constitution which are required to be notified to the registrar.

The section includes any special resolutions (**CA 2006, s. 29(1)(a)**) and any resolution or agreement agreed to by all the members of a company that, if not so agreed to, would not have been effective for its purpose unless passed as a special resolution: **s. 29(1)(b)**.

The reference to the constitution and the special resolution is obvious since the company may amend its articles—and thus its constitution—by special resolution: **s. 21(1)**. The reference to agreements agreed to by all the members of a company that, if not so agreed to, would not have been effective for its purpose unless passed as a special resolution, refers to the possibility that the articles of a company can be changed by a unanimous decision of the members.

This links to a number of cases where the courts have been willing to bypass the strict legal formality of the Companies Acts. Thus, in *Re Duomatic Ltd* [1969] 2 Ch 365 Buckley J said: 'I proceed on the basis that where it can be shown that all shareholders who had a right to attend and vote at a general meeting of the company assent to some matter which a general meeting … could carry into effect, that assent is as binding as a resolution in general meeting would be.' This principle is sometimes known as the 'unanimous consent rule'. The principle was followed in *Cane v Jones* [1981] 1 All ER 533. In this case, two brothers formed a company to run the family business. Each was a director and the shares were equally divided between the members of their family. The case concerned a claim that the constitution, which had originally given the chairman a casting vote, had been amended as a result of a unanimous decision of the members. The court held that the informal agreement had had the same effect as a special resolution altering the articles.

The decision in *Cane v Jones* was followed in *Re Home Treat Ltd* [1991] BCLC 705 where a company, in administration, was carrying on a business outside its objects. The administrator wished to continue the business and to sell it as a going concern. The court held that, since the company's only shareholder had agreed to the change of activity, it must be deemed to have changed its objects.

Although the unanimous consent rule has been criticised from a theoretical perspective (see, eg Grantham, R., 'The unanimous consent rule in company law' [1993] CLJ 245), it is clearly a pragmatic rule that recognizes the reality of informal decision-making in many small companies. Although the rule remains non-statutory, the **CA 2006** recognizes its continuing existence in **s. 281(4)**.

The **CA 2006** also contains an equivalent provision to **s. 29(1)(b)** in respect of a decision by the members of a class of shareholders (**s. 29(1)(c)**) which presupposes that a unanimous decision of the members of a class could as effectively amend the class rights as the statutory requirements: consent in writing of the holders of three-quarters in nominal value of the issued shares of that class, or a special resolution passed at a separate general meeting of the holders of that class: **s. 630(4)**.

Articles may be supplemented by a shareholders' agreement—usually a formal contract entered into at the time of the company's formation or subsequently. To be effective, all of the members for the time being should be parties to the agreement, which restricts their use in practice to small companies.

There are cases where the existence of a shareholder agreement is implied by the court. In *Pennell Securities Ltd v Venida Investments Ltd* (unreported, 25 July 1974) the directors proposed to call a general meeting to increase the company's capital by a rights issue on a nine-for-one basis. They knew that the claimant (with a 49 per cent shareholding) would not be able to take up the issue, reducing his minority holding to below 10 per cent. The court granted injunctions against the directors as violation of a tacit agreement between the members that the claimant's minority stake should remain at 49 per cent unless they otherwise agreed.

The company itself may be a party to such an agreement, but there are dangers in that the company may be held to have fettered its statutory powers. In *Russell v Northern Bank Development Corpn Ltd* [1992] 3 All ER 161, a company was set up in 1979. Soon after incorporation, an agreement was entered into between the five shareholders and the company that no further share capital would be issued without the consent of each party. In 1988, the board proposed an increase in capital by way of a rights issue.

Russell, a shareholder, obtained a declaration that the agreement was binding on his fellow shareholders (although not on the company itself since this would restrict the company's statutory right to increase its capital).

Agreement may be to the effect that each shareholder should be entitled to appoint a director. In *Re A & BC Chewing Gum Ltd* [1975] 1 All ER 1017 the agreement was that the petitioner, a corporate investor holding one-third of the capital, should have a fifty–fifty say in management. The agreement was in effect enforced on the equitable principles established in *Ebrahimi v Westbourne Galleries Ltd* [1973] AC 360 but it could, and should, have been enforced by injunction as a legally binding shareholder agreement. The terms may also provide that no shareholder should vote for alteration of articles or capital unless all members agreed, or that shareholders would not demand repayment of loans to the company except in certain circumstances. In *Snelling v John G Snelling Ltd* [1973] QB 87, the shareholders had lent money to the company and had agreed with each other that none of them would require repayment by the company while certain other funding arrangements were in place. The court refused to allow one of the shareholders to sue the company for repayment in breach of the agreement.

Shareholders may enter valid agreements restricting or determining the way in which they exercise their voting rights. These may be enforced by mandatory injunction. In *Greenwell v Porter* [1902] 1 Ch 530 the defendants agreed to do all within their power to secure election of two named persons as directors and to vote for their re-election. They later tried to oppose re-election of one of the two. The court granted an injunction restraining them from voting against the terms of their agreement.

The main advantage of a shareholder agreement is that the terms of the agreement cannot be altered by majority vote or special resolution and that the terms are, in principle, enforceable as of right—where appropriate by injunction—whereas rights under the articles may not be enforceable by shareholder minority. Shareholder agreements offer some protection to a minority shareholder whose avenues for redress (such as the unfair prejudice remedy under CA 2006, s. 994) are otherwise fairly limited. *Westcoast (Holdings) Ltd v Wharf Land Subsidiary (No. 1) Ltd* [2012] EWCA Civ 1003 shows the importance of clear drafting if an agreement is to be relied upon in a shareholder dispute.

The disadvantage of shareholder agreements is that they are binding on immediate parties only—not persons subsequently becoming shareholders. Such agreements bind only the parties to the agreement. In *Greenhalgh v Mallard* [1943] 2 All ER 234 it was held: 'If the contract ... only imposes an obligation to vote in respect of whatever shares the parties happen to have available, it follows that directly they sell their shares the contract is at an end—until possibly they acquire more shares ... If the contract ... ceases to operate when the shares are sold, then in the hands of the purchaser there can be no question of a continuing obligation which runs with the shares.' (Lord Greene MR)

Shareholder agreements are standard practice for joint ventures and management buy-outs.

Question 5

'By virtue of **s. 14** [now **CA 2006, s. 33**] the articles of association become, upon registration, a contract between a company and members. It is, however, a statutory contract of a special nature with its own distinctive features' (per Steyn LJ, ***Bratton Seymour Service Co Ltd v Oxborough [1992] BCLC 693***).

Discuss.

Commentary

There are many ways in which it can be said that the contract contained in the articles is of a special nature, many of which were highlighted in ***Bratton Seymour Service Co Ltd v Oxborough [1992] BCLC 693*** itself. Of these, the most significant are the fact that the terms of the contract can be varied by special resolution and that the members of the company can only enforce their contract rights to a limited extent, but other issues such as implication of terms and contractual remedies should also be touched upon.

Examiner's tip

Where, as here, there has been significant academic debate about an issue, an examiner will give you credit for some explicit consideration (or at least recognition) of this in your answer.

Answer plan

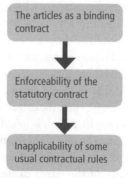

Suggested answer

Section 33(1) of the Companies Act 2006 (CA 2006) provides: 'The provisions of a company's constitution bind the company and its members to the same extent as if there were covenants on the part of the company and of each member to observe those provisions.' This establishes the nature of the legal effect of the articles of the company once registered. This is the equivalent provision to that of **s. 14 of the Companies Act 1985** and before that **s. 20 of the Companies Act 1948**, modified slightly to recognize that the memorandum is no longer a part of the company's constitution.

The contract contained in the articles (sometimes referred to as 'the statutory contract' or the 'section 33 contract') can be enforced by the company against the members of the company; by a member against a member; and by a member against the company.

So, it has been held that the company can enforce compliance with an obligation to refer disputes between the company and a member to arbitration if the articles contain a valid reference to an arbitration clause as in *Hickman v Kent or Romney Marsh Sheep-Breeders' Association* [1915] 1 Ch 881, while in *Pender v Lushington* (1877) 6 Ch D 70 the plaintiff sued to enforce his right as a member to have his vote recorded. In *Rayfield v Hands* [1960] Ch 1 the court established that a member could enforce against another member the obligation to acquire shares which that member wished to sell where such an obligation was contained in the articles.

Complications arise in respect of quite which provisions of the articles are enforceable under the statutory contract. In *Hickman v Kent or Romney Marsh Sheepbreeders' Association* [1915] 1 Ch 881, Astbury J stated that 'An outsider to whom rights purport to be given by the articles in his capacity as such outsider, whether he is or subsequently becomes a member, cannot sue on those articles treating them as contracts between himself and the company to enforce those rights.' While it is in accordance with normal principles of contract law that an outsider cannot generally sue on a contract to which he is not party, the statutory contract takes this a step further in denying that right even to an 'insider' if he is seeking to enforce rights in his capacity as an 'outsider'. Accordingly, in *Beattie v E & F Beattie Ltd* [1938] Ch 708 the court refused a stay of action in a case brought against the company by the plaintiff—a director and shareholder—since the dispute was in his capacity as a director not as a member, while in *Eley v Positive Government Life Assurance Co Ltd* (1876) 1 Ex D 88 the plaintiff was not permitted to enforce a right contained in the company's articles that he should be the company's solicitor for life, only removable on grounds of misconduct. The definition of outsider rights is broad and includes remuneration rights of directors contained in the articles. In *Re New British Iron Co, ex p Beckwith* [1898] 1 Ch 324 the court held that the articles did not constitute a contract between the company and the directors (although, since the directors had accepted office on the basis of the article, the terms were incorporated as an implied term in their contract of service). A similar decision was *Swabey v Port Darwin Gold Mining Co* (1889) 1 Meg 385 which held that the implied term was subject to prospective alteration in the normal way of any article.

The position on enforceability of the terms of the articles is complicated further by other cases, particularly *Quin & Axtens Ltd v Salmon* [1909] AC 442. In that case the company's two managing directors, Salmon and Axtens, held between them the bulk of the company's ordinary shares. There was an article to the effect that no resolution of a meeting of the directors for acquiring or letting premises would be valid if either Salmon or Axtens dissented. The directors resolved to acquire and let certain properties and Salmon dissented. At a subsequent general meeting, the shareholders passed similar resolutions. The House of Lords held that the shareholders' resolutions were inconsistent with the articles and granted Salmon an injunction restraining the company from acting on them. Lord Wedderburn has explained this as showing that members have an enforceable right for the company to be managed in accordance with its constitution (see Wedderburn, K. W., 'Shareholder rights and the rule in *Foss v Harbottle*' [1957] CLJ 194) and, provided that they sue in their capacity as such, members can thus indirectly enforce outsider rights by enforcing their right to have all the provisions of the constitution observed. However, the difficulty of reconciling the cases in this area has led to significant academic discussion with Lord Wedderburn's analysis subjected to further refinements by Goldberg, Prentice, and Gregory (see Goldberg, G. D., 'The enforcement of outsider-rights under section 20(1) of the Companies Act 1948' (1972) 35 MLR 362), Prentice, G. N., 'The enforcement of "outsider" rights' (1980) 1 Co Law 179, and Gregory, R., 'The section 20 contract' (1981) 44 MLR 526). Drury argues that the statutory contract should be viewed as a dynamic 'relational contract' characterized by longevity and incompleteness (see Drury, R. R., 'The relative nature of the shareholder's right to enforce the company contract' [1986] CLJ 219). While this analysis does not fully reconcile the cases, it provides a basis for understanding why rights in the articles should not be absolutely and uniformly enforceable, and an appreciation of the limits of contractual analysis in relation to the articles.

Quite apart from the complicated nature of the enforceability of the terms of the articles, there are other ways in which the statutory contract has its own special nature and distinctive features. First, it is clear that not all contractual remedies apply to the statutory contract. In *Scott v Frank F Scott (London) Ltd* [1940] Ch 794, the court rejected a request for the rectification of the articles to make them accord with the intention of the three brothers at the time of the company's registration. As regards alteration by way of an implied term, the court will not imply a term to change the articles by implication from extrinsic facts known only to some of the people involved in the formation of the company. In *Bratton Seymour Service Co Ltd v Oxborough* [1992] BCLC 693, the Court of Appeal rejected a request to imply a term, Steyn LJ stating:

> 'Just as the company or an individual member cannot seek to defeat the statutory contract by reason of special circumstances such as misrepresentation, mistake, undue influence and duress and is furthermore not permitted to seek rectification, neither the company nor any member can seek to add to or to subtract from the terms of the articles by way of implying a term derived from extrinsic surrounding circumstances.'

A term can, however, be implied to give business efficacy to the language of the articles in their commercial setting: *Equitable Life Assurance Society v Hyman* [2002] 1 AC 408. The power of the court to imply a term into the articles to give them business efficacy has been approved by the Privy Council in *Attorney General of Belize & ors v*

Belize Telecom Ltd & Anor [2009] UKPC 10 and in *Cream Holdings Ltd v Davenport* [2010] EWHC 3096 (Ch) the court stated that articles were to be construed like any other contract in the context of their commercial purpose.

Another way in which the statutory contract is of a special nature, distinct from a traditional contract, is the way in which the contract can be amended. Unlike a standard contract, the articles can be altered by means of a special resolution under **CA 2006, s. 21**, that is by majority vote rather than agreement of all the parties. Although articles can now be entrenched (**CA 2006, s. 22**), and this entrenchment can provide for unanimity, this would obviously be the exception rather than the rule. While the court has imposed restrictions on the alteration of the articles, such that they can only be altered 'bona fide in the interests of the company as a whole' (*Allen v Gold Reefs of West Africa Ltd* [1900] 1 Ch 656), this is obviously not equivalent to requiring the consent of all parties to the contract and so alteration of the statutory contract is quite distinct from contractual alteration more generally.

Accordingly, while **CA 2006, s. 33** gives contractual force to the articles of association, and a contractual basis seems appropriate in the context of the voluntary relationship that is the hallmark of a company, the contract is indeed of a special nature with some distinctive features.

Further reading

Cheung, R., 'The use of statutory shareholder agreements and entrenched articles in reserving minority shareholders' rights: a comparative analysis' (2008) 29 Co Law 234

Drury, R. R., 'The relative nature of the shareholder's right to enforce the company contract' [1986] CLJ 219

Goldberg, G. D., 'The enforcement of outsider rights under s. 20(1) Companies Act 1948' (1972) 35 MLR 362; (1985) 48 MLR 158

Grantham, R., 'The unanimous consent rule in company law' [1993] CLJ 245

Gregory, R., 'The section 20 contract' (1981) 44 MLR 526

Prentice, G. N., 'The enforcement of outsider rights' (1980) 1 Co Law 179

Rixon, F. G., 'Competing interests and conflicting principles: An examination of the power of alteration of articles of association' (1986) 49 MLR 446

Savirimuthu, J., 'Thoughts on *Russell*—killing private companies with kindness' (1993) 14 Co Law 137

Scanlan, G., and Ryan, C., 'The accrual of claims for breach of contract under s. 14 Companies Act 1985 and s. 33 Companies Act 2006: the continuing obligation' (2007) 28 Co Law 367

Sealy, L. S., 'Shareholders' agreements—an endorsement and a warning from the House of Lords' [1992] CLJ 437

Wedderburn, K. W., 'Shareholder rights and the rule in *Foss v Harbottle*' [1957] CLJ 194

Company contracts

Introduction

This chapter concerns the important topic of company contracts including pre-incorporation contracts, contracts beyond the company's capacity, and contracts outside the directors' authority—a topic that is a frequent subject of both problem and essay questions in examinations. This is an area that was changed significantly by the **First Company Law Directive 68/151/EEC (9 March 1968)** which was transposed into UK law initially by the **European Communities Act 1972**. The relevant provisions are now to be found in the **Companies Act 2006 (CA 2006)**.

Pre-incorporation contracts

At common law, companies could not be bound by pre-incorporation contracts and neither could the contracts be ratified after incorporation. That remains the case but following the implementation of the **First Company Law Directive** 'the person purporting to act for the company or as agent for it' is personally liable on the contract (**CA 2006, s. 51(1)**). The role of the **Contracts (Rights of Third Parties) Act 1999** is also of potential relevance in this area.

Contracts beyond the company's capacity

The *ultra vires* doctrine, established in *Ashbury Railway Carriage & Iron Co v Riche* **(1875) LR 7 HL 653,** decided that contracts outside a company's objects (the statement of a company's area of business contained in the company's memorandum of association until **CA 2006**) were illegal, void, and unratifiable. Over the next century, lawyers drafting multi-objects clauses managed to limit its effect so that by the 1960s the doctrine could be said to have been largely sidestepped apart from the odd exceptional decision.

Although the **Companies Act 1989** added **s. 3A** to the **Companies Act 1985** allowing companies to register 'to carry on a business as a general commercial company' able to 'carry on any trade or business whatsoever', and 'do all such things as are incidental or conducive to the carrying on of any trade or business' this was generally viewed to have been ineffective in reducing lengthy objects clauses.

The **CA 2006** dealt with this by giving companies unrestricted objects unless specifically restricted by the articles: **s. 31(1)**. Accordingly, for most new companies, it will not be possible for a company to contract outside its capacity. However, companies incorporated under previous legislation retain their old objects (now in the articles: **CA 2006, s. 28**) and, of course, companies may choose to restrict their objects (**s. 31**). In these situations **CA 2006, s. 39** ensures the validity of the transaction: 'The validity of an act done by a company shall not be called into question on the ground of lack of capacity by reason of anything in the company's constitution.'

Contracts beyond the powers of directors to bind the company

Companies may restrict the directors' power to bind the company. At common law, companies could avoid contracts beyond the directors' authority, making third parties vulnerable unless protected by the rule in *Royal British Bank v Turquand* (1856) 6 El & Bl 327 (*Turquand's Case*) and the doctrine of ostensible authority.

Here statute has also come to the protection of third parties dealing with companies, again due to EU intervention. Under **CA 2006, s. 40**, provided a person is dealing with the company in good faith, the power of the directors to bind a company (or authorize others to do so) is deemed to be free of any limitation in the company's constitution. This protection is removed where the parties include directors of the company or its holding company, or connected persons; here the transaction is voidable by the company: **s. 41**.

Contracts are made by a company, by writing under its common seal, or on its behalf by persons with express or implied authority: **CA 2006, s. 43**. Documents are executed by affixing its common seal or if signed by two authorized signatories or a director in the presence of a witness: **CA 2006, s. 44(2)**. The authorized signatories are every director or the company secretary. In favour of a purchaser, a document is deemed duly executed if it purports to be signed in accordance with **subs. (2)**. Thus in *Lovett v Carson Country Homes Ltd* [2009] EWHC 1143 (Ch) where a director forged the signature of another director on a debenture, the document was still valid. Companies are not required to have a common seal: **CA 2006, s. 45(1)**.

 Question 1

How effectively has the **Companies Act 2006, s. 51** dealt with the problem of pre-incorporation contracts?

Commentary

The topic of pre-incorporation contracts is relatively popular and fairly self-contained (although it can easily be combined with company formation and company contracts questions). The main issues here relate to the scope of the section and the limited protection it offers, particularly the inability to ratify pre-incorporation contracts.

Examiner's tip

Use your further reading to develop your ideas and raise issues and problems.

Answer plan

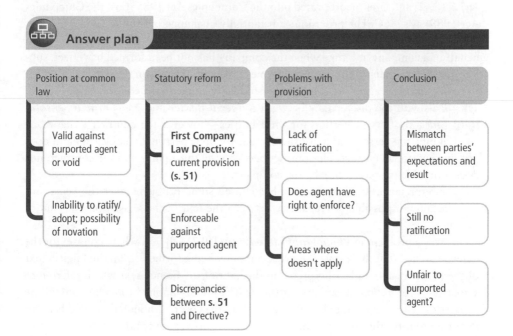

Position at common law	Statutory reform	Problems with provision	Conclusion
Valid against purported agent or void	**First Company Law Directive**; current provision **(s. 51)**	Lack of ratification	Mismatch between parties' expectations and result
Inability to ratify/ adopt; possibility of novation	Enforceable against purported agent	Does agent have right to enforce?	Still no ratification
	Discrepancies between **s. 51** and Directive?	Areas where doesn't apply	Unfair to purported agent?

Suggested answer

At common law, companies cannot be bound by pre-incorporation contracts and cannot 'by adoption or ratification obtain the benefit of a contract purporting to have been made on its behalf before the company came into existence': *Natal Land Co & Colonization Ltd v Pauline Colliery and Development Syndicate Ltd* [1904] AC 120. However, in *Kelner v Baxter* (1866) **LR 2CP 174** the court held that those contracting on behalf of the company purported to be agents of a non-existent principal and were, therefore, personally liable on the agreement. The position became more complicated following the decision in *Newborne v Sensolid (GB) Ltd* [1954] 1 QB 45 where a contract for the sale of goods was signed in the name of the unincorporated company followed by the signature of the founder and 'director'. The court held that the contract purported to be made by the company (the individual's signature merely authenticating that of the company) and as the company was not in existence when the contract was signed it was void. This was particularly problematic because a company is unable to ratify a pre-incorporation contract (as the company was not in existence at the time of the contract). While a company can enter into a post-incorporation contract on the same terms as the original contract (novation), this requires the agreement of both parties to the contract, which will not always be forthcoming.

The position was improved with the implementation of **First Company Law Directive 68/151/EEC (9 March 1968), Article 7** initially in the **European Communities Act 1972, s. 9(2)** and later incorporated into the **Companies Act 1985** (post the **Companies Act 1989**) as **s. 36C**. The provision, substantially unchanged, is in the **Companies Act 2006 (CA 2006), s. 51** and provides that: 'A contract that purports to be made by or on behalf of a company at a time when the company has not been formed has effect, subject to any agreement to the contrary, as one made with the person purporting to act for the company or as agent for it, and he is personally liable on the contract accordingly'. This deals with the discrepancy between *Kelner v Baxter* and *Newborne v Sensolid (GB) Ltd* and offers protection for third parties—however the contract is signed or entered into, the person acting for the company will be personally liable. What it does not do is create an enforceable contract between the third party and the contract; nor does it provide for ratification by the company.

The interpretation of the provision has caused some problems over the years, not least because of possible discrepancies between the text of the legislation and that of the Directive.

This was a problem in *Phonogram Ltd v Lane* [1982] QB 938 where counsel for the defence argued that the phrase 'before a company being formed …' in the English text of the Directive should be interpreted in the light of the French text which referred to a *société en formation*, meaning that the provision only applied to a company in the process of being incorporated. In the case before the court, although there had been an intention to form the company, no steps had been or were ever taken towards its formation. The contention was rejected by the court; the provision should apply whenever there is an intention to create a company, even before the incorporation process has commenced and even if the company is never actually formed.

There remain concerns over the scope of **CA 2006, s. 51**. The Directive presupposed the possibility of the company ratifying the contract and it can be argued that the intention of the Directive was that liability to the third party should primarily fall on the company and only in the absence of this should the persons acting on its behalf be personally liable. This also fits with the recommendations of the **Report of the Jenkins Committee (Cmnd 1749, 1962)** which recommended that 'a company should be enabled unilaterally to adopt contracts which purport to be made on its behalf or in its name prior to incorporation'. This has been adopted by many Commonwealth countries and was included in the abortive Companies Bill 1973. Nothing has since been done in this direction.

The **Contracts (Rights of Third Parties) Act 1999** could cover pre-incorporation contracts since it allows a non-party to enforce a contract provided that person is sufficiently identified and **s. 1(3)** of the 1999 Act specifically states that the person need not be in existence when the contract is entered into. The Law Commission acknowledged that changes to the doctrine of privity of contract could impinge on pre-incorporation contracts but was of the opinion that the matter should be left to be dealt with separately as part of the reform of company law. This matter was not in fact considered in the recent review of the subject, but the Act could enable a company to claim the benefit of contracts entered into on its behalf.

CA 2006, s. 51 deals exclusively with the liability of the parties in respect of pre-incorporation contracts and ignores the question of any rights of enforcement that these parties may have. While this is understandable in its origins as a protection for third parties, it is unfortunate as it created uncertainty as to the precise contractual position. This situation was resolved in *Braymist Ltd v Wise Finance Co Ltd* [2002] Ch 273 which held that the contract was enforceable by the person purporting to act for the company as well as enforceable against him.

There have been further instances which have shown the limitations of **CA 2006, s. 51**. **Section 51** applies only to pre-incorporation contracts and does not apply more generally to the problem of non-existent or misnamed companies, which has led to some criticism (eg Griffiths, A., 'Agents without principals: pre-incorporation contracts and section 36C of the Companies Act 1985' (1993) 13 LS 241). The section has been held not to apply where a company trades under a new name before the change is operative: *Oshkosh B'Gosh Inc v Dan Marbel Inc & Craze* [1989] BCLC 507—once a company is in existence (even if not using its intended name) **s. 51** cannot operate, which is obviously an issue where companies are purchased 'off-the-shelf'. Similarly it does not apply where a company had been described by an incorrect name: *Badgerhill Properties Ltd v Cottrell* [1991] BCLC 805. It was also held not to apply where a person contracted in the name of a company that had been struck off the register and a new company of the same name was subsequently incorporated to continue the business as there had been no intention to create the new company at the time of the contract: *Cotronic (UK) Ltd v Dezonie* [1991] BCLC 721. Furthermore, the common law position still applies to companies registering outside the UK (in this case Guernsey): *Rover International Ltd v Cannon Films Ltd* [1989] 1 WLR 912.

The law on pre-incorporation contracts is still an area where further reform would be beneficial. It is also questionable whether the spirit of the Directive has been fully transposed into UK law. Far from getting what the third party expects (a contract with the company), instead a binding contract is formed with the purported agent. This is enforceable against the third party as well as simply providing protection for the third party. Furthermore, the company has no easy route by which it can adopt the contract formed for its benefit, unlike in many other countries. Although Savirimuthu raises the issue of whether the 'agent' could assign the contract to the company (see Savirimuthu, J, 'Pre-incorporation contracts and the problem of corporate fundamentalism: are promoters proverbially profuse?' (2003) 24 Co Law 196) and the **Contracts (Rights of Third Parties) Act 1999** may also offer a way forward, these routes are clearly less straightforward than ratification.

While at first sight it appears entirely reasonable to impose liability on the person purporting to act on the company's behalf (particularly if this is a 'fallback' liability as seems to have been envisaged by the Directive), it may not always be fair to impose personal liability on such a person, particularly if there were several founding company members and it was simply chance that this individual was the person arranging that contract, particularly as he may not be in a position to ensure novation after the company's incorporation. While **s. 51** offers the opportunity to exclude liability (provided this is clear and express: *Phonogram Ltd v Lane*), it is unlikely that someone purporting to act on behalf of the company in this pre-incorporation stage will have sufficient legal awareness to take such a step. **Section 51** thus offers some protection to third parties, and is effective to that extent, but falls a long way short of dealing with all the problems of pre-incorporation contracts.

 Question 2

Tardis Ltd carries on business as a travel agent. There is no restriction on the company's objects in the articles of association. The articles provide that the board may delegate authority to a managing director or to individual directors who may contract on behalf of the company up to a limit of £50,000, beyond which the board's prior authority must be obtained.

The following agreements have been entered into on behalf of the company:

(a) The board agreed to sponsor a local student to attend a three-year course at a nearby university at a cost of £10,000. The course is unrelated to the business of the company.

(b) Adam, who acts as the managing director without having been formally appointed as such, contracted with Itma Ltd for the installation of a computer network for £55,000. He had not obtained the prior authority of the board for this.

Advise about the validity of these transactions and of the liability of the company and/or the board and the individual directors.

 Commentary

This problem question requires you to apply the law relating to contracts beyond the company's capacity and beyond the authority of the directors. While it is relatively straightforward, it does require an analysis of aspects of the statutory rules and consideration of their effectiveness to achieve the intentions of the **First Company Law Directive** which they are intended to implement. In this respect, you should consider whether it is necessary to fall back on the common law protection. It is also necessary in this area to consider aspects of the general duties of directors.

Answer plan

- Identification of the legal problems raised and the relevant statutory provisions
- Consideration of the law relating to contracts beyond the company's capacity and the capacity of Tardis Ltd
- Application of relevant statutory provision and consideration of the validity of the agreement and the liability of the company and the directors
- Consideration of the effectiveness of the relevant statutory provision relating to contracts beyond the directors' authority
- Discussion of the need to rely on common law protection of the rule in **Turquand's Case** and ostensible authority
- Application of relevant statutory provision relating to transactions involving directors or their associates and liability of the parties
- Conclusion

Suggested answer

The validity of contracts entered into by a company has traditionally depended upon questions of the company's capacity and the directors' authority. The first of these issues has been significantly eroded by statute, particularly the **Companies Act 2006 (CA 2006)** while the impact of the latter issue has also been reduced by statute.

We are told that there are no restrictions on the objects of the company. Since the coming into effect of the **CA 2006**, the problem of *ultra vires* (*Ashbury Railway Carriage & Iron Co v Riche* (1875) LR 7 HL 653) has been significantly reduced. Under the *ultra vires* doctrine, acts outside a company's capacity (which was determined by the company's objects) were void—this would have put the company's agreement to sponsor a student in doubt, as such an *ex gratia* agreement for a course unrelated to the company's business would be unlikely to be covered by the company's objects. However, **CA 2006, s. 31(1)** provides: 'Unless a company's articles specifically restrict the objects of the company, its objects are unrestricted.' This means that questions of the company's capacity do not arise. Even if the company did have restrictions in its objects the agreement would still be valid by virtue of **CA 2006, s. 39** which provides that the validity of an act done by the company shall not be called into question on the ground of lack of capacity by reason of anything in the company's constitution. This is wide enough to cover both contractual and *ex gratia* payments. Had the agreement been outside any restriction on the company's objects however, the directors would have acted in breach of their duties in failing to act in accordance with the company's constitution under **CA 2006, s. 171(a)** and would be liable to account to the company for the loss to the company as a result of the misuse of the company's assets, unless the agreement was ratified.

In respect of the contract with Itma Ltd for the computer system, Adam has clearly exceeded the limitation in the company's articles restricting the contractual authority of managing and individual directors to £50,000, beyond which the prior authority of the board is required and cannot therefore have actual authority to enter into this transaction. However, a company can be bound by the acts of its agent even in the absence of actual authority if the agent is found to have apparent (or ostensible) authority. The third party could argue that Adam has been held out as being the managing director of the company, that they acted in reliance on this holding out and that, since the contract would be within the potential authority of a managing director, it is enforceable against the company: *Freeman & Lockyer v Buckhurst Park Properties (Mangal) Ltd* [1964] **2 QB 480**. The issue then arises as to the effect of the limitation in the company's articles. Apparent/ostensible authority cannot be relied upon if the third party is aware of or is put on inquiry as to the limitation, and this could include constructive notice of the articles. However, here the legal position is now potentially covered by **CA 2006, s. 40**. This provides: 'In favour of a person dealing with a company in good faith, the power of the directors to bind the company or authorize others to do so, is deemed to be free of any limitation under the company's constitution': **CA 2006, s. 40(1)**. For the purposes of the section a person deals with a company if he is a party to any transaction or other act to which the company is a party (**CA 2006, s. 40(2)(a)**); and a person dealing with the company is not bound to enquire as to any limitation on the powers of the directors to bind the company or authorize others to do so, is presumed to have acted in good faith, and is not regarded as having acted in bad faith even if he knew that the act was 'beyond the powers of the directors under the company's constitution': **CA 2006, s. 40(2)(b)**.

From this it would appear that the company is liable on the contract to Itma Ltd. The only potential problem arises from the drafting of **CA 2006, s. 40(1)** as there have been questions as to whether the law is adequate to protect third parties dealing with a company through an individual director (except the managing director) acting without board authority. It has been suggested that, in order to be effective, the wording should be 'the power of the directors or an individual director to bind the company, or authorize others to do so'. A broad approach to interpreting the provision can be seen in the judgment of Browne-Wilkinson VC where, referring to **European Communities Act 1972, s. 9(1)**, he stated: 'the manifest purpose of both the directive and the section is to enable people to deal with a company in good faith without being adversely affected by any limits on the company's capacity or its rules for internal management' (*TCB Ltd v Gray* [1988] 1 All ER 108).

In contrast, in *Smith v Henniker-Major & Co* [2002] EWCA (Civ) 762 a narrow approach to the provision was taken in relation to the validation of an act by an inquorate board. Despite the approach in *Smith v Henniker-Major & Co* it seems probable that **CA 2006, s. 40** would apply in the current situation. This view is strengthened by the slight change in wording between **CA 1985, s. 35A** and **CA 2006, s. 40** so that **s. 40** refers to 'the power of the directors' rather than 'the power of the board of directors'. This is thought to expand the scope of **s. 40** so that it would cover the acts of individual directors such as Adam in this case.

This interpretation of **s. 40** means that third parties are unlikely to need the protection at common law of the Rule in *Royal British Bank v Turquand* (1856) 6 El & Bl 327 (*Turquand's Case*). Under *Turquand's Case*, it could be argued that persons dealing with the company are entitled to assume that the internal management rules of the company have been complied with; and that Adam has obtained the prior authorization as required by the constitution. This would allow the third party to enforce the contract against the company, provided they were not aware of the limitation nor put on inquiry as to the limitation.

It appears, therefore, that the company is bound by the agreement with Itma Ltd. Although **CA 2006, s. 40(4)** retains a shareholder's ability to restrain actions beyond the directors' powers, it seems from the question that the contract has already been entered into. Although the company is bound and so Itma Ltd is protected, Adam will still be in breach of his duty to the company under **CA 2006, s. 171(a)**. **CA 2006, s. 40(5)** makes clear that the fact that a contract is valid under **s. 40** does not affect any liability incurred by the directors by reason of their exceeding their powers.

Thus, in respect of the two situations the company would appear to be bound by both agreements but the directors could be liable to indemnify the company for any loss in respect of the second agreement.

? Question 3

Acts done by the organs of the company shall be binding upon it even if those acts are not within the objects of the company, unless such acts exceed the powers that the law confers or allows to be conferred on those organs.

However, Member States may provide that the company shall not be bound where such acts are outside the objects of the company, if it proves that the third party knew that the act was outside those objects or could not in view of the circumstances have been unaware of it; disclosure of the statutes shall not of itself be sufficient proof thereof.

(First Company Law Directive 68/151/EEC (9 March 1968), Article 9(1))

Analyse the problems in transposing Article 9(1) into UK law and the extent to which the doctrine of *ultra vires* has been abolished for registered companies.

Commentary

This essay question requires you to analyse the problems in the UK in implementing the **First Company Law Directive, Article 9(1)** and explain the current protection offered by the **CA 2006** in this respect. This requires consideration of the previous attempts to legislate and an analysis of where and why this legislation failed.

Answer plan

- Historical introduction to the *ultra vires* doctrine and the evolution of the traditional multi-objects clause
- Implementation of **Article 9(1) in the ECA 1972, s. 9(1)** and problems arising from the drafting of the legislation
- External abolition of the doctrine following the **Companies Act 1989** in respect of 'acts done'
- Internal retention in respect of proposed acts and liability of directors
- Analysis of the position post-**CA 2006**
- Continued liability of directors for breach of general duties under **CA 2006, s. 171**

 Suggested answer

At common law, contracts outside a company's objects were illegal, void, and un-ratifiable: *Ashbury Railway Carriage & Iron Co v Riche* (1875) LR 7 HL 653. This led to the draftsmen of company memoranda developing the multiple objects clause by which, in a series of sub-clauses, the company's objects extended to all sorts of potential activities. In addition, things which had previously been left to be implied as powers ancillary to the company's objects were specified as independent objects. These included the power to borrow. The courts fought back against this development, ostensibly for the protection of investors and lenders, and where the court identified the company's main object and found that this had been abandoned, it was able to wind up the company on the grounds of the failure of its *raison d'être*. This approach was finally defeated in *Cotman v Brougham* [1918] AC 514 where the court was forced to recognize the validity of a clause to the effect that all of the objects in each of the sub-clauses of the objects clause were equal and independent. A further development in *Bell Houses Ltd v City Wall Properties Ltd* [1966] 1 QB 207 recognized the validity of the subjective objects clause whereby companies could carry on any other trade or business which 'in the opinion of the directors' could be carried on alongside the other business of the company. Finally, *Re Horsley & Weight Ltd* [1982] 3 All ER 1045 recognized the possibility of the inclusion into the objects clause of non-commercial objects: charitable and political donations, etc. Political donations are now regulated by **Companies Act 2006 (CA 2006), Part 14, ss. 362–79**. *Ex gratia* payments to employees and ex-employees are also covered by statute: **CA 2006, s. 247**.

As a result, it could be said that by the end of the twentieth century—and even before—the problem of the *ultra vires* doctrine had been largely drafted out of existence apart from some problems. Thus in *Re Introductions Ltd* [1970] Ch 199, a company that had started out providing facilities for foreign visitors to the 1951 Festival of Britain and which was now engaged in pig farming, borrowed money on a secured loan from a bank for the purpose of this new, *ultra vires*, activity. In seeking to enforce its rights as a secured creditor, the bank relied on an independent object contained in a sub-clause empowering the company to borrow. The court held that the power to borrow could not be an independent object in itself, it was merely a power that had to be exercised for the legitimate purposes of the company. The distinction between objects and powers was largely removed by the decision in *Rolled Steel Products (Holdings) Ltd v British Steel Corpn* [1986] Ch 246. In effect, had the bank in *Re Introductions* been properly advised, they would have based their case on the validity of a subjective objects clause within the company's objects.

The impetus for reform came from **First Company Law Directive, Article 9(1)**. Since the UK was not a Member State of the then EEC at this time, there was no official English text of the Directive and—more importantly—no input concerning UK company law. As a result, the transposition of the Directive into UK law has taken a long time and it is still questionable as to whether it has been effectively implemented. The main problem concerned the term 'organs' of the company, which is a direct translation of the French '*organes*'. Since English company law limits the concept of directors as 'organs' to the identification theory for corporate criminal and tortious liability, the term was translated as 'directors' and also as 'board of directors'.

Article 9 was first transposed into English law by the **European Communities Act 1972, s. 9(1)** which referred to 'any transaction decided on by the directors' as being deemed to be within the capacity of the company. It also stated that the power of the directors to bind the company shall be deemed to be free of any limitation under the memorandum or articles of association. The use of the word 'directors' was held to exclude acts by one or some members of the board (except where there was only one board member) but was later extended to cover acts by the 'sole effective director'. The reference to a 'transaction' was held to exclude *ex gratia* payments, while the requirement of good faith was only resolved by way of a broad interpretation of the text in the light of the spirit of the Directive: *TCB Ltd v Gray* [1986] Ch 621. In spite of being regarded as generally ineffective, it was, however, replaced in virtually the same terms in **CA 1985, s. 35**.

The legislation was significantly revised by the **Companies Act 1989** with a revised **s. 35** and the removal of the doctrine of deemed notice in **CA 1985, s. 35B** and **s. 711A** (the latter not implemented for various reasons). The section was largely effective in abolishing the external aspects of the doctrine in so far as they related to third parties dealing with a company, largely by way of ignoring the concept of 'organs' and leaving it untranslated. Thus the provision became: 'The validity of an act done by a company shall not be called into question on the ground of lack of capacity by reason of anything in the company's memorandum.'

The *ultra vires* doctrine was not, however, abolished on an internal level and the section provided that a member of a company 'may bring proceedings to restrain the doing of an act which, but for subs. (1) would be beyond a company's capacity': **CA 1985,**

s. 35(2). The section further provided that the company could ratify an *ultra vires* action by special resolution, but that the directors were liable to indemnify the company in respect of any loss suffered by it irrespective of this ratification unless relieved of their liability by a separate special resolution: s. 35(3).

The legislation failed to take advantage of the second paragraph of **First Company Law Directive, Article 9(1)** and recognized the validity of all acts done in respect of third parties, even where they were aware of the fact that the act was beyond the company's capacity. The only exception was in respect of contracts where the third parties dealing with the company included the directors of the company (or its holding company) and persons connected with them: **CA 1985, s. 35(4)**. In such a situation the company could avoid the contract and, whether avoided or not, the parties to the contract were obliged to indemnify the company for any loss suffered by it and to account for any profits made—directly or indirectly—as a result of the transaction: **CA 1985, s. 322A**.

Thus, after the implementation of the **Companies Act 1989**, the *ultra vires* doctrine no longer posed a problem for third parties who had dealt with the company, and those contracts were able to be enforced by and against the company, but the company's directors were liable to indemnify the company in respect of losses. Members could still, however, prevent proposed actions by the company as being beyond the company's objects. The *ultra vires* doctrine continued to operate in respect of registered companies that were charities: **CA 1985, s. 35(4)**.

The **CA 2006**, based on a recommendation of the Company Law Review (Final Report, paras 9, 10) has adopted a completely different approach. Instead of companies being required to state their objects, companies have unrestricted objects unless the objects are specifically restricted by the articles. This means that unless a company makes a deliberate choice to restrict its objects, the objects will have no bearing on what it can do. Where the company has objects and acts beyond its capacity, the position is now covered by a simplified replacement to **CA 1985, s. 35** which states: 'The validity of an act done by a company shall not be called into question on the ground of lack of capacity by reason of anything in the company's constitution': **CA 2006, s. 39(1)**. In place of imposing liability on the directors in further subsections, the issue of liability of the directors is now covered by **CA 2006, Chapter 2 of Part 10** relating to the general duties of directors. Under **CA 2006, s. 171**, directors of a company must 'act in accordance with the company's constitution'. Should they enter into any dealings beyond the capacity of the company, liability to account to the company for any losses will now arise under this section.

An exception to this is charitable companies which will need to restrict their objects under charities legislation and in addition some community interest companies may also choose to restrict their objects. The Act makes separate provision for charitable companies which are covered by **CA 2006, s. 42**.

In conclusion, it took the UK government 17 years to draft legislation to implement the **First Company Law Directive** in respect of contracts beyond the company's capacity. This is continued in the **CA 2006** which in a radical step sidesteps the problem by offering companies the possibility of unlimited capacity.

Question 4

Jerry set up Ecotours organizing ecological tourism in the UK. Jerry brought in Lewis, an investor who did not want to be involved in the business. It was agreed to buy an off-the-shelf company and rename it Ecotours Ltd. Jerry was the principal shareholder and managing director; Lewis a non-executive director. The articles required the board's prior consent for contracts over £10,000.

Jerry found an ideal location for the agency and agreed to acquire the lease. He instructed Lee, his solicitor, to take the assignment in the name of Ecotours Ltd. The assignment was completed in January 2008 and a company was acquired and renamed Ecotours Ltd in February 2008.

The assignor, having received a better offer, sought to avoid the assignment in March.

In February, without the board's prior approval, Jerry contracted with Infocon Ltd for a £15,000 computer system. Jerry's wife is a major shareholder in Infocon Ltd.

Advise Jerry and Lewis of the legal position regarding these dealings.

Would your answer be different if, when the assignment was completed, an off-the-shelf company had already been acquired but the company's name had not been changed, and if the major shareholder in Infocon Ltd had been the child of Jerry's girlfriend from her previous marriage?

Commentary

This problem question concerns the topic of pre-incorporation contracts and contracts beyond the authority of directors where the parties include a director of the company or persons connected with him. In respect of pre-incorporation contracts, this requires the application of **CA 2006, s. 51**. For contracts beyond the authority of directors, you are required to apply the appropriate sections of the Companies Acts, including those concerning the identification of persons connected with directors.

Answer plan

- Identification of the problems raised by the question
- Application of **s. 51(1)** to the assignment of the lease to Ecotours Ltd
- Application of **_Braymist v Wise Finance Co Ltd_** concerning the enforcement of the contract
- Application of **s. 40(1)** to the contract between Ecotours Ltd and Infocon Ltd and recognition of the potential application of **s. 41**
- Analysis of the sections relating to the identification of Infocon Ltd as a person with whom the director of Ecotours Ltd is connected
- Application of **s. 41** and recognition of the legal position of Ecotours Ltd and the liability of the contracting parties
- Consideration of the changed circumstances

Suggested answer

This problem raises the issue of pre-incorporation contracts and their validity and enforceability and the issue of directors acting beyond their authority in respect of transactions with directors or their associates.

In respect of the assignment of the lease, the solicitor has been instructed by Jerry, the managing director of Ecotours Ltd, to take the assignment in the name of Ecotours Ltd at a time before the acquisition by Jerry and Lewis of an off-the-shelf company and its renaming as Ecotours Ltd. This is clearly a pre-incorporation contract on the interpretation of *Phonogram Ltd v Lane* [1982] QB 938. The **Companies Act 2006 (CA 2006), s. 51(1)** will apply making the person purporting to act for the company or as agent for it personally liable.

The legislation merely deals with the issue of liability on the contract and does not concern itself with the issue of the validity and the enforceability of the contract. This was, however, settled by the decision in *Braymist v Wise Finance Co Ltd* [2002] Ch 273. In a similar situation to this, concerning a contract for the sale of property by an as yet unincorporated company, the buyers attempted to escape from the contract by arguing that, as a pre-incorporation contract, it was void. The court rejected this argument and held that the contract was validated by **Companies Act 1985, s. 36C** (now **CA 2006, s. 51(1)**).

The main issue then to be resolved was whether the person was able to enforce the contract on behalf of the unincorporated company. In that case, on behalf of the company, it was argued that the contract should be enforceable by—among others—the controlling shareholder of the group of companies who had instructed the solicitor to draw up the contracts in the name of the unincorporated company. This was based on the 'identification theory' and the claim that he represented the mind and will of the company: *Tesco Supermarkets Ltd v Nattrass* [1971] 2 All ER 127. The court rejected this argument and held that the solicitor alone was the 'deemed contracting party' to the contract and that only he could enforce the contract.

Applying this decision to the facts of the present case, the assignment of the lease is valid and it can be enforced against the assignor by Lee, the solicitor instructed by Jerry.

The second aspect of the question involves an unauthorized contract since it is beyond the authority of Jerry as managing director but not beyond the company's capacity. The articles of the company require the prior approval of the board for contracts in excess of £10,000. Jerry has contracted with Infocon Ltd for a computer system costing £15,000. In this respect the contract can be validated under **CA 2006, s. 40**. This section provides that in favour of a person dealing with the company in good faith, the power of the directors to bind the company, or authorize others to do so, is deemed to be free of any limitation under the company's constitution: **s. 40(1)**.

A further complication here, however, is that the section applies subject to **s. 41** in respect of transactions with directors or their associates: **s. 40(6)**. Where a company enters into a transaction whose validity depends on **s. 40**, and the parties to the transaction include: (a) a director of the company or of its holding company; or (b) a person connected with any such director, the transaction is voidable by the company at the instance of the company: s. 41(2).

Persons connected with directors are as specified in CA 2006, ss. 252–6: s. 41(7). Under s. 252, connected persons include members of the director's family (s. 253) and a body corporate with which the director is connected (as defined in s. 254): s. 252(2)(a) and (b). Members of the director's family include the director's spouse or civil partner: s. 253(2)(a). As regards a body corporate with which the director is connected, s. 254 provides that a director is connected with a body corporate if, but only if, he and the persons with whom he is connected: (a) are interested in shares comprised in the equity share capital of that body corporate of a nominal value to at least 20 per cent of that share capital; or (b) are entitled to exercise or control the exercise of more than 20 per cent of the voting power at any general meeting of that body: s. 254(2)(a) and (b).

The question informs us that Jerry's wife is a major shareholder in Infocon Ltd. If this shareholding amounts to more than 20 per cent of the equity, Infocon Ltd is a body corporate connected with Jerry and s. 41 applies. The result of this is that the contract is voidable by Ecotours Ltd (s. 41(2)). Whether the contract is avoided or not, Jerry and Infocon Ltd are liable to account to Ecotours Ltd for any direct or indirect gain, and to indemnify the company for any loss or damage: s. 41(3). In respect of Infocon Ltd there is the possibility that the company would escape liability if it could be established that at the time of the transaction it did not know that Jerry was exceeding his powers: s. 41(5).

If, when the assignment had been completed, Jerry and Lewis had already acquired an off-the-shelf company but had not yet changed the company's name to Ecotours Ltd, the position would be as in the case of *Oshkosh B'Gosh Inc v Dan Marbel Inc & Craze* [1989] BCLC 507 and there would be no application of s. 51(1). In that case, Craze acquired an off-the-shelf company, E Ltd, and later changed its name to DM Ltd. Before the change was registered, the company acting through Craze bought goods from the plaintiff. In an action under European Communities Act 1972, s. 9(2) (now CA 2006, s. 51(1)), it was held that the section could not be applied to make Craze personally liable because the company had been formed when the contract was made. The issue of an amended certificate of incorporation did not imply that the company had been re-formed or reincorporated. If this was the case, the assignment of the lease in the question case could be enforced by the company under its new name, Ecotours Ltd.

If the major shareholder in Infocon Ltd had been the son of Jerry's girlfriend's previous marriage the situation would be different, depending on the child's age. Jerry's girlfriend would be connected with him if they lived together in an enduring family relationship: s. 253(2)(b). In addition, any children or step-children of Jerry's girlfriend would also be connected with Jerry, but only if they live with the director and have not attained the age of 18: s. 253(2)(d). If this was the case, the situation would still fall within CA 2006, s. 41; otherwise the situation would be that the validity of the contract would be covered by s. 40(1).

Further reading

Ferran, E., 'The reform of the law on corporate capacity and directors' and officers' authority: Parts 1 and 2' (1992) 13 Co Law 124 and 177

Gilmore, P., 'The execution of deeds by a company: the current position in England and Wales' (2010) 31 Co Law 3

Griffiths, A., 'Agents without principals: pre-incorporation contracts and section 36C of the Companies Act 1985' (1993) 13 LS 241

Milman, D., 'Company contracts: a review of the current and restated law' (2008) 240 Co LN 1

Savirimuthu, J., 'Pre-incorporation contracts and the problem of corporate fundamentalism: are promoters proverbially profuse?' (2003) 24 Co Law 196

Talbot, L.E., 'A contextual analysis of the demise of the doctrine of ultra vires in English company law and the rhetoric and reality of enlightened shareholders' (2009) 30 Co Law 323

5

Share capital

Introduction

The different categories of share capital are defined in the **Companies Act 2006 (CA 2006)**: issued and unissued capital (**s. 546(1)(a)**); called-up capital (**s. 547**); and uncalled capital (**s. 257**). In practice most companies issue shares fully paid up.

The aggregate nominal value of the issued share capital is credited to the share capital account (SCA). On formation, this is equal to the net assets of the company. Once the company begins to trade, the net assets fluctuate according to the success or otherwise of the business. The SCA, however, remains unchanged until the company formally increases or reduces its capital in accordance with powers in the **CA 2006**.

The company's share capital can be viewed as the creditors' guarantee fund, in that creditors of limited liability companies can only claim against the company's capital, and not the capital of the company's members. The doctrine of capital maintenance ensures: (a) the company has raised the capital it claims to have raised; and (b) the capital is not subsequently returned, directly or indirectly, to the shareholders. This principle gives rise to much, often complex, statutory law, based to a great extent on principles developed in earlier cases.

Raising capital

The most important topic under this heading is the issue of the allotment of shares for non-cash consideration. The legal position for public and private companies can be illustrated as set out below.

Public companies

(a) No issue against performance of future personal services (**s. 585**)

(b) Minimum payment pre-allotment—one-quarter of nominal value and all of any premium paid up (**s. 586**)

(c) Time limit for long-term undertaking, performed or performable within five years (s. 587)

(d) Valuation with report to company six months before allotment (ss. 593 and 597)

Private companies

(a) Shares can be issued in consideration of an undertaking to perform future services

(b) No minimum payment on issue/allotment

(c) No time limits for transfer of assets/performance of undertaking

(d) No control on valuation: *Re Wragg Ltd* [1897] 1 Ch 796

Capital maintenance

The rule in *Trevor v Whitworth* (1887) **12 App Cas 409** established that a company could not buy its own shares. The rule, now subject to important exceptions, is restated in **CA 2006, s. 658(1)**. The exceptions are:

- Acquisition of fully paid shares otherwise than for valuable consideration: **s. 659(1)**
- Acquisition of shares in a reduction of capital: **ss. 641–57**
- Purchase in pursuance of a court order under various sections including **ss. 994–6** (protection of members against unfair prejudice): **s. 659**
- Purchase of own shares as treasury shares: **ss. 724–32**

The rules also cover:

- Payment of dividends: **ss. 830–47**
- Financial assistance for the acquisition of shares in a public company: **ss. 678–80**

Shares may be issued for more than their nominal value: shares issued at a premium. The aggregate amount or value of the premiums must be transferred to a Share Premium Account: **s. 610(1)**. This account is also subject to the capital maintenance provisions (**s. 610(3)**) subject to statutory exceptions. The same is true for the Capital Redemption Reserve: **s. 733**.

 Question 1

Commenting on the law regulating the issue of shares in a public company for a non-cash consideration, L. S. Sealy (2001) called it 'a very elaborate (and costly) procedure…: a pretty large sledgehammer to crack a fairly small nut'.

Explain the procedure and the consequences of breach for the company, the allottees, and subsequent shareholders and consider to what extent Sealy's comment is fair.

Commentary

This question picks up the topic of raising capital and the regulation of the allotment of shares for non-cash consideration with particular concern for the position of public companies. You should be aware of the slack regulation of this area at common law from the end of the nineteenth century right up to the implementation in the **Companies Act 1980** of the **Second Company Law Directive 77/91/EEC (13 December 1976)**. In addition to explaining the operation of the regulatory system now in **CA 2006**, you are called upon to comment on whether indeed such complex and expensive regulation can be justified.

Answer plan

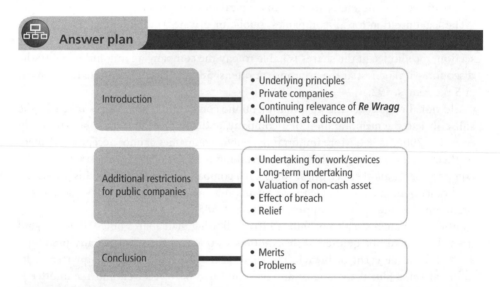

Introduction
- Underlying principles
- Private companies
- Continuing relevance of *Re Wragg*
- Allotment at a discount

Additional restrictions for public companies
- Undertaking for work/services
- Long-term undertaking
- Valuation of non-cash asset
- Effect of breach
- Relief

Conclusion
- Merits
- Problems

Suggested answer

The courts recognized the importance of a company's share capital as the creditors' guarantee fund even before the decision in *Salomon v A Salomon & Co Ltd* [1897] **AC 22** settled the fact that the incorporators of a company were not liable to indemnify the company's creditors. They elaborated detailed rules to ensure that companies raised the capital they claimed to have raised and then retained that capital in the business and did not return it—directly or indirectly—to the shareholders.

In relation to raising capital, *Ooregum Gold Mining Co of India v Roper* [1892] **AC 125** established that companies could not issue shares at a discount to their nominal value so the company could not issue preference shares credited as paid up to 75 per cent of their nominal value even though the company's ordinary shares were already trading below their nominal value. In *Re Eddystone Marine Insurance Co* [1893] 3 **Ch 9** the court held that companies could not allot their shares for past consideration since past consideration was no consideration. The protection offered by these decisions was weakened, however, when the Court of Appeal accepted that companies could allot shares in return for property and services and held that, in the absence of fraud, the value received by the company in respect of its shares could not be inquired into: *Re Wragg Ltd* [1897] **1 Ch 796**.

This continued to be the position until the UK was obliged to implement strict capital raising regulations in respect of public companies by the **Second Company Law Directive**. It remains the position for private companies. The Second Directive was implemented in the **Companies Act 1980** and the provisions are now in **CA 2006, Chapters 5 and 6 of Part 17, ss. 580–609**. The rationale of the rules is to ensure that the company receives the aggregate nominal capital and any premium.

The legal position for all companies, public or private, is that shares cannot be allotted at a discount: **CA 2006, s. 580(1)**. If shares are allotted in contravention of this section, the allottee of the shares is liable to pay the company an amount equal to the discount, with interest at the appropriate rate: **s. 580(2)**. The appropriate rate is fixed at 5 per cent: **s. 592**.

Additional rules cover the position for public companies. Thus, shares taken by the subscriber to the memorandum of a company, and any premium, must be paid up in cash: **CA 2006, s. 584**. More importantly, public companies cannot accept in payment of their shares or any premium an undertaking to work or perform services for the company or for another person: **s. 585(1)**. If a company acts in breach of this provision, the holder of the shares is liable to pay an amount equal to their nominal value and any premium plus interest at the appropriate rate: **s. 585(2)**.

Public companies are also prohibited from allotting their shares unless they are paid up at least as to one quarter of their nominal value and the whole of any premium: **s. 586(1)**. In the event of breach, the share is to be treated as if one-quarter of its nominal value plus the whole of any premium had been received and the allottee is liable to pay the minimum amount which should have been received by the company, with interest at the appropriate rate: **s. 586(3)**. Public companies must also not allot shares otherwise than in cash if the consideration is or includes an undertaking which is to be, or may be, performed more than five years from the date of the allotment: **s. 587(1)**. In the event of breach, the allottee is liable to pay the company an amount equal to the aggregate of their nominal value and the whole of any premium, with interest at the appropriate rate: **s. 587(2)**.

Subsequent holders of any shares issued in breach of these provisions will be joint and severally liable, with the exception of persons who are purchasers for value who, at the time of their acquisition, did not have actual notice of a contravention of the law, or who acquired the shares from a subsequent holder who was not liable: **s. 588(1) and (2)**. The Act provides that the breach of any provision in **Chapter 5 of the CA 2006** constitutes an offence by the company and every officer of the company in default and that persons convicted are liable to a fine: **s. 590**.

A further control over public companies is the requirement for valuation of any non-cash consideration, which is the area specifically referred to by Sealy. A public company must not allot shares as fully or partly paid up as to nominal value or any premium unless the consideration has been independently valued, with a copy of the valuer's report given to the company within six months immediately preceding the allotment and a copy to the allottee: **s. 593**. The very detailed legal regulations relating to the valuation are laid down in **s. 596**, with **ss. 1150–3** setting out the qualifications and independence of the valuer. A copy of the valuation report must be sent to the registrar of companies: **s. 597**. In the event of breach of **s. 593**, the allottee is liable to pay the company an amount equal to the aggregate of the nominal value of the shares, the whole of any premium plus interest at the appropriate rate: **s. 593(3)**. The valuation requirement is subject to exceptions under **s. 594** (arrangement with another company) and **s. 595** (merger).

Even more stringent regulations (both independent valuation (**s. 599**) and approval of the members (**s. 601**)) apply to agreements for transfer of a non-cash asset to a company within the company's initial period (two years from the date of issue of a trading certificate under **s. 761**) where the transferor is a subscriber to the memorandum and where the transfer is equal in value to one-tenth or more of the company's issued share capital: **s. 598**. The need for independent valuation under **s. 599** does not affect the need for an independent valuation under **s. 593** where the transfer is in consideration of shares.

In respect of non-compliance with **s. 593**, the Act makes subsequent holders of the shares jointly and severally liable with any other person subject to exemption for a purchaser for value without notice or a person acquiring from such a person: **s. 605**. The Act also provides for the criminal liability of the company and every officer in default: **s. 607**.

The harshness of the law is softened by the power of the court to grant relief in the event of liability in respect of contravention of these provisions (**s. 589(1)** and **s. 606(1)**). The court can grant exemption if and to the extent that it is just and equitable having regard to whether the applicant has paid or is liable to pay any amount in respect of any other liability in respect of those shares; whether any other person has paid or is likely to pay any such amount or whether the applicant or any other person has performed in whole or in part, or is likely to perform any such undertaking, or has done or is likely to do any other thing in payment or part payment for the shares: **s. 589(3), s. 606(2)**. An example of an unsuccessful application for relief is *Re Bradford Investments plc (No. 2)* [1991] BCLC 688. In this case, four members of a partnership transferred the partnership business to the company in consideration of the allotment of 1,059,000 fully paid £1 ordinary shares. Subsequently, the company claimed £1,059,000 from them as the issue price. Relief was refused as the court was not satisfied that the business had any value when it was transferred to the company. However, in *Re Ossory Estates plc* [1988] BCLC 213 relief was granted as there was clear evidence that the company had received property equal to (and probably exceeding) the value of the shares.

The question of whether the current regulation of public companies is excessive in this respect will probably depend upon the stance of the commentator. The law certainly imposes complex and costly obligations on the company which will be seen as excessive by company officers, particularly given that a company's share capital is no longer seen as a decisive factor in a lender's decision to do business with a company.

In the light of the current stress on transparency and corporate governance, however, the rules can be seen as a means of improving investor confidence in public companies.

It is clear that the regulations provide protection against obvious areas of potential abuse and, in so doing, ensure that the company does receive the capital that it declares it has received. While this capital may subsequently be lost in the course of business, at least investors can be confident that the company has commenced trading with the stated capital.

Some aspects of the provisions seem unnecessary, particularly the need for copies of the valuation report to be circulated to the allottee: **CA 2006, s. 593**. In addition, making the company criminally liable for breach of provisions is illogical and contradictory. While imposing a fine on officers in default can be defended, there is no logic in fining the company.

 Question 2

In March 2008, Utopia plc issued 2,500,000 £1 ordinary shares to Adam in consideration of the transfer to the company of four printing machines valued at £750,000 each and Adam's services as a design consultant for one year valued at £50,000. The first machine was delivered when the shares were allotted, but the others are to be delivered over the next two years as Adam's own printing business is run down. Adam transferred 500,000 of these shares to his wife, and 100,000 to each of his four children.

Consider the legality of the share issue and the potential liability of the parties.

 Commentary

This problem question requires you to apply the law relating to the allotment of shares in a public company for non-cash consideration to a factual situation. In particular it concentrates on the requirement that a public company cannot allot shares unless it receives as a minimum one-quarter of the aggregate nominal value and all of any premium.

 Answer plan

- Statement of the law relevant to the question: issue of shares at a premium, issue for less than the statutory minimum, absence of statutory valuation
- Liability of the allottee and subsequent holders
- Possibility of relief by the court
- Criminal liability of company and directors in default

Suggested answer

The legal issues raised by this question concern the law relating to the allotment of shares by a public company for non-cash consideration. The relevant law is contained in **Chapters 5 and 6 of Part 17 of the Companies Act 2006 (CA 2006)** and in particular in **ss. 585, 586, 588, 589, and 590**.

In this case, a public company has agreed to allot shares to Adam with an aggregate nominal value of £2.5m in return for a transfer to the company by Adam of four printing machines valued at £750,000 each and an undertaking to act as a design consultant for one year valued at £50,000. The aggregate value of the consideration for the share issue is on the face of it £3,050,000. Since the aggregate nominal value of the shares allotted is less than the apparent value of the non-cash consideration, it is clear that this is an issue of shares at a premium of £550,000.

In accepting an undertaking to do work or perform services as consideration for the allotment, the company is in breach of **CA 2006, s. 585(1)**. As a result, Adam would be liable to pay to the company an amount equal to the nominal value of the shares, together with the whole of the premium, and to pay interest at the appropriate rate as fixed by **s. 592: CA 2006, s. 585(2)**.

The company has allotted 2.5 million shares to Adam against the transfer to it of only one of the machines, with the remaining three machines to be transferred to it over the next two years. The performance of the service as a design consultant may also be postponed to a future date. The company has as a result transferred shares with an aggregate nominal value of £2.5m in return for an immediate consideration of £750,000. As a result, the company is also in breach of a prohibition from allotting shares except as paid up at least to one-quarter of their nominal value and the whole of any premium: **s. 586(1)**. If the company allots shares in breach of this provision, the shares are to be treated as if one-quarter of their nominal value, together with the whole of any premium, had been received and the allottee is liable to pay the company the minimum amount which should have been received in respect of the allotment: **s. 586(3)**. The minimum amount that should have been transferred to the company on allotment is one-quarter of £2.5m, namely £625,000 plus the total amount of the premium of £550,000, ie a total of £1,175,000. The company must credit the amount of £625,000 to the share capital account and £550,000 to the share premium account and Adam must pay an amount to bring his contribution to the company up to the required minimum—a contribution of a further £425,000.

A further complication is that we are told that the machines are valued at £750,000 each but there does not appear to have been a valuation report in accordance with **CA 2006, s. 593** in respect of an independent valuation in accordance with **s. 596(1)**; a valuer's report to the company in the six months immediately preceding the allotment of the shares and a copy of the report to the allottee. There is also no mention of a copy of such a report having been delivered to the registrar in accordance with **s. 597**.

If there has been a breach of **s. 593(1)**, Adam, the allottee, is liable to pay the company the aggregate amount of the nominal value of the shares, the whole of the premium, and interest at the appropriate rate: **s. 593(3)**.

Adam's wife and four children have since received 900,000 of these shares. The fact that some of these shares have been transferred to Adam's wife and children means that the wife and children will be jointly and severally liable along with Adam in respect of the amounts for which he is liable under **CA 2006, ss. 585 and 586** unless they are purchasers for value without notice of the shares: **s. 588**. There is also joint and several liability for breach of **s. 593: s. 605**. The court has power to grant relief to Adam and his wife and children under both **s. 589** and **s. 606** and the sections clearly rule out any double jeopardy for Adam and his wife and children.

If this agreement to transfer four machines and to provide advice as a design consultant has been honoured, or is likely to be honoured, there is a probability that Adam and his wife and children will be exempt from liability in whole or in part. The burden of proof would be on Adam and his family to establish that the company has received either total or partial consideration for the share allotment. A successful claim was made under *Re Ossory Estates plc* [1988] BCLC 213. In this case the vendor of property to the company received eight million shares as part of the consideration for the sale. No report and valuation of the property had been made in accordance with the **Companies Act 1985 (CA 1985), s. 103** (equivalent to **CA 2006, s. 593**) and a claim was made against the allottee for payment of £1.76m for the price of the shares. The court, however, granted relief under **CA 1985, s. 113** (now **CA 2006, s. 606**) on the grounds that the company had sold some of the property at a substantial profit and had undoubtedly received at least money or money's worth equal to the aggregate nominal value of the shares and any premium.

Even if Adam and his family escape liability in whole or in part, the company and any officers of the company in default have committed criminal offences for contravention of the provisions against allotment in return for personal services, non-compliance with the minimum payment requirement, and the failure to undertake a valuation in accordance with **CA 2006, s. 593**. This means that they are liable to a fine on conviction under **s. 590** (for offences in **Chapter 5 of Part 17**) and **s. 607** (for offences in **Chapter 6 of Part 17**).

Question 3

The rules relating to maintenance of capital of a limited liability company with a share capital are designed to protect the company's creditors for whom the company's capital is a guarantee fund.

In this context, analyse the function of the law relating to—

(a) The role of the capital redemption reserve in the redemption or purchase by a company of its own shares, and

(b) Controls on the payment of dividends for public and private companies

Commentary

This question relates to the rule in *Trevor v Whitworth* since the passing of the **Companies Act 1981**. This allows companies to acquire their own shares but subject to stringent rules to ensure that there is no breach of the doctrine of maintenance of capital. As an aspect of the same doctrine, it also concerns the regulation of the payment of dividends post the **Companies Act 1980** recognizing the legal distinction between private and public companies.

You are required to show understanding of the common law rules and the ways in which those rules were deficient in that they were either too rigid (in the case of companies acquiring their own shares) or too lax (in respect of the payment of dividends).

Having analysed the pre-1981 common law position, you must cover the reform of the law and show in what way it is relevant to and acts to promote the protection of creditors.

 Answer plan

* The doctrinal basis of the common law rule in *Trevor v Whitworth* and the regulation of the payment of dividends
* The changes introduced post **Companies Act 1981** and the relaxation of the rule in *Trevor v Whitworth*
* The need for the capital redemption reserve where the company redeems or buys its shares out of distributable profits as opposed to the proceeds of a fresh issue of shares
* The position regarding companies holding shares as treasury shares
* The basis of the reform of the law relating to the payment of dividends and the relevance of the distinction made between the regulation of public and private companies
* As a conclusion, an analysis of how effectively the regulation of these two areas operates to protect the company's creditors

 Suggested answer

The rules relating to capital maintenance have their origin in the common law. The rule in *Trevor v Whitworth* (1887) 12 App Cas 409 established that a company could not buy its own shares since this would be a reduction of capital which could only be achieved through a formal, statutory procedure. The common law also established that companies were prohibited from paying dividends out of capital since this was also a way of returning capital to shareholders: *Re Exchange Banking Co, Flitcroft's Case* (1882) 21 Ch D 519. The common law rules relating to dividends were flawed, however, in that there was no restriction against the payment of dividends out of current trading profits without making provision for the depreciation of fixed assets: *Lee v*

Neuchatel Asphalte Co (1889) 41 Ch D 1. Companies could also pay dividends out of profits without making good losses in fixed capital: *Verner v General & Commercial Investment Trust* [1894] 2 Ch 239; or to make good past revenue losses: *Ammonia Soda Co Ltd v Chamberlain* [1918] 1 Ch 266. The court also decided that dividends could be paid out of unrealized profits: *Dimbula Valley (Ceylon) Tea Co Ltd v Laurie* [1961] Ch 353.

The position changed when the **Second Company Law Directive 77/91/EEC (13 December 1976)** was transposed into UK law in the **Companies Act 1980.** This imposed stringent controls over public companies. In respect of the payment of dividends, the common law rules were replaced by statutory provisions which distinguished between private and public companies with the latter being more severely regulated to ensure capital maintenance.

The **Companies Act 1981** created a further radical change in the law by allowing companies to purchase their own shares in controlled circumstances. The rule in *Trevor v Whitworth* had already been modified in 1929 when the law was changed to allow companies to redeem (buy back and cancel) shares issued as redeemable preference shares. After the **Companies Act 1981,** the power to issue redeemable shares was extended to cover shares of all categories: ordinary, preference, and deferred. A further modification to the rule came in the decision in *Re Castiglione's Will Trusts* [1958] Ch 549 where fully paid shares gifted to the company but held by a nominee on the company's behalf were held not to violate the rule in *Trevor v Whitworth*. In a further major change to the law, the blanket prohibition on companies acquiring their own shares was made subject to numerous exceptions when companies could buy their own shares subject to complex regulatory rules. The effect of these regulations was to ensure creditor protection while allowing companies greater flexibility.

The capital redemption reserve (CRR) relates to the cancellation of shares redeemed under **CA 2006, s. 688(b)** or the cancellation of shares purchased under **s. 706(b)(ii)** and is designed to ensure respect for the capital maintenance rules.

Companies redeeming or purchasing their own shares can finance the purchase by the proceeds of a fresh issue of shares or out of distributable profits, defined as profits out of which the company could lawfully make a distribution: **s. 736.**

If the shares are purchased or redeemed out of the proceeds of a fresh issue of shares, then there is no reduction in the company's share capital account since the new issue takes the place of the old. Thus, if a company wishes to redeem an issue of 1 million 7 per cent preference shares and does so by issuing 1 million 3 per cent preference shares and using the capital raised to redeem the 7 per cent issue, the company's capital is maintained since the aggregate nominal value of the new issue replaces the cancelled issue.

Where, however, the redemption or purchase is out of distributable profits, the company's capital is reduced. In order to maintain its capital, the company must transfer the aggregate nominal value of the redeemed or purchased issue to the CRR: **s. 733(2).** The same is true where the redemption or purchase is wholly or partly out of the proceeds of a fresh issue and the aggregate amount of those proceeds is less than the aggregate nominal value of the shares redeemed or purchased. In that event, the amount of the difference must be transferred to the CRR: **s. 733(3)**. The CRR is a capital account and the provisions relating to the reduction of a company's share capital apply as if the capital redemption reserve were part of its paid up share capital: **s. 733(6)**. The company may, however, use the capital redemption reserve to pay up new shares to be allotted to members as fully paid bonus shares: **s. 733(5)**.

Companies may hold their own market traded shares as treasury shares subject to **s. 724**. The holding is limited to 10 per cent of the nominal value of the issued capital of the company where the company has only one class of share (**s. 725(1)**) or to 10 per cent of the aggregate nominal value of each class of shares where the share capital is divided into shares of different classes: **s. 725(2)**. If the company subsequently cancels shares held as treasury shares, the company's capital is reduced by the nominal amount of the shares cancelled: **s. 729(4)**. In this event, the company is also required to transfer to the CRR the amount by which the company's share capital is diminished: **s. 733(4)**.

The statutory rules relating to distributions, the payment of dividends, are now in **CA 2006, Part 23**. Distributions can only be made out of profits available for the purpose: **s. 830(1)**. These are its 'accumulated, realised profits, so far as not previously utilised by distribution or capitalisation, less its accumulated, realised losses, so far as not previously written off in a reduction or reorganisation of capital duly made': **s. 830(2)**. There are special rules for investment companies—accumulated revenue profits, see **ss. 832–5**.

A public company is subject to more stringent rules and may only make a distribution if: (a) the amount of its net assets is not less than the aggregate of its called-up share capital and undistributable reserves; and (b) if, and to the extent that, the distribution does not reduce the amount of those assets to less than that aggregate: **CA 2006, s. 831(1)**. A company's undistributable reserves are its share premium account, capital redemption reserve, revaluation reserve (the amount by which its accumulated, unrealized profits exceed its accumulated, unrealized losses), and other reserves that the company is prohibited from distributing by any enactment, or by its articles (**s. 831(4)**).

Shareholders are liable to repay any distribution if they know or have reasonable grounds for believing that the distribution was illegal: **s. 847(2)**.

In conclusion it can be seen that the function of the capital redemption reserve serves to maintain the company's share capital in the event of the company redeeming or purchasing shares wholly or partly out of distributable profits by ensuring that the company transfers the aggregate of that amount to an account that is subject to the rules on capital reduction. In so doing, it operates to protect the company's creditors. In respect of the payment of dividends, public companies cannot make a distribution that would reduce their net assets to below the aggregate of their undistributable reserves. This operates so as to maintain the company's capital. The position for creditors of private companies is less protected but certainly the anomalies of the position under the common law by which distributions could potentially be made out of capital have been removed.

Question 4

Owen, the MD of Grand Designs (GD) plc, a property development company, is the major shareholder with 5 million shares. In negotiations to bring into the company Peter, a wealthy businessman, Owen agreed on behalf of GD plc to acquire a property with planning permission for commercial development from Peter for £3m. Peter then obtained an unsecured loan of £2m from the South Bank and purchased 50 per cent of Owen's shareholding in GD plc for £5m.

Peter joined the board of GD plc, and shortly after, GD plc created a floating charge over its property portfolio to secure Peter's loan from the South Bank.

Consider:

(a) the legality of these transactions entered into by GD plc, and

(b) the rights and liabilities of Owen, Peter, and the South Bank

Commentary

This question calls upon you to show familiarity with and the ability to apply the law prohibiting public companies from giving financial assistance for the acquisition of their shares or the shares in their holding company. The law in this area has been simplified by **CA 2006** but many of the judicial decisions under previous Companies Acts are of relevance in analysing the situation and reaching a conclusion.

The question requires you to recognize and distinguish between contemporaneous and subsequent financial assistance and consider the principal purpose defence that can be raised by the company. It also requires you to consider the criminal and civil liability of the parties and the validity of charges issued in the course of any financial assistance.

Answer plan

- Definition of financial assistance and the distinction between contemporaneous and subsequent financial assistance
- Identification of the transactions that are potential breaches of the law and the possibility of their falling within the scope of the principal purpose defence
- Analysis of the limitations imposed on this defence by the decision in *Brady v Brady*
- Civil liability of the parties and the validity of the floating charge
- Criminal liability of the company and directors in default

Suggested answer

This problem raises the question of whether GD plc has been guilty of the offence of financial assistance under **Companies Act 2006 (CA 2006), ss. 677–83** in respect of facilitating the financing of Peter's purchase of 50 per cent of Owen's shareholding in the company. There are two situations which could constitute financial assistance: the purchase by GD plc of the commercial property from Peter for £3m and the creation of a floating charge over the company's property portfolio to secure Peter's previously unsecured loan of £2m from the South Bank. Although the **CA 2006** abolished financial assistance for private companies, it remains applicable to public companies (and private companies in a group with public companies).

According to *British and Commonwealth Holdings plc v Barclays Bank plc* [1996] **1 WLR 1** the provision 'requires that there should be assistance or help for the purpose of acquiring shares and that that assistance should be financial' (Aldous J). Financial assistance is defined in **CA 2006, s. 677** as including financial assistance given by way of a guarantee, security, or indemnity: **s. 677(1)(b)(i)** (which covers the creation of the floating charge) and any other financial assistance given by the company where the net assets of the company are reduced to a material extent by the giving of the assistance: **s. 677(1)(d)(i)** (this could potentially cover the purchase of Peter's property if the purchase price is in excess of the value of the property acquired). In *Belmont Finance Corpn Ltd v Williams Furniture Ltd* [1979] **Ch 250** four directors of the defendant company, with the connivance of two of the three directors of the plaintiff company, had sold its property worth £60,000 for the price of £500,000. The four directors then used the money to purchase all the issued shares in the plaintiff company for £489,000. The Court of Appeal held that the transaction was illegal financial assistance and a breach of what is now **CA 2006, s. 678(1)**. Even if the purchase of the property is at a fair value it could be argued that, if the principal purpose of the purchase was to provide Peter with the funds to acquire Owen's shares, this could constitute illegal financial assistance. This was the point made by Hoffmann J in *Charterhouse Investment Trust Ltd v Tempest Diesels Ltd* [1986] **BCLC 1**.

The law recognizes two types of financial assistance: contemporaneous financial assistance and subsequent financial assistance, and both are prohibited: **CA 2006, s. 678**.

As regards contemporaneous financial assistance, the offence is described as follows: 'Where a person is acquiring or proposing to acquire shares in a public company, it is not lawful for that company, or a company that is a subsidiary of that company, to give financial assistance directly or indirectly for the purpose of the acquisition before or at the same time as the acquisition takes place' (**CA 2006, s. 678(1)**). This could potentially cover the purchase of the commercial property from Peter which occurred prior to Peter's acquisition of Owen's shares.

Subsequent financial assistance is where a person has acquired shares in a company, and a liability has been incurred for the purpose of the acquisition by that or another person. In such a situation, it is not lawful for that company, or a subsidiary of that company, to give financial assistance directly or indirectly for the purpose of reducing or discharging the liability if, at the time the assistance is given, the company in which the shares were acquired is a public company: **CA 2006, s. 678(3)**. By issuing a floating charge to secure Peter's previously unsecured loan from the South Bank, GD plc is guilty of subsequent financial assistance since, in the event of Peter defaulting on the loan, the South Bank could enforce the floating charge against GD plc's assets. This is an example of indirect financial assistance in that the charge is created in favour of the South Bank rather than the actual person benefiting from the financial assistance.

Exceptionally, the law does not prevent a subsidiary which is a foreign company from giving financial assistance for the acquisition of shares in its holding company: *Arab Bank plc v Mercantile Holdings Ltd* [1994] 2 All ER 74.

Both of these offences are subject to the purpose exceptions under which the company can escape liability on the ground that either the company's principal purpose in giving the assistance is not to give it for the purpose of any such acquisition (in the case of contemporaneous financial assistance) or to reduce or discharge any liability incurred (in the case of subsequent financial assistance) and the assistance is given in good faith in the interests of the company, or that the giving of the assistance (or the reduction or discharge) is only an incidental part of some larger purpose of the company and the assistance is given in good faith in the interests of the company: **CA 2006, s. 678(2) and (4)**.

The scope of this was severely restricted by the House of Lords' decision in *Brady v Brady* [1989] AC 755 where it rejected the decision of the High Court and the Court of Appeal that financial assistance as part of a major company reorganization to resolve the conflict and deadlock between the two brothers who controlled it and to avoid its likely liquidation fell within the exception. The House of Lords distinguished between a purpose and the reason why a purpose is formed and held that the larger purpose must be something more than the reason why the transaction was entered into. This decision has significantly limited the scope of the purpose exceptions, although the exception was held to have been satisfied in *Re Uniq plc* [2011] EWHC 749.

Applying the cases and the reasoning in *Brady v Brady* it is highly unlikely that GD plc could argue that the financial assistance is to achieve the larger purpose of bringing Peter and his expertise into the company, even if this were in the interests of the company.

In respect of the purchase of Peter's property, if this was a purchase at a substantial overvaluation, Owen could be liable to account to the company for any loss to the company in breach of his fiduciary duties. In addition, if Peter received the consideration knowing that the transaction was improper and an abuse of Owen's fiduciary duties, he could also be liable as a constructive trustee to account to GD plc: *Belmont Finance Corpn Ltd v Williams Furniture Ltd* (No. 2) [1980] 1 All ER 393; *Royal Brunei Airlines Sdn Bhd v Tan Kok Ming* [1995] 2 AC 378. It is also possible for the company to sue Owen and Peter for damages for conspiracy, despite the company being a party to the transaction: *Belmont Finance Corpn Ltd v Williams Furniture Ltd* [1979] Ch 250. It could also be illegal financial assistance even where the purchase was not at an overvalue if the principal purpose behind the purchase was not the acquisition of a property for the company but to facilitate Peter's share acquisition.

In respect of the creation of the floating charge over GD plc's assets to secure the unsecured loan obtained by Peter from the South Bank, the charge will be illegal and unenforceable against the company by the bank: *Heald v O'Connor* [1971] 1 WLR 497.

Prohibited financial assistance is a criminal offence committed by the company and every officer of the company who is in default: CA 2006, s. 680(1). A person convicted on indictment is liable to imprisonment for a term not exceeding two years and/or a fine. On summary conviction they are liable in England and Wales to imprisonment for a term not exceeding 12 months and/or a fine not exceeding the statutory maximum: s. 680(2). It has also been held that causing a company to give financial assistance is evidence of unfitness under the **Company Directors Disqualification Act 1986, s. 6**: *Re Continental Assurance Co of London plc* [1997] 1 BCLC 48.

Further reading

Dachnert, A., 'The minimum capital requirement—an anachronism under conservation: Parts 1 and 2' (2009) 30 Co Law 3 and 34

Ferran, E., 'Corporate transactions and financial assistance: shifting policy perceptions but static law' [2004] CLJ 225

Ferran, E., 'Creditors' interests and "core" company law' (1999) 20 Co Law 314

Judge, S., 'When is the capital maintenance rule breached?' [2011] F. & C.L.P 5

Pickering, M. A., 'Shareholder voting rights and company control' (1965) 81 LQR 248

Proctor, C., 'Financial Assistance: new proposals and new perspectives?' (2007) 28 Co Law 3

6

Loan capital

Introduction

This chapter deals with long-term borrowing by companies. For most companies share capital meets only a small part of their capital needs and loan capital is therefore of huge importance. This chapter introduces the following important topics:

(a) The legal nature of and the various forms of debentures issued by companies

(b) The legal distinction between fixed and floating charges created by companies over their assets as security for loans

(c) The registration of charges and the consequences of non-registration or late registration, and

(d) The priority of charges on insolvency and the avoidance of charges under the **Insolvency Act 1986**

This is a complex area of the law not least because there is no real legal or commercial definition of a debenture, and the distinction between fixed and floating charges has not always been clear. The criteria for identifying fixed and floating charges is an area of great importance for students of company law.

The registration of charges has seemingly been on the point of reform for decades, with major reform in the **Companies Act 1989** never implemented. Although the **Companies Act 2006 (CA 2006)** initially largely re-enacted the position under the **Companies Act 1985**, significant amendments have been made subsequently by the **Companies Act 2006 (Amendment of Part 25) Regulations 2013 (SI 2013/600)**. Accordingly, from 6 April 2013, **CA 2006, Part 25, Chapters 1** and **2** have been replaced with a new **Chapter A1** applying to charges created on or after 6 April 2013 (charges created before that date remain subject to the former **Chapters 1** and **2**).

The topic obviously overlaps with share capital in considering the financing of a company, but it also overlaps with corporate insolvency in the sense that it is possible for the liquidator of a company to set aside charges created by companies in the run up to the commencement of insolvency. The importance of this is that it releases assets that would otherwise be the preserve of the secured creditor to be distributed to unsecured creditors. In this respect, it is important to understand the increased vulnerability of floating charges as against fixed charges. In the context of corporate insolvency, it is also important to be aware of the clear advantage of the secured creditor with a fixed charge over the secured creditor with a floating charge. The former ranks above all other creditors, including the expenses of the liquidation, while the latter ranks in a lowly position just above the ordinary, unsecured creditors.

? Question 1

'In my opinion a debenture means a document which either creates a debt or acknowledges it, and any document which fulfils either of these conditions is a "debenture". I cannot find any precise legal definition of the term, it is not either in law or commerce a strictly technical term, or what is called a term of art.' (Per Chitty, J: *Levy v Abercorris Slate and Slab Co* **(1887) 37 Ch D 260**)

Discuss.

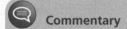 Commentary

This essay question requires you to consider this definition of a debenture and compare and contrast it to the statutory definition in order to see whether something more precise can emerge. In effect, the statutory definition is even less informative than this judicial pronouncement of 125 years ago. The problem essentially is the wide range of debentures that can be identified and you need to analyse the differences between them. An essential area of confusion is that the term can be used to cover the acknowledgement of unsecured loans as well as referring to a document that identifies and creates a charge over the company's assets as security for the charge.

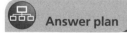 Answer plan

- Statutory definition of debenture and different types of debenture: single, debentures in a series, and debenture stock
- Secured and unsecured debentures
- Perpetual, redeemable, and convertible debentures
- Registered and bearer debentures
- Priority of debenture holders in company insolvency

Suggested answer

The statutory definition of a debenture as including 'debenture stock, bonds and any other securities of a company, whether or not constituting a charge on the assets of the company' (**Companies Act 2006 (CA 2006), s. 738**) is every bit as non-informative as this judicial attempt at a definition at the end of the nineteenth century. The source of the problem in establishing a clear definition is that the term 'debenture' covers an enormous spectrum of instruments in connection with corporate borrowing—simply any document evidencing a debt of any kind.

The most confusing aspect of the definition is the reference to the existence of an instrument as a debenture 'whether or not constituting a charge on the assets of the company'. In spite of this, both in commercial usage and as generally understood, the term refers to a document evidencing a loan secured by charges over the company's assets. In recognition of this, the Listing Rules require that any issue of unsecured debentures should be referred to as an 'unsecured debenture' and in practice it is more common in that situation to avoid the term altogether and use a term such as 'loan stock' or 'loan notes' as an alternative.

The definition also encompasses single debentures where the company issues an instrument acknowledging its indebtedness to a single lender. This is a typical transaction between a company and the company's bank and the instrument will generally be in the standard form of the bank. A debenture can also be created in favour of a single loan raised from a number of creditors. In this case there will be a number of instruments issued by the company in a series evidencing the company's indebtedness and usually secured by charges over the company's assets. This is called a debenture in a series and the individual debenture holders will rank as creditors equally (*in pari passu*) in the event of the default or insolvency of the company. If this form of loan is secured on the company's assets, the instrument will create charges in favour of a trustee for the debenture holders; normally a trust corporation or an insurance company by means of a trust deed.

The most complex form of debenture is debenture stock (sometimes referred to as bonds). This will concern a quoted company whose securities are listed on the Stock Exchange or a secondary market. The company will raise a loan which will be converted to stock in the sense that the total loan will be divided into units of currency (£1). Investors advancing money to the company will be issued debenture stock certificates evidencing their total personal loan to the company forming part of the total loan. The advantage to the investor is that the debenture stock can be traded on the stock market in the same way as shares. The statutory provisions for transfer of securities apply to shares and debentures: **CA 2006, ss. 770–8 and 783–7**. If the issue is secured, the company will once again create charges over its assets by way of a trust deed to a trust corporation or insurance company which will hold the charges on trust for the debenture stock holders.

The advantage of a trust deed in both debentures in a series and debenture stock is that the company can deal with the trustee should it wish to amend the details of the charged property. It is also an advantage to the debenture holders since the trustee could also be appointed a director of the company to oversee and protect the debenture holders' interests.

The major difference between a debenture secured by a charge over the company's property rather than a mortgage is that a debenture can be perpetual. The **CA 2006** provides that debentures or a deed for securing debentures is not invalid simply because the debentures are: (a) irredeemable; or (b) redeemable only: (i) on the happening of a contingency (however remote); or (ii) on the expiration of a period (however long), any rule of equity notwithstanding: **s. 739**.

The reference to the rule of equity is to the rule against 'clogging' the equity of redemption of a mortgage. This refers to inserting terms into the mortgage restricting the mortgagor's right to redeem the mortgage beyond a reasonable time. In *Knightsbridge Estates Trust Ltd v Byrne* [1940] AC 613, the House of Lords held that a mortgage of a freehold property by the appellants to Byrne, with a covenant to repay the money by 80 half-yearly instalments, was a debenture and not a mortgage, and that the postponement of the right to redeem for 40 years was not void as a clog on the equity of redemption.

A further distinction is that there can be registered debentures and bearer debentures, although bearer instruments are extremely rare in the UK. If the debentures are registered, then the company has a legal obligation to register an issue of debentures as soon as practicable but in any event within two months of their allotment: **CA 2006, s. 741**. Where the company issue is debenture stock, the company must issue debenture stock certificates within two months of the allotment: **s. 769**. There is no statutory requirement for companies to keep a register of debenture holders, but if such a register is kept then it must be available for inspection at the company's registered office or a place permitted under regulations made under **s. 1136**: **s. 743**. (The same applies to the obligatory registers of members: see **s. 114**).

Debentures (more normally debenture stock) can be expressed to be redeemable or convertible into shares. Redeemable debentures allow the company to buy them back in and cancel them in accordance with the terms of the debenture. Convertible debentures have the possibility of being converted into shares of the same nominal value. If debentures are convertible, they cannot be issued at discount in order to ensure compliance with the rules of raising and maintenance of share capital. Non-convertible debentures can be issued at a discount to their nominal value.

In respect of debentures and debenture stock, the debenture holder/debenture stockholder will receive a return on the loan in the form of fixed interest. This is a charge on the company and is payable by the company whether or not the company has made a profit and can therefore pay out a dividend in respect of its shares.

The priority of the debenture holder as a creditor in the event of the insolvent liquidation of the company depends on the nature of the charges—if any—securing the loan. Where the loan is secured by a fixed charge over specific assets of the company, the debenture holders will rank ahead of all the other creditors of the company, including the expenses of the liquidation. Where secured by a floating charge over the company's assets, the debenture holder will rank after the preferential creditors of the company and above the ordinary unsecured creditors of the company. In many cases the debenture will be secured by a combination of fixed and floating charges.

 Question 2

'A specific charge, I think, is one that without more fastens on ascertained and definite property or property capable of being ascertained and defined; a floating charge, on the other hand, is ambulatory and shifting in its nature, hovering over and so to speak floating with the property which it is intended to affect until some event occurs or some act is done which causes it to settle and fasten on the subject of the charge ...' (Per Lord Macnaghten: *Illingworth v Houldsworth* **[1904] AC 355**)

Analyse the judicial application of the distinguishing characteristics of fixed and floating charges, particularly in the context of fixed charges over fluctuating assets and book debts.

 Commentary

This is one of the most complex aspects of company borrowing. Creditors will generally require some form of security in respect of advances to the company and companies (and limited liability partnerships) have the choice of creating fixed and/or floating charges over their assets as opposed to sole traders and general partnerships which cannot create floating charges. Once floating charges were recognized and their characteristics were identified at the beginning of the twentieth century, there was for a long time no problem in distinguishing between fixed and floating charges. This all changed in the 1980s when creditors tried to create fixed charges over fluctuating assets including book debts and chattels. You need to analyse the problems faced by the court regarding attempts by legal draftsmen to extend fixed charges beyond their original scope and the decision of the House of Lords in this respect.

 Answer plan

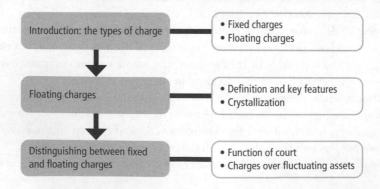

Introduction: the types of charge	• Fixed charges • Floating charges
Floating charges	• Definition and key features • Crystallization
Distinguishing between fixed and floating charges	• Function of court • Charges over fluctuating assets

Suggested answer

Fixed (or specific) charges are legal or equitable charges created by the company over specific, identified assets. The fundamental characteristic of fixed charges is that the company cannot deal with or dispose of the charged asset without the chargee's consent. A fixed charge can be created over present and future assets but in the case of future assets, the asset must be sufficiently described so as to be identifiable when it is finally acquired.

A fixed charge is generally created over freehold or leasehold property, fixed plant and machinery although fixed charges can be created over less permanent assets including receivables (or book debts). Secured creditors will always favour a fixed over a floating charge wherever possible for the advantage that gives them in priority on the insolvency of the company and this has led to complex attempts to create fixed charges in ever-widening circumstances.

The floating charge is 'an equitable charge on the assets for the time being of a going concern' (*Governments Stock and Other Securities Investment Co Ltd v Manila Railway Co Ltd* [1897] AC 81), first legally recognized in *Re Panama, New Zealand and Australian Royal Mail Co* (1870) 5 Ch App 318. The most commonly accepted definition is given by Romer LJ in *Re Yorkshire Woolcombers Association Ltd* [1903] 2 Ch 284:

> '…if a charge has the three characteristics that I am about to mention, it is a floating charge: (1) If it is a charge on a class of assets of a company present and future; (2) if that class is one which, in the ordinary course of the business of the company, would be changing from time to time; and (3) if you find that by the charge it is contemplated that, until some future step is taken by or on behalf of those interested in the charge, the company may carry on its business in the ordinary way as far as concerns the particular class of assets I am dealing with.'

Accordingly the main characteristics of a floating charge are that it is a charge on some or all of the assets of the company present and future where the assets change in the ordinary course of the company's business, and until crystallization the company may treat the assets as if uncharged. It is this third aspect that is the essential characteristic of a floating charge that distinguishes it from a fixed charge.

Crystallization is the event that causes the charge to cease to float over the body of assets covered by the charge and to attach to those assets comprising that class at the time of crystallization. This will usually be a formal act taken by the chargeholder (such as the appointment of a receiver or administrator or the giving of notice) but it can also be the happening of an event not directly triggered by the chargeholder (such as the commencement of the winding up, or where the company ceases to be a 'going concern'(*Re Woodroffes (Musical Instruments) Ltd* [1985] 3 WLR 543)). Crystallisation can also occur under the terms of an automatic crystallization clause (*Re Brightlife Ltd* [1987] Ch 200) although the **Insolvency Act 1986, s. 251** provides that charges created as floating charges rank as such and so cannot change their position in the order of priority of creditors even if crystallized before commencement of the liquidation, administration, or receivership. Until crystallisation the floating charge is not a charge on any individual asset of the company: *Evans v Rival Granite Quarries Ltd* [1910] 2 KB 979.

It is for the court to determine whether a charge is a fixed charge or a floating charge, irrespective of the description of the charge in the instrument creating the charge: *Re Armagh Shoes Ltd* [1984] BCLC 405. This is particularly important in respect of attempts to create fixed charges over a range of assets not previously thought capable of being so charged. In *Siebe Gorman & Co Ltd v Barclays Bank Ltd* [1979] 2 Lloyd's Rep 142, the court recognized a fixed charge over receivables (book debts) due to the fact that the charging instrument required the debts to be credited to a specific bank account and restricted the company's right to dispose of the monies paid into this account. In this case, there was no problem since the chargeholder was a bank. Even for banks, however, the situation has not always been straightforward. In *Royal Trust Bank v National Westminster Bank plc* [1996] 2 BCLC 682 the chargee bank was given the right under the charging instrument to demand that the company should open a dedicated account into which it should pay all monies received on collection of debts. In effect, the monies collected went into the company's ordinary trading account. As a result, the charge was held to be a floating rather than a fixed charge. In *William Gaskell Group Ltd v Highley* [1994] 1 BCLC 197 it was held that a charge on book debts requiring them to be paid into an account from which withdrawals could only be made with the chargee's consent was a fixed charge.

There were problems with creditors seeking to obtain fixed charges over receivables where the chargeholder, not being a bank, was unable to restrict the chargor's right to deal with or dispose of the funds once paid: *Re Brightlife Ltd* [1987] Ch 200.

Problems in creating fixed charges over receivables led to attempts to create hybrid charges. These were recognized in *Re New Bullas Trading Ltd* [1993] BCC 251 where the court approved a charging instrument creating a fixed charge over receivables while they remained outstanding but a floating charge over the monies once they had been collected by the company. In *Agnew v Commissioner of Inland Revenue* [2001] 2 AC 710 (also known as *Re Brumark Investments Ltd*) the Privy Council held that *Re New Bullas Trading Ltd* was wrongly decided. In *Re Spectrum Plus Ltd* [2005] 2 AC 680 the House of Lords unanimously overruled *Siebe Gorman & Co Ltd v Barclays Bank Ltd* and *Re New Bullas Trading Ltd* holding that a debenture which required the proceeds of book debts to be paid into a bank account, but which placed no restriction on the use of the balance of the account, had to be regarded as a floating charge. The decision means that, in order to create a fixed charge, the relevant assets must be permanently appropriated to the payment of the debt for which the charge is a security.

Attempts to create fixed charges over chattels have generally been recognized as floating charges in the absence of a restriction of chargor's right to deal in or dispose of assets charged. However, in *Re Cimex Tissues Ltd* [1994] BCC 626 a charge over plant and machinery was held to be a fixed charge even though the charge envisaged that some of the charged items might be changed from time to time as they wore out. In *Re GE Tunbridge Ltd* [1994] BCC 563 the charging instrument prohibited the company from disposing of the assets without the chargee's consent but there was no requirement that, if they were sold, the proceeds should be paid into a designated account. This was held to be a floating charge.

In *Re CCG International Enterprises Ltd* [1993] BCLC 1428 a contract giving a bank a floating charge on a company's assets required the company to insure the charged property and required any money received under the policy to be paid into an account designated by the bank and used as the bank directed either to reduce the debt secured by the charge or the replacement of the lost assets. It was held that this created a fixed charge over the insurance money.

In *Agnew v Commissioner of Inland Revenue* the Privy Council made clear that in order to determine whether a charge is fixed or floating the court must first identify the rights the parties intended to create (looking at the rights rather than the label attached to the charge by the parties) and then decide, as a matter of law, whether those rights create a fixed or floating charge. In making that determination, it is clear that the third characteristic—the ability to deal with the assets charged in the ordinary course of trading—is more important than the other two characteristics. In *Re Spectrum Plus Ltd* Lord Scott said this was 'the essential feature of the floating charge, the characteristic that distinguishes it from a fixed charge'. The other characteristics are thus non-esssential, so in *Re Bond Worth Ltd* [1980] Ch 228 the assets affected by a floating charge were not 'present and future' but present in respect of the goods and future in respect of the proceeds of sale, while in *Welch v Bowmaker (Ireland) Ltd* [1980] IR 251 a charge was held to be a floating charge although there was no anticipation of the assets being turned over in the course of the company's business.

Question 3

'The reforms to the registration of charges introduced into the **Companies Act 2006** by the **Companies Act 2006 (Amendment of Part 25) Regulations 2013** were extremely limited and not worth the wait.'

Discuss.

Commentary

Although reform in this area had been long anticipated, the 2013 changes, which apply to charges created on or after 6 April 2013, are not particularly extensive. In many respects the law has not altered, although there have been some notable changes to improve the registration system. In order to evaluate the new provisions you will need to have an appreciation of both the pre- and post-2013 law. You should explain clearly how the new provisions have changed the law, and where the law remains unchanged.

Examiner's tip

Rather than discussing the original law and then explaining the new law, a more effective technique is to identify important features of the registration system and assess within these areas what changes, if any, have been made.

 Answer plan

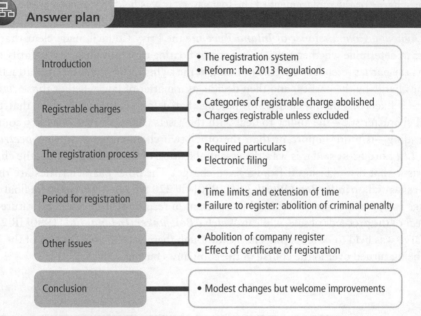

Introduction	• The registration system • Reform: the 2013 Regulations
Registrable charges	• Categories of registrable charge abolished • Charges registrable unless excluded
The registration process	• Required particulars • Electronic filing
Period for registration	• Time limits and extension of time • Failure to register: abolition of criminal penalty
Other issues	• Abolition of company register • Effect of certificate of registration
Conclusion	• Modest changes but welcome improvements

Suggested answer

The registration system enables those dealing with a company to check what charges exist over a company's assets and a failure to register can affect the priority of lenders in the event of a company's insolvency. Registration is thus of great significance to companies and those dealing with them. This essay will explain the system of registration for company charges, assessing where the 2013 Regulations have altered the law and evaluating the significance of these changes.

After several abortive attempts at reform, the system of registration in the **Companies Act 2006 (CA 2006), Part 25** was largely unchanged from the **Companies Act 1985** and based on a system dating from 1901. However, **CA 2006, s. 894** empowered the Secretary of State to make regulations altering **Part 25** and, following a series of consultations during 2010–12, the **Companies Act 2006 (Amendment of Part 25) Regulations 2013 (SI 2013/600)** came into force on 6 April 2013. This replaces **CA 2006, Part 25,**

Chapter 1 (which governed companies registered in England, Wales, and Northern Ireland) and **Chapter 2** (governing companies registered in Scotland) with **Chapter A1** which applies to all parts of the UK. **Chapter A1** only applies to charges created on or after 6 April 2013; for charges created before then the old law applies.

Registrable charges

One of the most significant changes brought about by the 2013 Regulations is the type of charges that are registrable.

Before 2013, **CA 2006, s. 860** provided a list of registrable charges in nine categories that included charges on land or any interest in land, other than a charge for any rent or other periodical sum issuing out of land; charges for the purpose of securing any issue of debentures; and charges on book debts.

Only if a charge fell within one of these categories was a charge registrable. Since the effect of non-registration of a registrable charge is that the charge is void against the liquidator, administrator, or any creditor, it could be essential to prove that an unregistered charge was not registrable if it were to be enforceable. This made the categories critical and could provide an additional incentive to draft charges in the form of fixed rather than floating charges as all floating charges were registrable, but not all fixed charges were (eg a charge on shares: *Arthur D Little Ltd (In Administration) v Ableco Finance LLC* [2003] Ch 217).

Chapter A1 does not provide a list of registrable charges, instead making all charges registrable except for those specifically excluded in **s. 859A(6)**, which are (a) a charge in favour of a landlord on a cash deposit given as a security in connection with the lease of land; (b) a charge created by a member of Lloyd's to secure its Lloyd's underwriting obligations; and (c) a charge specifically excluded by another Act. During consultation, consideration was given to exclusion of charges arising by operation of law, but these have not been included in the **s. 859A(6)** list and so such charges (eg a vendor's lien: *London and Cheshire Insurance Co Ltd v Laplagrene Property Co Ltd* [1971] Ch 499) are now registrable.

Registration

Registration can be by the company or a person interested in it, and is usually by the chargeholder as they have more to lose in the event of a failure to register. Under **Chapter A1, s. 859D** the company or interested person sends a certified copy of the charge instrument together with a 'statement of particulars' to the registrar and the registrar is then under a duty to register that charge (**s. 859A**). This is an improvement on the old system that required delivery of more detailed 'prescribed particulars' together with the original charge instrument, with the registrar then having to check the particulars against the instrument before returning the original instrument of charge. The new system allocates a unique reference code to each charge, displayed on the charge certificate, which should allow easier tracking of charges by those searching the register.

In a distinct improvement on the former, paper-based system, charges and statements of particulars (and statements of full or partial satisfaction) can now be filed electronically.

As under the previous provisions, the charge and particulars are to be delivered to the registrar within 21 days from the day after the day on which the charge is created, CA 2006, s. 859(4). (The new provisions, s. 859E, provide a table identifying the date of creation of the charge depending on its type and the date of delivery.) The system thus continues the risk of the 21 day 'invisibility period' during which anyone searching the register would not be aware of all existing charges, and demonstrates the limits of the 2013 reforms.

It is possible to apply for an extension to the time for delivery by virtue of s. 859F(3), echoing the previous system in the former s. 873. This allows the court (on application of the company or person interested) to extend the period for delivery if satisfied the failure to deliver the documents was 'accidental or due to inadvertence or to some other sufficient cause', or is 'not of a nature to prejudice the position of creditors or shareholders of the company', or that on other grounds it is just and equitable to grant relief. The courts have generally been willing to extend the period for registration, provided that rights acquired in the meantime are not prejudiced, although the courts may refuse to extend the period after a long delay: *Re Teleomatic Ltd* [1994] 1 BCLC 90.

Failure to register

A failure to register results in the charge being void against the company's liquidator, administrator, or any creditor (s. 859H). This position is unchanged (formerly in s. 874). This does not affect the validity of the debt itself which remains payable (*Re Monolithic Building Company* [1915] 1 Ch 643), but will rank as an unsecured debt on a company's liquidation. In *Re Cosslett (Contractors) Ltd* [2002] 1 BCLC 77 it was made clear that the charge is not void against the company while it is not in administration or winding up. When a charge becomes void, the money secured by the charge becomes immediately payable (s. 859H(4), formerly s. 874(3)).

There is no longer a duty on the company to register a charge. The former s. 860 stated the company 'must' deliver the documents to the registrar; and a failure to register was a criminal offence by the company and every officer in default. The new s. 859A is phrased in terms of the obligation being on the registrar to register the charge once the documents are filed within the delivery period. Of course, as an unregistered charge is invalid against the liquidator, etc in practice the company (or lender) will be commercially obliged to register in any event, but the 2013 Regulations have removed the criminal sanction.

Other issues

One complaint of the old system was that variations in a registered charge could only be made by effectively registering anew. Under s. 859O, where a charge is amended by adding a negative pledge clause (restricting creation of charges ranking ahead or equal to the charge) or varying the ranking of the charge in relation to any other charge, either the company or the person taking the benefit of the charge can register the amendment.

Before 6 April 2013 companies had to keep their own register of charges (which was open to inspection) (**CA 2006, s. 876**) but this requirement has been abolished. Companies do need to keep copies of instruments creating or amending charges (**s. 859P**) which will be open to inspection (**s. 859Q**) so the impact of this change is limited.

The 2013 Regulations have not made changes in respect of the effect of the certificate of registration. Accordingly the certificate remains conclusive evidence that documents were delivered to the registrar before the end of the delivery period (as extended): **s. 859I (7)**. This applies even if the certificate is demonstrably inaccurate, as in *Re Mechanisations (Eaglescliffe) Ltd* [1966] Ch 20, where the amount secured was incorrectly stated, and *Re CL Nye Ltd* [1971] Ch 442 where the date of creation of the charge was wrong.

Conclusion

While seven years passed between enactment of the **CA 2006** and reform to the company charge registration system, given the lost decades before that, few will be inclined to complain. Those that favour a different system (the US-style 'notice filing' system is most frequently cited, eg by the Company Law Review ('Modern Company Law for a Competitive Economy' Final Report)) may be disappointed and the changes are certainly not ambitious. Nonetheless, the changes at least reduce confusion over what charges are registrable, introduce a UK-wide system, remove the unnecessary criminal penalty for failure to register, and allow electronic filing. Furthermore, by taking a fairly cautious approach to reform in such a commercially important area, users can adapt to the changes without significant difficulty.

  Question 4

Hernando's Hideaway Ltd (HH Ltd) operated a nightclub. In June 2013, Lola Bank plc (LB plc) agreed to allow HH Ltd an overdraft on the security of a combination fixed and floating charge over the whole of HH Ltd's assets. The debenture was executed on 21 June 2013. The company secretary of HH Ltd meant to register the debenture but forgot to do so. The failure to register the debenture was discovered in January 2014.

In December 2013, HH Ltd created a second fixed charge over its leasehold premises in favour of Ravers Ltd (R Ltd) to finance the installation of a sound system. R Ltd was informed of the earlier charge to LB plc and noticed that the charge had not been registered when it applied for registration of its charge.

Advise the company secretary of HH Ltd how best to secure the validity of the charge to LB plc and of the priority in respect of the two charges and of any unsecured creditors to whom the company became liable before the charge was late registered.

Commentary

This is a problem concerning the consequences of failure to register within the requisite period and the possibilities open to the company secretary of HH Ltd to rectify the matter. It also raises the issue of the priority of charges. You are required to consider the occasions when out-of-time registration is possible and consider any alternative course of action open to the company secretary and the consequences for LB plc.

Answer plan

- Identification of the legal problems raised by the question
- Discussion of the possibility of late registration and the effect of such action
- Consideration of the possibility of inserting a new date and registering the charge within 21 days of the new date
- In respect of Ravers (R) Ltd, discussion of the significance of R Ltd being aware of the existence of LB plc's charge and its non-registration prior to the registration of their own charge
- Application of the law to the problem and advice concerning the legal position of the parties and unsecured creditors

Suggested answer

This question raises legal issues concerning the effect of failure to register charges within the requisite statutory period, the possibility and legal effect of late registration and the priority of charges.

In respect of the charge to Lola Bank (LB) plc, the charge was created on 21 June 2013 and so is governed by the new **Chapter A1** of the **Companies Act 2006 (CA 2006)**, inserted by the **Companies Act (Amendment of Part 25) Regulations 2013** which has effect for charges created on or after 6 April 2013. As it does not fall within the very limited categories of excluded charges in **s. 859A(6)**, the charge should have been registered with the registrar of companies within the period of 21 days from the day after the date of its creation. As this has not been done the charge is void as against a liquidator, administrator, or any creditor (**s. 859H**) and the money advanced by the bank against the security of the charge is immediately repayable. Under the previous law the failure to register the charge would have been a criminal offence by the company and every officer in default but this is no longer the case following the 2013 reforms.

There are two possible courses of action open to the company secretary to salvage the situation. The most obvious solution would be to apply to the court for late registration of the charge under **s. 859F**, which echoes the previous provision found in **s. 873**. A high court judge can only order that the period allowed for registration can be extended if satisfied that the failure to register the charge falls within the terms of **s. 859F**. In this respect, the situation would appear to be covered in that it was accidental or due to inadvertence. It would be necessary to satisfy the court that the failure to register the charge was not motivated by the desire to delude persons dealing with the company into thinking that it was in a better financial position than was in fact the case.

In *Re Kris Cruisers Ltd* [1949] Ch 138, the company secretary of the company thought that the solicitor had registered the charge and the solicitor thought the company secretary had done so. In the event, the charge was unregistered. The court, however, allowed its late registration under the equivalent provision. Where none of the grounds is established, late registration is refused: *Re Teleomatic* [1994] 1 BCLC 90.

The effect of late registration is that the charge becomes void through failure to register and that it remains void until it is registered. The effect of this would be that, whereas the charge held by LB plc would have enjoyed priority from the date of its creation, the charge will only become valid once the late registration is achieved. This is important in respect of priority over subsequent charges.

Out-of-time registration can be on such terms and conditions as are just and expedient and is generally subject to the following formula: 'That ... this order is to be without prejudice to the rights of any parties acquired prior to the time when the said debenture is to be actually registered.'

The effect of this formula was considered in *Watson v Duff Morgan and Vermont (Holdings) Ltd* [1974] 1 All ER 794. In January 1971, the company created a first debenture in the plaintiff's favour to secure £10,000 and a second debenture in favour of the defendant to secure £5,000. The debentures were secured by floating charges covering all undertakings and property, present and future including uncalled capital. The second charge was made subject to and ranked immediately after the first charge. The second debenture was registered within 21 days but the first was not registered. In October 1971, the plaintiff applied for late registration and the order was made subject to the above condition. In the event, the company went into liquidation with insufficient assets to provide even £5,000. The plaintiff successfully claimed that his debenture ranked in priority to the other, the proviso only applied to the period when the first debenture was void for non-registration. The defendant's rights had not been acquired during that period but when the second debenture was executed.

In spite of this formula, if other chargees have agreed that their charges are to rank after a charge that was not registered through inadvertence, etc the court will respect the contractually agreed priorities between the parties: *Barclays Bank plc v Stuart Landon Ltd* [2001] 2 BCLC 316. There is no protection to persons becoming unsecured creditors of the company during the time that the charge was unregistered. The court takes the view that unsecured creditors run the risk that the company might subsequently create a charge over its assets: *Re MIG Trust Ltd* [1933] Ch 542.

If the charge to LB plc were not dated except in pencil, it would always be open for the company secretary to falsify the date on which the charge was created and to register it within 21 days of the false date. In *Esberger & Son Ltd v Capital and Counties Bank* [1913] 2 Ch 366, the company deposited with its bank an undated but signed memorandum of charge on 17 September 1910. On 14 June 1911, the bank manager filled in that date onto the document and registered it with the registrar of companies on 3 July. The court held that the charge was void as not having been registered in time.

It was only in *National Provincial and Union Bank of England v Charnley* [1923] 1 KB 431 that the matter of the conclusive nature of the registrar of companies' certificate of registration was raised and recognized. The conclusive nature of the registrar's certificate has subsequently been recognized in *Re Eric Holmes (Property) Ltd* [1965] Ch 442 where the court recognized the validity of a charge created on 5 June and not registered within the 21 days of its creation but subsequently dated 23 June and registered within 21 days of that date. This could also be a route for the company secretary.

In respect of the charge created in favour of Ravers (R) Ltd over the leasehold premises in December 2013, the fact that R Ltd was aware of the existence of the unregistered combined fixed and floating charge in favour of LB plc does not affect the validity and priority of their registered charge. A registered charge has priority over an earlier unregistered charge, even though the holder of the registered charge has notice of the unregistered security: *Re Monolithic Building Co* [1915] 1 Ch 643.

As regards the priorities between the two charges, the charge in favour of LB plc is only registered after January 2014 whereas the charge in favour of R Ltd is registered within 21 days of its creation in December 2013. This means that the fixed charge in favour of R Ltd will rank in priority over the fixed charge of LB plc. Since the charge to LB plc is a combined fixed and floating charge, the floating charge will always rank after a subsequent fixed charge over the same asset. Any persons who became unsecured creditors of the company between the charge to LB plc becoming void for non-registration and being registered out-of-time will not be protected by the subsequent validation of the charge.

Question 5

Paradise Ltd is a wholly owned subsidiary company of Eden Ltd which is itself controlled by Adam, the principal shareholder and managing director. Paradise Ltd suffered a financial crisis in 2004 and it was agreed in January 2005 that Eden Ltd would pay off its outstanding debts and advance a further £50,000 on the security of a floating charge on Paradise Ltd's assets. Eden Ltd settled the debts and made the first payment to Paradise Ltd in March 2005, although the debenture containing the charge was not actually executed until July 2005. The charge was registered within 21 days of its creation.

The company had a major supplier, Viper plc, which in September 2005 refused to make further deliveries to Paradise Ltd on credit since it was already owed £40,000 for previous deliveries. Following talks between the directors of Paradise Ltd and Viper plc, Viper plc agreed to continue to supply Paradise Ltd on condition that Paradise Ltd created in its favour a fixed charge over its freehold premises to cover the existing debt of £40,000. The charge was created in October 2005 and registered within 21 days.

Paradise Ltd went into creditors' voluntary liquidation in March 2006.

Advise the liquidator of the validity of the charges to Eden Ltd and Viper plc.

Commentary

This problem question shows how great an overlap there is between the topics of charges and corporate insolvency where the company creating the charge becomes insolvent after having created the charge. In this question, you are not being asked primarily to discuss issues relating to insolvency proceedings but merely to consider how they can impinge on the validity of company charges.

Answer plan

- Identification of the legal problems raised by the question
- Discussion of the law relating to the avoidance of floating charges and the interpretation of **s. 245(2)**
- Application of the law to the facts of the case involving Paradise Ltd and Eden Ltd
- Discussion of the law relating to voidable preferences and the interpretation of **s. 239**
- Application of the law to the fixed charge created by Paradise Ltd in favour of Viper plc

Suggested answer

This question raises problems connected with the avoidance of floating charges under **Insolvency Act 1986 (IA 1986), s. 245** and charges being avoided as voidable preferences under **IA 1986, s. 239**.

Floating charges created in favour of outsiders within one year before the onset of insolvency are invalid under **s. 245(3)(b)** unless the chargee can prove that the company was not unable to pay its debts at that time or became so as a consequence: **s. 245(4)(a) and (b)**. For connected persons, the period is extended to two years (**s. 245(3)(a)**) and is not conditional upon the company being unable to pay its debts at the time of the creation of the charge. The onset of insolvency is precisely determined for administrations and liquidations: **s. 245(5)**. Connected persons are defined in **IA 1986, s. 249** and by reference to **IA 1986, s. 435**.

There are exceptions to the charges being avoided as regards the extent of the aggregate of:

(a) the value of money paid, or goods or services supplied to the company at the same time as, or after, the creation of the charge

(b) the value of the discharge or reduction at the same time as, or after, the creation of the charge of any debt of the company, and

(c) any interest payable in pursuance of (a) or (b): **s. 245(2)(a)**.

The exceptions under (a) and (b) are both subject to the proviso that the cash, goods, and services paid or supplied to the company, or the value of the discharge or reduction of any debt of the company took place 'at the same time as, or after, the creation of the charge'.

In an early decision under earlier equivalent sections, the court took a very relaxed view of the definition of 'at the same time'. Thus in *Re F & E Stanton Ltd* [1929] 1 Ch 180 M advanced money to an insolvent company on the security of debentures creating a floating charge. The company passed a resolution to issue the debenture before the loan was advanced but the debentures were not issued until five days after the last instalment of the advance and 54 days after the first instalment. The company went into liquidation within five days of the creation of the charge. The court nevertheless held that the charge was created 'at the same time' as the advance and the charge was valid.

In interpreting this proviso in respect of **IA 1986, s. 245** in *Re Shoe Lace Ltd* [1992] BCLC 636, the court decided that the degree of contemporaneity depended upon the ordinary meaning of the words used. On that basis, although loans had been made between April and early July in consideration of the proposed creation of a debenture, they could not be said to have been made at the same time as the creation of the debenture, which was finally executed on 24 July. The floating charge was, therefore, invalid. This decision was criticized by the court in *Re Fairway Magazines Ltd* [1993] BCLC 643 where the judge followed the approach of *Re F & E Stanton Ltd*. The Court of Appeal, however, endorsed the High Court's decision in *Re Shoe Lace Ltd* on appeal under the name *Power v Sharp Investments Ltd* [1994] 1 BCLC 111.

The result of this is that an advance made before the formal execution of a debenture, but in anticipation of it, will not be regarded as being made at the same time as the creation of the charge unless the interval is so short that it can be regarded as minimal.

In respect of the floating charge to Eden Ltd by Paradise Ltd, Eden Ltd is a person connected with Paradise Ltd since it is the parent company of Paradise Ltd. The floating charge is therefore vulnerable under **IA 1986, s. 245(2)** for a period of two years from the date of its creation in July 2005 in the event of Paradise Ltd going into liquidation within that period. In the event, Paradise Ltd went into insolvent liquidation in March 2006. As a result, the floating charge is avoided unless it falls within one of the exceptions in **s. 245(2)(a)–(c)**. Since Paradise Ltd's debts were discharged and money was advanced to it by way of a loan before the date of the creation of the charge, the liquidator can avoid the charge under **s. 245(2)**.

The result is that Eden Ltd is no longer a secured creditor of Paradise Ltd and the charged property is released for the benefit of unsecured creditors. Eden Ltd will be an unsecured creditor and will have to claim alongside the other unsecured creditors.

In respect of the fixed charge created in favour of Viper plc to secure an existing debt, the charge is potentially vulnerable to be set aside as a voidable preference under **IA 1986, s. 239**. Under this provision, administrators or liquidators may be able to set aside payments and charges created in the period prior to the onset of insolvency which put a creditor or guarantor or surety of a creditor into a better position in the event of the company going into an insolvent liquidation or administration. Changing the status of Viper plc from that of an unsecured creditor to a secured creditor with a fixed charge is a major improvement in status.

In order to be set aside, such transactions must have taken place within the relevant time prior to the onset of insolvency, which is two years for connected persons and six months for outsiders: **s. 240(1)(a)** and **(b)**, and the company must at the time of the transaction have been unable to pay its debts within the meaning of **IA 1986, s. 123**. Preferences are only voidable where it can be established that the company creating the charge or making the payment was motivated by a desire to confer a benefit on the person preferred. For connected persons, an intention to advantage the person is presumed: **s. 239(6)**; *Re DKG Contractors Ltd* [1990] BCC 903; and *Re Beacon Leisure Ltd* [1991] BCC 213. In the event of charges or payments being avoided, the court may order retransfer of property, release or discharge of security, repayments to administrator or liquidator, revival of guarantees, and so on: **s. 241**. Third parties who are bona fide purchasers in good faith and for value are protected: **s. 241(2)** and **(2A)**. Proceeds of a successful claim are held on trust for the unsecured creditors: *Re Yagerphone Ltd* [1935] 1 Ch 392.

In *Re MC Bacon Ltd* [1990] BCLC 324, the company had an unsecured overdraft limit of £300,000. In 1986 it lost its major customer and two of the directors retired from active management. In May 1987 a bank report found the company to be technically insolvent. As a condition of continuing to operate the bank account, the bank demanded fixed and floating charges over the company's assets. In September 1987 the company went into liquidation and the liquidator sought to set aside the charge as a transaction at an undervalue or as a voidable preference.

Having rejected the submission that the charge could be avoided as a transaction at an undervalue, the court considered the question of whether it was void as a voidable preference. It concluded that the company did not necessarily desire that which it intended to achieve and held that the charge was not voidable. Banks and suppliers under the terms of a current account are in an advantageous position in respect of this. In *Re Yeovil Glove Co Ltd* [1965] Ch 148, a bank met company cheques totalling some £110,000 subsequent to the creation of a secured debenture to secure an existing debt. This was held to be a new advance even though the overdraft remained virtually unchanged. This was due to the operation of the rule in *Clayton's Case* (1816) 1 Mer 572 in the bank's favour. The rule provides that credits to a current account discharge debts in the order in which they were incurred in the absence of specific appropriation.

In conclusion, the floating charge in favour of Eden Ltd can be avoided by the liquidator of Paradise Ltd. The fixed charge in favour of Viper plc is, however, valid since it was created as a result of pressure from the chargee which prevents the liquidator claiming that Paradise Ltd intended to prefer Viper plc as required by the legislation.

Further reading

Atherton, S., and Jameel Mokal, R., 'Charges over assets: issues in the fixed/floating jurisprudence' (2005) 26 Co Law 10

Capper, D., 'Fixed charges over book debts—the future after *Brumark*' (2003) 24 Co Law 325

Law Commission, 'Company security interests' (2005) Law Comm No 296, Cm 6654

McCormack, G., 'Extension of time for registration of company charges' [1986] JBL 282

Pennington, R., 'The vulnerability of debenture holders' (2004) 25 Co Law 171

Pennington, R., 'Recent developments in the law and practice relating to the creation of security for companies' indebtedness' (2009) 30 Co Law 163

Smart, P., 'Fixed or floating? *Siebe Gorman post-Brumark*' (2004) 25 Co Law 331

Walters, A., 'Statutory redistribution of floating charge assets: Victory (again) to Revenue and Customs' (2008) 29 Co Law 129

Wild, L., '*Spectrum* and *Leyland DAF*: the spectre of new claims' (2006) 27 Co Law 151

7

Shares and shareholders

Introduction

'Share' means a share in the company's share capital: **Companies Act 2006 (CA 2006),
s. 540(1)**. Shares are personal property (**s. 541**) and must have a fixed nominal value:
s. 542. This can, however, be in any currency, and different classes of shares in the same
company may be in different currencies: **s. 542(3)**.

An important legal distinction is the difference between registered and bearer shares
as regards title, transfer, and the legal significance of the share certificate (share warrant
for bearer shares). In practice, bearer shares are rarely met in the UK, and in 2013 the
Department for Business, Innovation and Skills consulted on whether they should be
abolished ('Transparency and trust: discussion paper' (BIS/13/959), July 2013).

In this area of the company law syllabus, it is particularly important to understand
the rights associated with the different classes of share that can be issued by a company:
ordinary, preference, and deferred shares. It is important to realize at the outset that the
preference share—despite its name—is one whose holders are generally disadvantaged.
They have sometimes been described as 'hybrid securities' meaning that they combine
the characteristics of shares and debentures. This is due to the fact that the holders of
preference shares have few of the powers of shareholders—generally no voting rights—
while enjoying few of the advantages as creditors—security and priority in liquidation.

Associated with this is the major topic of variation of class rights—concerning statutory
restrictions on the right of the company directors to vary the rights of a particular class of
share without the consent of the majority of the holders of that class of share. In respect
of this, it is important to be aware of the significance of the judicial definition of what
constitutes variation of class rights and its damaging effect on the statutory protection.

Other important topics in this area of the syllabus include existing shareholders' rights
of pre-emption in respect of new issues of equity shares (**ss. 560–77**); restrictions on
the directors' power to allot shares (**ss. 549–51**); certification and transfer of shares
(**ss. 768–82**); and the register of members (**ss. 113–28**).

Question 1

What is a share?

 Commentary

This is a potentially broad question that you could take in slightly different directions, depending on the particular focus of your course. So, for example, if your course looks in detail at the legal rules relating to different types of share and transfer of shares, you could address this in some depth; or if your course looks more closely at the legal nature of shares, then you can focus on this. Examiners will want to see a balance of legal knowledge, practical understanding, and some engagement with cases and academic discussion, in order to answer the question fully. As well as recognizing different types of share, you need to consider the different elements of a share and how the relative importance of these elements may differ according to the type of share and the interests of the shareholder. The question also allows you to show your understanding of the statutory contract and the interests of shareholders.

 Examiner's tip

Don't just describe different types of share—to get the higher marks you need to show that you have really thought about the complexity of a share and its various features.

 Answer plan

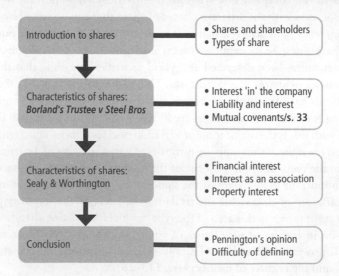

| Introduction to shares | • Shares and shareholders
• Types of share |

| Characteristics of shares:
Borland's Trustee v Steel Bros | • Interest 'in' the company
• Liability and interest
• Mutual covenants/s. 33 |

| Characteristics of shares:
Sealy & Worthington | • Financial interest
• Interest as an association
• Property interest |

| Conclusion | • Pennington's opinion
• Difficulty of defining |

Suggested answer

Despite shares being fundamental to company law (the vast majority of companies are limited by shares), it is difficult to define a share both comprehensively and concisely. That is because, as well as there being different types of share, a share has distinct features that differ in importance depending on the interests of the shareholder. Shareholders may be as diverse as an owner-manager in a one-person company, or an investor holding shares in multiple companies on a largely disinterested basis, and the nature of a share looks very different from those different perspectives. Accordingly, while the general notion of a share (and shareholder) is tolerably clear, finding a workable and meaningful definition is another matter. This essay will consider existing definitions and descriptions of shares and their features, and assess whether it is possible to state with any certainty 'what is a share'.

A share measures a shareholder's interest in the company—the shareholder's proportional share in a company's share capital and (assuming the articles of association provide for one vote per share) proportional voting power. Although shares must have a nominal value by virtue of **Companies Act 2006 (CA 2006), s. 542(1)** (often a small amount, eg 10p or £1), this is not the 'value' of the share, which is worth what someone is willing to pay for it (assuming a market exists in the shares) or, in the event of a solvent winding up, the proportional share of the company's assets less its liabilities.

Most shares are ordinary shares, the residual category of shares. If a company has only one class of shares, this class is ordinary shares, and every company must have at least one ordinary share. These usually carry a right to a variable dividend (declared lawfully in accordance with the **CA 2006** and the company's articles) and a right to share in the company's assets on winding up (after payment of the company's liabilities). The other main type of share is preference shares. These are very different in nature to an ordinary share and typically carry rights to a fixed (and usually cumulative: *Webb v Earle* **[1875] LR 20 Eq 556**) dividend and a preferential right to return on capital on winding up. These rights are described as 'preferential' as they are dealt with in priority to the rights of ordinary shareholders; they are not 'better' than ordinary shares, simply different. Outside these two main types of share, companies may issue any number of different classes of share provided the articles allow, potentially carrying different nominal values (even in different currencies: *Re Scandanavian Bank Group plc* **[1988] Ch 87**) and different rights (including redeemable shares: see **s. 684**). Any rights that attach to a particular class of shares, but not generally, are regarded as 'class rights' (see *Cumbrian Newspapers Group Ltd v Cumberland & Westmoreland Herald Newspapers and Printing Co Ltd* **[1987] Ch 1**) and provisions (**ss. 630–5**) exist to protect shareholders in respect of variations to these rights.

A share does not give its holder any share in the company's property (*Short v Treasury Commissioners* **[1948] AC 534**); the company as a separate entity owns its assets (*Macaura v Northern Assurance Co* **[1925] AC 619**). The member's share is in the company's share capital (**s. 540(1)**). The **CA 2006** also provides that shares are personal property (**s. 541**) and transferable in accordance with the articles (**s. 544(1)**).

These statutory provisions indicate some features of a share but do not explain what a share is.

The classic analysis of a share comes from *Borland's Trustee v Steel Brothers & Co Ltd* [1901] 1 Ch 279: 'A share is the interest of a shareholder in the company measured by a sum of money, for the purpose of liability in the first place, and of interest in the second, but also consisting of a series of mutual covenants entered into by all the shareholders *inter se* in accordance with [CA 2006 s. 33]' (Farwell J). It is clear, as Professor Pennington points out (see Pennington, R., 'Can shares in companies be defined?' (1989) 10 Comp Law 140), that this is a partial description rather than a complete definition but it is helpful to investigate further the features identified by Farwell J.

First, and importantly, Farwell J recognizes that the interest of a shareholder is 'in' the company. This indicates how the shareholders are very much part of the company—unlike a creditor, whose interests are 'against' the company. A share thus creates a different type of interest to that of a purely contractual interest.

Secondly, a share is an interest measured by a sum of money, but is not itself a sum of money. As discussed earlier, shares have a nominal value, measured in monetary terms, but this is a method of proportional measurement rather than a statement of monetary value. Farwell J talks of the share having both elements of liability and interest. Liability arises from the taking up of the shares—a shareholder is liable to pay for the shares, either on issue or on later call, but beyond that a shareholder has no further financial liability (shareholders are not liable for the company's debts: *Salomon v A. Salomon & Co Ltd* [1897] AC 22). In terms of interest, the shareholder's financial interest or return on his investment (whether by distribution of dividends or return of capital) is measured by reference to his proportional share.

The reference to 'mutual covenants' relates to the rights of shareholders under the articles—commonly known as the 'statutory contract' under what is now **CA 2006, s. 33.** This statutory deeming provision creates a contract between the company and the shareholders (and the shareholders *inter se*). This relationship is not identical to a traditional contract (*Bratton Seymour Service Co Ltd v Oxborough* [1992] BCLC 693); for example contractual remedies of rescission and mistake are not available, and not all provisions of the articles are directly enforceable by members (see, eg *Hickman v Kent or Romney Marsh Sheepbreeders' Association* [1915] 1 Ch 881: only membership rights can be enforced). Nonetheless this statutory contract indicates the voluntary and binding nature of the relationship and the importance of the provisions of the articles. A shareholder of course has further rights and obligations arising from the provisions of the **CA 2006.**

A share then is essentially a bundle of different rights and obligations. This is supported by Sealy and Worthington (see *Cases and Materials on Company Law* (10th edn, 2013)) who identify three key aspects of a share. The first is a reflection of the shareholder's financial stake in the company; it indicates the member's level of financial interest and liability—the share measures the amount a shareholder might have to contribute to a company's capital, and provides the proportional measurement for financial returns. Secondly, a share is a measure of the shareholder's interest in the company as an association of members—a share gives its holder rights as a member of an association, including voting rights, as set out by the articles. Thirdly, a share is a species of property in its own right. This aspect is not included in Farwell J's analysis (but is reflected in **CA 2006, s. 541**)—a share is an item of property and thus capable of being bought, sold, charged and split into legal and beneficial interests.

This analysis shows that the importance of these features will differ according to the type of share and reasons for holding it. As a shareholder in a small private company, the second element—rights in the association—is likely to be more important, while the share being an item of property may seem irrelevant. As the holder of preference shares the first element—the financial return by way of a fixed dividend payment—is likely to be most important. For an investor in a listed public company, the third element is the most important as financial gains are often made through purchase and sale of shares rather than dividend payments, and voting rights are largely irrelevant (as each shareholding is a tiny proportion of the company's shares).

It is similarly difficult to define shares by way of contrast with other investments in companies such as debentures (loans, usually secured on a company's assets). While in essence the concepts are very different, in practice, the two concepts can become blurred. For example, preference shares providing for a fixed return and no voting rights in many ways look more like a loan than a share and are often termed 'hybrid securities'.

Professor Pennington's conclusion is that shares are 'a species of intangible movable property which comprise a collection of rights and obligations relating to an interest in a company of an economic and proprietory character, but not constituting a debt'. Although this definition is not one many shareholders would find illuminating, this may be the closest we can come to an all-encompassing definition, recognizing that a more meaningful answer to 'what is a share' depends on quite who is the shareholder.

Question 2

Distinguish between ordinary shares and preference shares. Why are preference shares described as a hybrid between debt and equity?

Commentary

This is an important topic that, in an examination paper, would generally appear in the form of an essay question. You need to have the distinctions between the shares at your fingertips and to be able to make the distinction between the two classes of share in a cogent fashion. While preference shares only represent a small percentage of the number of shares issued, it is important to realize how they are used, particularly in respect of venture capital and corporate financing of quoted companies where they are frequently issued as an alternative to borrowing. Because of the rights generally attaching to them, preference shares are a hybrid between debt and equity.

Answer plan

- General introduction and characteristics of ordinary and preference shares
- Dividend rights of preference and ordinary shares
- Rights to return of capital of preference and ordinary shares
- Voting rights of preference and ordinary shares
- Function of preference shares as an alternative to borrowing
- Characteristics rendering preference shares a hybrid between debt and equity

Suggested answer

Many companies divide their share capital into different classes of shares and refer to one class or more as preference shares as opposed to the ordinary shares issued by the company. Shareholder rights relate to dividend, return of capital, and voting rights. The rights will depend entirely on the terms of issue or the articles; there are no statutorily defined rights.

The characteristic of preference shares is that they rank ahead of ordinary shares as to either dividend or return of capital or both. Thus, the preference dividend will be paid in priority to the ordinary dividend and, on the company's dissolution, the preference shareholders will have priority in respect of the return of their capital: preference shareholders carry 'priority as to dividend and capital' *Re EW Savory Ltd* [1951] 2 All ER 1036.

The preferential dividend payable on a preference share is generally a fixed percentage of the nominal value of the share and is an identifier of the share: for example shares might be described as '7 per cent preference shares'. If the shares were issued at a premium, however, the dividend is normally expressed in pence per share or as a percentage of the total subscription price.

Occasionally, particularly for venture capital transactions, preference shares may have a right to a particular percentage of the company's profits. There must be a clear definition of profits in the document creating the rights which must set out how the percentage of profits should be divided. This will usually be proportionately according to the shareholding.

In addition, unless otherwise stated, the shares are deemed to be cumulative preference shares so that the failure to pay a dividend in a financial year means that the right will be carried forward or 'accumulate' until it is paid: *Webb v Earle* [1875] LR 20 Eq 556. The presumption can be rebutted by providing that the dividend is only 'payable out of net profits of each year': *Staples v Eastman Photographic Materials Co* [1896] 2 Ch 303.

The date at which the dividend is due depends on the articles. Dividends can become payable: by resolution of the shareholders, by a resolution of the directors, automatically on specified dates provided that (and to the extent that) the company has profits available for distribution. The advantage of the latter is if the company has distribut-able profits, the dividend becomes a debt due on the specified date and the shareholder can sue the company if it is not paid.

If a company is wound up with arrears of preference dividend, difficulties arise as to whether a right to arrears of dividend has arisen. Preference shareholders may have no right to a dividend at least until it has been declared and arrears of undeclared dividend will not be paid on a winding up. In *Re Roberts and Cooper Ltd* [1929] 2 Ch 383 the holder of 4 per cent cumulative preference shares was entitled on winding up to be paid the amount paid up on their shares and arrears of dividend due at the date of winding up. The company went into liquidation with surplus assets; it was held that the share-holders were not entitled to payment of arrears since dividends were not due until de-clared. To avoid this, the rights should provide for the payment of arrears of preference dividend whether declared or not. The problem would still arise if the dividend fell due on a specified date if the company had distributable profits.

In contrast, ordinary shares have unlimited rather than fixed dividend rights and those rights are not cumulative. Thus, if the company is successful, there is no limit to the amount of dividend that can be declared but if it is unsuccessful the shareholder loses the dividend for that financial year. The right to a dividend arises where the com-pany makes a distributable profit ('accumulated, realised profits ... less ... accumu-lated, realised losses ...' (CA 2006, s. 830)) and declares a dividend.

In respect of return of capital, all shares are presumed to have equal rights to a return of capital unless specifically provided. If preference shareholders enjoy a priority, how-ever, the effect is that they have no right to a share of surplus assets: *Scottish Insurance Corporation Ltd v Wilsons & Clyde Coal Co Ltd* [1949] 1 All ER 1068. Repayment of capital is limited to the nominal value of the shares and not to any premium element unless there is a right to be paid the issue price in priority to the other shareholders.

Ordinary shareholders will generally be postponed to any preference shareholders in respect of return of capital but will then have the sole right to share in any surplus assets unless there are deferred or founders' shares with a deferred right of return of capital and exclusive claims over surplus assets.

As regards voting rights, preference shareholders will be deemed to have equal vot-ing rights with all other shareholders. In practice, the right to vote will generally be restricted to certain specified matters: if the preference dividend is in arrears beyond a specified period; if the shares are redeemable and redemption has not taken place on a specified date; and if there is a proposal to wind up the company. In respect of the non-payment of a dividend, if the articles are appropriately drafted, the voting rights can arise even where the company was unable to pay the dividend because there were no available profits: *Re Bradford Investments plc* [1990] BCC 740.

Preference shares will often be a preferred way for a venture capital firm to invest in companies. The company's bankers and creditors may find the issue of preference shares more acceptable than a large loan and the preference shares rank after all creditors in a winding up. In addition, the company's balance sheet will be less highly geared and look more solid to potential suppliers and customers. For the venture capitalist the advantages are a potential dividend stream and the possibility of weighted voting rights in given situations so that they will be able to vote down a resolution to wind up the company or be able to appoint and remove directors on the company's failure to achieve performance targets. The risk is that if a corporate preference shareholder has a majority of the votes or can remove or appoint a majority of the board, the company could become a subsidiary of the corporate preference shareholder: **CA 2006, s. 1159(1)**.

Ordinary shareholders generally enjoy voting rights in the general meeting and will participate in the decision making. In the event of a takeover bid for the company, their shares will be sought after and will potentially show an increase in value.

Listed companies can issue preference shares as part satisfaction of consideration due in respect of a share or business acquisition or as a means of raising capital at cheaper rates than for a loan. They are also sometimes issued on a company refinancing with debt being converted into preference shares. For the issuing company, preference shares have the advantage that the dividend payable may be lower than the rate of interest that would have been incurred had the capital been borrowed (although interest payments are tax deductible whereas dividends are not). The absence of voting rights prevents the preference shareholders from acquiring a voting stake in the company. The issue of preference shares may not count towards the calculation of gearing ratios under the company's finance documents. In addition, the issue of preference shares may be made without a pre-emptive offer to existing shareholders unless they are convertible into ordinary shares: **CA 2006, ss. 560–1**.

Even if not issued as an alternative to a loan, all preference shares are hybrid securities. In having a right to a fixed dividend they, like creditors, do not benefit materially from the company's success in respect of earnings. But unlike creditors with a right to interest on their loan, the dividend is only payable if the company has available distributable profits, whereas interest payments are payable even where the company makes a loss. As has been shown, even if the dividend is cumulative, in the event of the company's liquidation, the arrears of cumulative dividend may not be provable in the liquidation.

The same is true as regards capital value since the price of the preference share will only fluctuate in value during the company's lifetime in relation to the level of the fixed dividend as against the market rate of interest. On the company's liquidation, even if they enjoy priority in return of capital over ordinary shares, they are still below creditors in priority who can even be protected by charges over the company's assets.

Finally, the lack of voting rights means they have no right to participate in the decision making of the company. This is true for most creditors but important creditors may be given the right to nominate a director to represent their interests.

When one considers their vulnerability to selective reduction of capital and the lack of protection they receive in respect of variation of class rights, we can but agree with the statement in *Gower's Principles of Modern Company Law* (9th edn, 2012): 'Suspended midway between true creditors and true members they [preference shareholders] may get the worst of both worlds, unless the instrument creating the preference shares is carefully drafted.'

Question 3

Nick is the holder of registered shares in both Diabolo Ltd and Luciferous Ltd. In relation to the shares in Diabolo Ltd, last year Michelle stole the share certificate from Nick's study and, pretending to be Nick, deposited the certificate and a signed blank transfer form with South Bank as security for a loan. When Michelle defaulted on the loan, South Bank transferred the shares to Paolo. On receipt of the share certificate and the transfer form, Diabolo Ltd replaced Nick with Paolo on the register of members and issued a share certificate to him. Paolo later transferred the shares to Quentin. When Nick queried the fact he had not received any dividends from Diabolo Ltd, he was informed that he was no longer a shareholder.

In relation to the shares in Luciferous Ltd, Nick has learned that the directors have decided to allot a significant number of shares to Rafael. Nick is unhappy as this allotment will dilute his shareholding and he has not been offered the opportunity to buy any further shares. Luciferous Ltd has only one class of shares and Nick is a minority shareholder.

Advise Nick.

 Commentary

This question deals with the topic of estoppel by share certificate and requires an understanding of the rights and liabilities of the parties where a forged transfer has been used in a sequence of share transfers. You also need to consider statutory pre-emption rights in private companies including the effect of a failure to comply and the possibility of disapplication of these rights.

 Answer plan

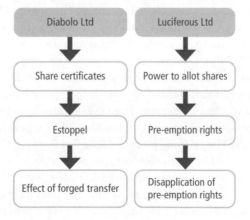

Suggested answer

This question concerns two main issues—estoppel by share certificate and a shareholder's rights of pre-emption.

In relation to Diabolo Ltd, a share certificate is prima facie evidence of title (**Companies Act 2006 (CA 2006), s. 768(1)**). While the evidence can be rebutted, if a company issues a certificate which contains incorrect information the company may be estopped from denying the truth of the certificate, if the certificate has been relied upon: see *Re Bahia and San Francisco Rly Co* (1868) LR 3 QB 584. Here the court held that, in giving the certificate to an individual, the company makes a representation that he is the true holder of the shares and that purchasers in the market should act upon this. The purchaser having relied upon the representation contained in the share certificate, the company was estopped from denying that those named on the certificate were the legal holders (see also *Balkis Consolidated Co v Tomkinson* [1893] AC 396). In *Bloomenthal v Ford* [1897] AC 156 the appellant lent money to a company on the security of shares where the certificates stated that the shares were fully paid. When the company went into liquidation, it was discovered that nothing had been paid on the shares and the liquidator, therefore, sought payment for the shares from Bloomenthal as a contributor. The court rejected this as the company was estopped from denying that the shares were fully paid.

A statement can only create an estoppel against the company if it is made with the company's authority. *Ruben v Great Fingall Consolidated* [1906] AC 439 concerned a deliberate forgery of a share certificate by the company secretary, who provided this to a firm of stockbrokers as security for a loan. The company refused to register the brokers as holders and they sued for damages. The House of Lords held that the company could not be liable as the forged certificate was a pure nullity. The same decision was reached in *South London Greyhound Racecourses Ltd v Wake* [1931] 1 Ch 496. However, this does not mean that a company can never be estopped from disputing the validity of a forgery. At the time of these decisions, the company secretary was thought to have no implied authority as agent to bind the firm. This has changed—*Panorama Developments (Guildford) Ltd v Fidelis Furnishing Fabrics Ltd* [1971] 2 QB 711 held that a company secretary has implied authority to bind the company in respect of administrative matters. A company secretary is also an authorized signatory to company documents under CA 2006, s. 44(3).

In the present case it is the transfer that is a forgery, with Diabolo Ltd issuing the certificate on the basis of that transfer. Where the company has acted in reliance on a forged transfer, it can claim an indemnity from the person sending in the forged transfer, even though the person is totally innocent: see *Sheffield Corporation v Barclay* [1905] AC 392 and *Yeung Kei Yung v Hong Kong & Shanghai Banking Corpn* [1981] AC 787.

Applying the law to the facts of the problem, since the transfer was a forgery it is void and Nick is still the registered holder of the shares now registered to Quentin. Diabolo Ltd must either pay damages to Nick, including dividend payments not received, or retransfer to his name the shares currently registered to Quentin. In respect of Quentin, however, Diabolo Ltd is estopped from denying that Paolo was the registered holder of the shares and Diabolo Ltd must issue him with equivalent shares or pay damages. Diabolo Ltd will be entitled to claim indemnity from South Bank in respect of the losses arising from the sending in of the forged transfer. South Bank could potentially claim indemnity against Michelle if they can trace her.

In relation to Luciferous Ltd, directors can generally only allot shares if authorized to do so by a resolution or the articles (**CA 2006, s. 551**). However, under **s. 550** directors of a private company with one class of shares have the power to allot shares without express authorization except to the extent they are prohibited from so doing by the company's articles. The question does not suggest any such prohibition so the **s. 550** power can be exercised. It must be remembered though that directors must 'only exercise powers for the purposes for which they are conferred': **s. 171(b)** and this duty (the 'proper purposes' rule) has often been invoked in relation to the allotment of shares (eg *Hogg v Cramphorn Ltd* [1967] Ch 254; *Bamford v Bamford* [1970] Ch 212). The reasons for the allotment would have to be examined, but provided the 'substantial purpose' (*Howard Smith Ltd v Ampol Petroleum Ltd* [1974] AC 821) is within the proper scope of the power (generally in relation to the allotment of shares this is the raising of capital) the directors will not be in breach of their duty to the company. If the directors were acting outside the scope of their powers then the allotment would be invalid. Directors must also be aware of their overriding duty to act in good faith to promote the success of the company (**s. 172**). The question does not suggest that the directors are acting otherwise than for a proper purpose and in a manner they believe will promote the success of the company and so in the absence of further information this does not seem to offer a route for Nick.

Nick is concerned that he has not been offered the chance to purchase more shares to maintain his proportional shareholding. Existing shareholders are given statutory pre-emption rights (**CA 2006, ss. 560–77**) in respect of an allotment of 'equity securities' (including ordinary shares). Before an allotment, **s. 561** requires a company to make an offer to each person holding ordinary shares (communicated in accordance with **s. 562**) to allot to him 'on the same or more favourable terms' a proportion of those securities matching his existing proportional shareholding. An allotment cannot be made until the period for acceptance of such an offer (at least 21 days) has expired or the company has received notice of acceptance or refusal of the offer.

If an allotment is made in contravention of **ss. 561/562**, the company and every officer who knowingly authorized or permitted the contravention are jointly and severally liable to compensate the person to whom an offer should have been made for any loss, damage, costs, and expenses sustained or incurred as a result: **s. 563(2)**. An allotment in contravention of **ss. 561/562** is not invalid, although an allotment made in favour of the directors themselves was set aside in *Re Thundercrest Ltd* [1995] 1 BCLC 117.

The important thing for Nick to be aware of is that **CA 2006, s. 561** is subject to several exceptions. Those relating to the issue of bonus shares (**s. 564**) and securities held under employee share schemes (**s. 566**) do not seem to apply here. However allotments for non-cash consideration are also excluded (**s. 565**) and this would be an easy way for the directors to avoid Nick's pre-emption rights. Furthermore, the articles of a private company can exclude all or any of the statutory pre-emption requirements whether generally or in relation to allotments of a particular description: **s. 567**.

There are also ways in which pre-emption rights can be disapplied. Particularly relevant here is the ability of private companies with only one class of shares to disapply the rights, giving the directors power by the articles, or by special resolution, to allot equity securities as if **s. 561** did not apply to the allotment, or applied as modified by the directors: **s. 569(1)**. (Rights can also be disapplied where a company has a provision in its articles to that effect (**s. 567**) or where the company's articles make separate provision for pre-emption rights in relation to a class (**s. 568**), while **ss. 570 and 571** provide for disapplication generally or for a specific allotment where the authority to allot arises under **s. 551**).

Accordingly, while it would seem that the directors' proposed allotment to Rafael would be in breach of Nick's rights of pre-emption, there are many routes by which these rights could be avoided or disapplied. If the rights have not been excluded or disapplied then Luciferous Ltd and its directors will be liable to compensate Nick. Nick should also be aware that the allotment may give him grounds to petition under **CA 2006, s. 994** as conduct that is unfairly prejudicial to his interests as a member: see, eg *Re Coloursource Ltd* [2005] BCC 627.

 Question 4

Utopia plc has a share capital of two million £1 ordinary shares and one million £1 7 per cent cumulative preference shares. The preference shares have the following rights under the articles:

(a) to participate rateably with the ordinary shareholders in the profits of the company,

(b) a preferential right to dividends and repayment of capital on winding up, and

(c) no right to attend meetings and to vote

Following the sale of its chain of 'Paradiso Hotels', the company has capital surplus to its requirements and the directors of Utopia plc decided that, operating a reduced business following the disposal, it will be difficult to support the payment of the preferential dividend. The board decided, therefore, to formally reduce the company's capital by buying in and cancelling the preferential shares.

In accordance with the procedure under **Companies Act 2006 (CA 2006), s. 645**, Utopia plc passed a resolution to reduce the issued share capital by repaying the preference shares at par. The preference shareholders did not receive notice of the meeting and the vote was passed by the holders of the ordinary shares. The preference shareholders have not yet received a dividend in respect of the previous financial year.

Advise the preference shareholders whether:

(a) they can prevent Utopia plc from going through with the reduction, and otherwise

(b) whether they are entitled to arrears of cumulative dividend prior to being bought out

Commentary

This problem raises the issue of the rights of preference shareholders, particularly the fact that, where shareholders are given preferential rights in respect of dividend and return of capital, these are held to be an exhaustive statement of their rights. This means that a preferential right to a return of capital on a winding up excludes the preference shareholders from a right to a share of surplus assets. This has been established in numerous decisions since the 1950s and you are required to show your familiarity with them and to understand their significance.

The question also raises the issue of the right of shareholders to claim arrears of undeclared preferential dividend.

Answer plan

- Rule relating to the interpretation of class rights and recognition of the exhaustive nature of any preferential right

- Explanation of the significance of the application of this rule of interpretation which makes the preference shareholder vulnerable to a selective reduction of company capital

- Recognition that such a selective reduction does not constitute a variation of class rights; neither would it enable a petition on the grounds of unfair prejudice

- Explanation of the position regarding arrears of undeclared dividend

Suggested answer

This problem raises the issue of the interpretation of class rights as set out in the company's articles and whether there has been a variation of those rights in breach of the requirements of the **Companies Act 2006 (CA 2006)**. It also concerns the date at which the right to a dividend vests and becomes an actionable right against the company.

The legal presumption in respect of the interpretation of class rights is that all shares have equal rights unless otherwise stated. The rights referred to are the right to a dividend, the right to attend and to vote at the general meetings of the company, and the right to the return of capital in the event of the winding up of the company. In contradiction of this statement of equality, however, it has been held that where a particular class of share has been given a preferential right in any one of these areas, this is an exhaustive statement of the shareholder's right in that respect.

This was first decided in respect of the right of preference shareholders to a preferential, fixed dividend paid in priority to the ordinary shareholders. Thus, in *Will v United Lankat Plantations Ltd* [1914] AC 11 the House of Lords affirmed a Court of Appeal decision that where shareholders were entitled to a fixed dividend of 10 per cent in preference to the payment of a dividend to the ordinary shareholders, they had no further right to participate when a higher dividend was paid to the ordinary shareholders. The decision was of great importance to the holders of preference shares which, previous to this decision, had been presumed to be participating preferential, or preferred ordinary, shares. This meant that, in addition to receiving their fixed dividend in priority to a payment of dividend to the ordinary shareholders, they could share in any payment of dividend in excess of their fixed dividend when the distribution was made to the ordinary shareholders.

This decision was later extended to cover the preferential right to a return of capital on winding up. In *Scottish Insurance Corporation Ltd v Wilsons & Clyde Coal Co Ltd* [1949] 1 All ER 1068 it was held that where preference shareholders enjoyed a preferential right to return of their capital on winding up, they had no further rights to share in the distribution of surplus assets. This meant that the rights in respect of any surplus assets were the sole preserve of the ordinary shareholders. In this case, the defendant company's business had been nationalized and the company proposed to pay off the preference capital in anticipation of liquidation. Once the company had paid off the preference shareholders, it intended to distribute as surplus assets to the ordinary shareholders the compensation received by the company for the transfer of the company's business and assets to the National Coal Board.

This scheme was opposed by the holders of the preference shares who believed that this would rob them of their right to participate in surplus assets in the liquidation. The shareholders also claimed that the proposed selective reduction was unfair since it deprived them of the right to continue to receive a favourable return (7 per cent) on their investment. The court equated the position of preference shareholders to that of a creditor stating: 'Whether a man lends money to a company at 7% or subscribes for its shares carrying a cumulative preferential dividend at that rate, I do not think that he can complain of unfairness if the company, being in a position lawfully to do so, proposes to pay him off.' The consequence of this decision was to allow companies to engage in a selective reduction of capital under **CA 2006, s. 641** by reducing their capital to repay the preference shares and to cancel them.

In another decision arising out of the nationalization of the coal industry, *Re Chatterley-Whitfield Collieries Ltd* [1948] 2 All ER 593, the company proposed to continue its mining activities in Northern Ireland but the loss of its principal business activity meant that it had capital surplus to its requirements. The company proposed to repay out of its reserves the whole of the preference capital at par and to cancel them. The articles entitled the preference shareholders to the return of their capital on a winding up in priority to the ordinary shareholders. The Court of Appeal held that a company that reached a decision that it could no longer support the dividend payments on its preferential capital would be guilty of financial ineptitude if it did not take steps to reduce its capital by paying off the preferential shares. It also stated that, in confirming a reduction of capital, the court will require the reduction to be effected by the repayment of capital in the first instance to those shareholders entitled to priority in a winding up. This decision was confirmed by the House of Lords in *Prudential Assurance Co Ltd v Chatterley-Whitfield Collieries Ltd* [1949] AC 512.

In *Re Saltdean Estate Co Ltd* [1968] 1 WLR 1844, the court approved of the statement by Lord Greene MR in *Prudential Assurance Co Ltd v Chatterley-Whitfield Collieries Ltd* that the risk of prior repayment on a reduction of capital 'is a liability that anyone has only himself to blame if he does not know it'. The court also stated that such prior payment was not a variation or abrogation of any right attached to such a share. This was approved by the House of Lords in *House of Fraser plc v ACGE Investment Ltd* [1987] AC 387 where, faced with the cancellation of preference shares, it approved the statement in the Court of Appeal: 'the proposed cancellation of the preference shares would involve fulfilment or satisfaction of the contractual rights of the shareholders, and would not involve any variation of their rights'. This is so even if preference shareholders have further rights of participation with regard to dividend (*Re Saltdean Estate Co Ltd*).

This means that it is impossible for shareholders in such a situation to claim that they are the victims of a variation of their class rights in breach of **CA 2006, s. 630(2)**, unless the articles expressly provided that the rights attached to a class of share shall be deemed to be varied by a reduction of the capital paid up on the shares, when a separate class meeting would be required. In *Re Northern Engineering Industries plc* [1994] 2 BCLC 704, the preference shareholders had sought to protect themselves by the insertion into the company's articles of a provision that a reduction of capital paid up on their shares was deemed to be a variation of their rights requiring approval in a separate class meeting. The company argued that the variation only covered a reduction in the paid up value not the extinction of the capital by repayment of the total amount. The Court held that 'reduction' included 'extinction'.

The company can, therefore, pass a resolution (voted by the holders of ordinary shares) to reduce the company's capital by cancelling the preference shares and repaying them (possibly at their nominal value) without the preference shareholders having a say in the matter. It is also clear that the court will confirm the decision under **s. 645**.

It would not be possible, either, for the preference shareholders to claim unfair prejudice under **CA 2006, s. 994**.

We are also asked to advise the preference shareholders as to whether they are entitled to their arrears of unpaid dividend before they can be bought in and cancelled. Claims in respect of arrears of undeclared cumulative preference dividend are not provable in a winding up. Arrears of declared cumulative dividend are a deferred debt in a winding up and only payable out of surplus assets remaining after repayment of other debts. It would, therefore, not be possible for the preference shareholders to claim payment of arrears of undeclared dividend.

In conclusion, Utopia plc can proceed with its scheme without fear of any intervention in favour of the rights of the preference shareholders as long as they comply with the statutory rules relating to reduction of capital.

? Question 5

To what extent can it be claimed that the law adequately protects shareholders against a variation of their class rights? Analyse the strengths and weaknesses of the current system with particular regard to preference shareholders.

Commentary

This question requires you to discuss the law relating to the protection of shareholders against a variation of their rights by the company. The position is that variation of class rights can only be achieved in accordance with express variation of class rights terms contained in the company's articles and, in the absence of such a provision, in compliance with the statutory provisions under **CA 2006**. An analysis of the effectiveness of the protection cannot be complete without discussion of the judicial interpretation of a variation of class rights. This severely reduces the potential protection offered by the statute.

Answer plan

- Statement of the statutory protection of class rights
- Judicial interpretation of class rights: positive and negative aspects
- Possibility of shareholders claiming that a variation could be successfully contested by a petition against unfair prejudice: **s. 994**
- Possible breach of directors' duty to act fairly between members of the company

Suggested answer

In order to increase the protection of shareholders against a variation of their class rights, there is statutory regulation of variation of class rights. As a result, class rights cannot be varied under the normal statutory provision relating to the alteration of the company's articles in general (a special resolution under **Companies Act 2006 (CA 2006), s. 21**), but can only be varied in accordance with a variation procedure in the company's constitution or in accordance with **CA 2006, ss. 630–40**. Although these provisions distinguish between companies with and without a share capital, this answer will consider only companies with a share capital.

Rights attached to a class of a company's shares can only be varied in accordance with a variation provision in the company's articles or with the consent of the holders of shares of that class in accordance with the section: **s. 630(2)**. The consent required for these purposes is consent in writing from the holders of at least three-quarters in nominal value of the issued shares of that class, or a special resolution passed at a separate class meeting: **s. 630(4)**. Any amendment of a provision in the company's articles for the variation of class rights, or the insertion of such a provision into the articles, is itself to be treated as a variation of those rights: **s. 630(5)**. Any reference in the section and in a provision in the articles to variation of rights shall include a reference to their abrogation: **s. 630(6)**.

This is without prejudice to any other restrictions on the variation of the rights (s. 630(3)) which allows for the possibility that variation may be restricted by entrenched provisions of the articles under **CA 2006, s. 22**.

As added protection, where rights attached to any class of share are varied under **s. 630**, the Act provides for the holders of not less in the aggregate than 15 per cent of the issued shares of the class in question (if they did not consent to or vote in favour of the resolution for the variation) to apply to the court to have the variation cancelled (s. 633(2)) on the ground that the variation would unfairly prejudice the shareholders of the class represented by the applicant (s. 633(5)). If an application is made, the variation has no effect unless and until it is confirmed by the court: s. 633(3). The application must be within 21 days of the giving of the consent or the passing of the resolution (s. 633(4)).

At first sight then there would appear to be adequate statutory protection of shareholders against variation of their class rights. However, it is necessary to look at the judicial interpretation of class rights to analyse the protection that the courts have been willing to recognize.

On the positive side, the court has held that a vote on a resolution to modify class rights must be exercised for the purpose, or dominant purpose, of benefiting the class as a whole: *British America Nickel Corpn Ltd v O'Brien* [1927] AC 369. In this case, the company had issued mortgage bonds secured by a trust deed that provided that a majority of bondholders, representing not less than three-quarters in value, could sanction a modification of the bondholders' rights. A scheme for reconstruction of the company was approved by the requisite majority, but it was held that one of the bondholders, without whose vote the proposal would have failed, had been induced to support the proposal by the promise of a large block of ordinary shares. The Privy Council held that the vote was invalid.

In the same way, it has been held that shareholders voting in a class meeting in connection with a reduction of capital must have regard to the interests of the class as a whole: *Re Holders Investment Trust Ltd* [1971] 1 WLR 583. In this case, the company sought confirmation from the court of a reduction of capital by which it proposed to cancel the redeemable preference shares and to allot the holders an equivalent amount of unsecured loan stock. The proposal was approved by an extraordinary class meeting of the preference shareholders at which 90 per cent of the votes cast were held by trustees who also held about 52 per cent of the ordinary shares and who, as such, stood to gain substantially from the reduction. The court held that the vote was ineffective because the majority preference shareholders had voted in their own interests without regard to what was best for the preference shareholders as a class.

A further positive step was to increase the scope of the definition of what constituted class rights, over and above the traditional notion of rights attached to particular shares concerning the right to vote, to participate in dividends and to return of capital on winding up. In *Cumbrian Newspapers Group Ltd v Cumberland & Westmorland Herald Newspaper & Printing Co Ltd* [1986] BCLC 286 the plaintiff had acquired

10.67 per cent of the ordinary shares and the articles of the defendant were altered to give the plaintiff:

(a) rights of pre-emption over the company's other ordinary shares;

(b) rights in respect of unissued shares; and

(c) the right to appoint a director for as long as the plaintiff continued to hold at least 10 per cent of the shares.

The court held that these were rights or benefits conferred on the beneficiary in the capacity of member or shareholder of the company and thereby rights attached to a class of shares which could not be altered or removed by a special resolution under what is now s. 21(1) but could only be varied under what is now s. 630.

In *Harman v BML Group Ltd* [1994] 1 WLR 893, a company had B shares and A shares. Under a shareholders' agreement the two classes of shares ranked equally except for certain specified pre-emption rights, and a shareholders' meeting could not be quorate unless a B shareholder was present or represented by a proxy. The Court of Appeal held that this right to be present for a quorum was a class right.

In other ways, however, the courts have significantly weakened the protection offered to holders of a particular class of shares by narrowing the very concept of 'variation', effectively making a distinction between direct and indirect variation of shareholders' rights. While a direct variation of class rights is protected by the law, the court has held that the rights of a class of shareholders are not 'varied' by a change in the company's structure or in the rights attached to other shares which affects merely the enjoyment of such rights. In *White v Bristol Aeroplane Co* [1953] Ch 65, the company's articles provided that the rights attached to any class of shares might be 'affected, modified, varied, dealt with, or abrogated in any manner' with the sanction of an extraordinary resolution at a class meeting. The company, which had an issued capital of £600,000 preference and £3.3m ordinary shares, proposed to issue to the existing ordinary shareholders 660,000 preference shares of £1 each and 2.64m ordinary shares at 50p each, financed from the company's reserves. This was held not to affect the rights of the existing holders of preference shares so as to require their approval. Their rights were as before although effectively swamped by the enlargement of the class of persons entitled to exercise them: see also *Re John Smith's Tadcaster Brewery* [1953] Ch 308.

In *Greenhalgh v Arderne Cinemas Ltd* [1946] 1 All ER 512 the company had two classes of share: one with a nominal value of 10p and the other with a nominal value of 50p; both shares had the right to one vote per share. The holder of the 10p shares was able to dominate the company's decisions. To destroy the power of this class of share, the company passed a resolution splitting the 50p shares into five 10p shares, each with a right to one vote per share. The court held that this was not a variation of the rights of the holder of the 10p shares. In an extraordinary decision, the court also held that a rateable reduction of all shares, including preference shares, was not a variation of the class rights of the preference shares, although it resulted in a reduction of the preference dividend while it did not affect the ordinary dividend: *Re Mackenzie & Co Ltd* [1916] 2 Ch 450.

In respect of these decisions, it is clear that the disadvantaged shareholders would now be able to bring a claim in respect of unfair prejudice under **CA 2006, s. 994**. It is also clear that, if it could be established that the directors were not acting fairly as between members of the company in accordance with **s. 172(1)(f)**, they could be in breach of their duty to the company which could give rise to civil penalties under **s. 178**, although it must be acknowledged that this duty is owed to the company and not the shareholders themselves.

Further reading

Milne, E., 'Joint venture shareholders: protecting your position' (2010) 21 PLC 45

Pennington, R., 'Can shares in companies be defined?' (1989) 10 Co Law 140

Pickering, M. A., 'The problem of the preference share' (1963) 26 MLR 499

Directors and their duties

Introduction

This topic is a major source of examination questions in all company law programmes. The first thing to be aware of is the extended definition of directors to include *de jure* and *de facto* directors. This has been particularly important for director disqualification cases but is also relevant to directors' duties more generally. The distinction—if any—between *de facto* and shadow directors has been a matter of some legal debate. Companies may have corporate directors, although the **Companies Act 2006 (CA 2006), s. 155** requires a company to have at least one natural director and the Department for Business, Innovation and Skills has recently consulted on abolishing corporate directors altogether (see 'Transparency and trust: discussion paper' (BIS/13/959), July 2013). The position of nominee directors is also of interest in relation to directors' duties.

One of the major changes of the **CA 2006** was the codification of directors' duties. The 'general duties' of directors are now set out in **ss. 171–7**, but, as **s. 170(3) and (4)** make clear, these are based on the preceding common law rules and equitable principles and regard should be had to those rules and principles in interpreting and applying the statutory duties, so pre-2006 decisions are still very much relevant. Furthermore, **s. 178** provides that the consequences of breach are the same as would apply if the corresponding common law rules and equitable principles applied.

The general duties of a director, as set out in **ss. 171–7**, are:

- Duty to act within powers
- Duty to promote the success of the company
- Duty to exercise independent judgment
- Duty to exercise reasonable care, skill, and diligence
- Duty to avoid conflicts of interest
- Duty not to accept benefits from third parties
- Duty to declare interest in proposed transaction or arrangement

The general duties are not in all points an exact replica of the pre-2006 law; although described as a codification of duties the **CA 2006** does make some changes. Some are quite significant (eg **s. 172**) while others clarify the legal position (eg **s. 174**).

As well as the general duties, further obligations and restrictions are applied in relation to specific situations, key amongst which are substantial property transactions (**ss. 190–6**); directors' long-term service contracts (**ss. 188–9**) and loans, quasi-loans, and credit transactions (**ss. 197–214**). It is also worth bearing in mind the ways in which a director may avoid liability, in particular through ratification (where **s. 239** now provides some clarity) and the ability of the court under **s. 1157** to relieve a director from liability if he has acted honestly, reasonably, and ought fairly to be excused.

Directors and their duties is a large and sometimes complex topic. In addition, because of the importance of directors to the company, directors' duties can overlap with lots (indeed most) other topics—particularly common links are with company contracts, minority protection, company management/corporate governance, share capital, and corporate insolvency.

 Question 1

Section 250 of the Companies Act 2006 gives an extended definition of 'director' to include not only *'de jure* directors' but also *'de facto* directors'. In respect of *'de facto* directors' and 'shadow directors' consider the ways in which the courts have attempted to distinguish between the two and whether there is a meaningful distinction between them.

 Commentary

This is a relatively straightforward question that requires appreciation of the different statutory definitions of shadow director in the statutes and the significance of the difference. It also calls for discussion and analysis of a number of judicial decisions to trace the evolution of the concepts of *de facto* and shadow directors.

 Answer plan

- Statement of the definitions of 'director' in UK legislation and analysis of the differences arising from those definitions
- Identification of the vulnerable parties
- Analysis of judicial decisions concerning attempts to define and distinguish between *de facto* and shadow directors
- Flexible approach of the UK courts stressing similarities

Suggested answer

A director is defined as including 'any person occupying the position of a director, by whatever name called': **Companies Act 2006 (CA 2006), s. 250.** There are three categories of director: *de jure* directors, *de facto* directors, and shadow directors. The last is defined as persons 'in accordance with whose directions or instructions the directors of the company are accustomed to act', but excluding persons giving advice in a professional capacity: **CA 2006, s. 251.** There is a proviso that 'a body corporate is not to be treated as a shadow director of any of its subsidiary companies by reason only that the directors of the subsidiary are accustomed to act in accordance with its directions or instructions'.

The **Company Directors Disqualification Act 1986** contains a similar definition of a director (s. 22(4)) and shadow director (s. 22(5)), as does the **Insolvency Act 1986 (IA 1986) (s. 251).** The proviso excluding parent companies in respect of their subsidiaries is missing, however, and parent companies can be shadow directors of subsidiaries for the purposes of **IA 1986, s. 214** (wrongful trading) and are subject to statutory disqualification. The parties most vulnerable to claims of being *de facto* or shadow directors are major shareholders, creditors (including banks), and consultants, and they are the subject of most of the legal decisions considered below.

UK decisions have attempted to define and distinguish between *de facto* and shadow directors. In *Re Lo-Line Electric Motors Ltd* [1988] Ch 477, Sir Nicolas Browne Wilkinson VC likened a shadow director to an *éminence grise*. And Harman J in *Re Unisoft Group Ltd* [1994] 1 BCLC 609 referred to the shadow director as 'the puppet master' and the board as the 'cat's paw' of the shadow director.

In *Re a Company (No. 005009 of 1987), ex p Copp* [1989] BCLC 13 it was claimed that a bank which imposed terms on a technically insolvent company allowing it to continue to trade was a shadow director. In *Kuwait Asia Bank EC v National Mutual Life Nominees Ltd* [1991] 1 AC 187, the Kuwait Bank and another company held 80 per cent of the shares in AIC Securities Ltd (AICS). By agreement, AICS was to have five directors, two nominated by the bank and three by the other company. The bank's nominees were bank employees. Rejecting a claim that the bank was a shadow director of ACIS, Lord Lowry stated: '[the bank's nominees] were two out of five directors ... And there is no allegation ... that the directors ... were accustomed to act on the direction and instruction of the bank'. This is authority that a person could only be a shadow director if the board as a whole was accustomed to act on their directions or instructions.

In *Re Hydrodam (Corby) Ltd* [1994] 2 BCLC 180, the liquidator of Hydrodam, a wholly owned subsidiary of Eagle Trust plc, applied for orders against 14 defendants under **IA 1986, s. 214** including Eagle Trust plc and all of its directors maintaining that they were shadow or *de facto* directors of Hydrodam, which only had two corporate directors. Millett J held there was an essential difference between the two, seeing them as alternatives and even 'in most ... cases ... mutually exclusive'.

According to Millett J, a *de facto* director is held out as a director, and claims to be a director although never actually appointed as such. He held that it was necessary to prove that they undertook functions which only a director could properly discharge, and not sufficient to be involved in the company's management or undertaking tasks performable by a manager. In contrast, a shadow director does not claim to be a director and is not held out as such. To be a shadow director, it was necessary to prove: (a) who are the directors of the company—*de facto* or *de jure*; (b) that the alleged shadow director directed them how to act; (c) that they acted in accordance with such directions; and (d) that they were accustomed to do so.

The main issue was whether the directors of a corporate director of another company were automatically shadow or *de facto* directors of that other company. Millett J held that something more would be required in order for this to arise such as active participation of the board member in making board decisions by the corporate director in relation to the actions of the subject company. This position has been endorsed by the majority of the Supreme Court in *Holland v Commissioners for Revenue & Customs*; *Re Paycheck Services 3 Ltd* [2010] UKSC 51 where it was held that an individual whose acts are wholly referable to his role as director of a corporate director of Company A is not a *de facto* director of Company A.

A clear distinction between *de facto* and shadow directors was not made in *Re Tasbian Ltd (No 3)* [1991] BCLC 792 where the Court of Appeal referred to a 'company doctor' as either a *de facto* or a shadow director for the purposes of disqualification proceedings.

In the Australian case of *Standard Chartered Bank of Australia Ltd v Antico* [1995] 18 ACSR 1 Hodgson J held that the mere fact that one company (Pioneer) held 42 per cent of another company's shares and three nominees on its board did not make it a shadow director of that company, but that it was a shadow director since the three nominee directors made decisions only in their capacity as directors of Pioneer in respect of funding and the granting of security.

Another Australian decision, *Australian Securities Commission v AS Nominees* [1995] 13 ACLC 1822, held that the issue was simply to identify the locus of effective decision making. If the power lay with a third party not claiming adviser protection, the court could find that person a shadow director.

In respect of *de facto* directors, Robert Walker LJ in *Re Kaytech International plc* [1999] 2 BCLC 351, stated that the court should take account of all external and internal factors as a question of fact rather than a single test. Shadow and *de facto* directors had in common the fact that they exercised real influence (otherwise than as professional advisers) in the governance of a company, and that this could be concealed or open and even a combination of both.

The Court of Appeal considered the definition of shadow director in *Secretary of State for Trade and Industry v Deverell* [2000] 2 WLR 907 in respect of disqualification orders against two men who claimed to be 'consultants'. It was established that both men regularly gave advice, which the board followed as a matter of course. Morritt LJ, finding that the two defendants were shadow directors, stated that the issue was who had real influence in the company regardless of labels and forms of communication and that 'shadow director' was to be broadly construed to give effect to the parliamentary intention of the protection of the public rather than strictly construed because of its quasi-penal consequences. The aim was to identify those, apart from professional advisers, with real influence in the company. He agreed with *Australia Securities Commission* and *Re Kaytech* that this did not have to be over the whole field of its corporate activities, but must cover essential matters of corporate governance including financial affairs. It was not a necessary requirement to prove that some or all of the directors placed themselves in a subservient role or surrender their discretion to the shadow director. Describing the board as the cat's paw, puppet, or dancer to the shadow director's tune was a degree of control in excess of the statutory requirement. Neither was it necessary for a shadow director to lurk in the shadows.

Later decisions have continued this debate and the distinction between shadow and *de facto* directors is increasingly blurred. In *Re Mea Corpn Ltd, Secretary of State for Trade and Industry v Aviss* [2006] **EWHC 1846** the court held that the role of the shadow director did not have to extend over the whole range of the company's activities and that there was no conceptual difficulty in reaching the conclusion that a person could be a *de facto* and shadow director at the same time. In *Gemma Ltd v Davies* [2008] **EWHC 546**, the court held that in order to be a *de facto* or shadow director, it had to be shown that the person had 'real influence' on the corporate decision making. In *Holland v Commissioners for Revenue & Customs; Re Paycheck Services 3 Ltd* the Supreme Court recognised the erosion between the concepts of *de facto* and shadow directors. In *Re Mumtaz Properties Ltd* [2011] **EWCA Civ 610** it was held that a person was a *de facto* director even though he had not held himself out to be a director.

In conclusion, while recognizing the value of the extended definition of directors, it is arguably counter-productive to attempt to distinguish between shadow and *de facto* directors.

Question 2

Taking into account **Companies Act 2006, s. 172**, is it true to say that a director owes his duties to the company alone?

Commentary

This question looks at an area of directors' duties where the **CA 2006** has moved away from a pure codification of the previous law. In **s. 172** the complex nature of a company as both a separate entity and an association of members comes to life, while also recognizing the involvement of other 'stakeholders' in a company. Accordingly, the question touches implicitly on an important company law debate: should a company be run purely in the interests of its members (shareholder primacy) or for the benefit of all those with a stake in the company (stakeholding)? You need therefore to have some understanding of this debate—particularly the discussion in, and surrounding, the Company Law Review about the benefits of the two approaches and the 'enlightened shareholder value' approach eventually adopted.

Examiner's tip

The focus of this question is to whom duties are owed rather than **CA 2006, s. 172** itself. This means that although the question specifically mentions **s. 172** you shouldn't provide a lengthy discussion of all aspects of the section (such as the 'good faith' point) that would be relevant in a more general analysis of **s. 172**

 Answer plan

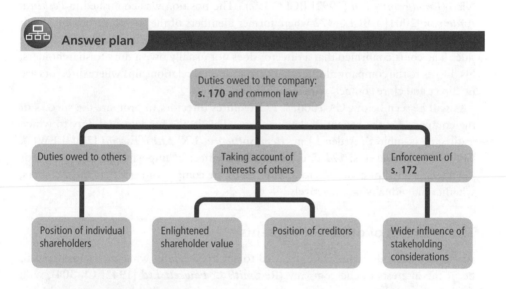

 Suggested answer

A director owes his duties to the company. **Section 170(1)** of the **Companies Act 2006 (CA 2006)** states: 'The general duties … are owed by a director of a company to the company'. This confirms the approach taken at common law prior to the codification of directors' duties in the **CA 2006** although it does not explain what 'the company' is in this context. Even nominee directors owe their duties to the company rather than the person appointing them and can only take account of the appointor's interests to a limited extent (*Hawkes v Cuddy* [2009] 2 BCLC 427).

However, the statement that a director owes his duties to the company does not do justice to the complexities of the relationship between directors, company, shareholders, and other stakeholders. First, there may be situations where a director owes duties to individual shareholders. Secondly, even where a director does not owe duties to others, the interests of other people may still be of significance when carrying out his functions.

Duties owed to shareholders

The circumstances in which a director owes a duty directly to someone other than the company are very limited. *Percival v Wright* [1902] 2 Ch 421 made very clear that directors do not owe duties to shareholders, whether individually or collectively. However, directors may owe duties directly to shareholders where they act as the shareholder's agent (*Allen v Hyatt* (1914) 30 TLR 444) or where the nature of the company and the director–shareholder relationship is such that the directors have taken on direct responsibilities to the shareholders (*Coleman v Myers* [1977] 2 NZLR 225; *Re Chez Nico (Restaurants) Ltd* [1992] BCLC 192). The position was confirmed in *Peskin v Anderson* [2001] 1 BCLC 372 where former members of the Royal Automobile Club Ltd claimed that the directors owed them a duty to disclose the details of a pending sale. The court confirmed that a director does not usually owe a duty to shareholders, his duty is to the company alone, other than in special relationships where directors are in 'direct and close contact' with shareholders.

As will be seen below, CA 2006, s. 172 requires directors to promote the success of the company for the benefit of the members. This is 'the fundamental duty to which a director is subject': Arden LJ in *Item Software (UK) Ltd v Fassihi* [2004] EWCA Civ 1244. However, s. 172 does not have the effect of imposing any duty towards members; a director continues to owe duties to the company rather than the members, whether individually or collectively.

The interests of other constituents

At common law directors were required to act bona fide in what they considered to be in the interests of the company (*Re Smith & Fawcett Ltd* [1942] Ch 304), with the interests of the company being the interests of the shareholders as a general body (*Gaiman v National Association for Mental Health* [1971] Ch 317). In a slight departure from this, s. 172 requires a director to 'act in the way he considers, in good faith, would be most likely to promote the success of the company for the benefit of its members as a whole ...'. This recognizes the dual nature of the company—first as a separate entity that can succeed or fail, and secondly as an association of members who will benefit from the company's success. Section 172(1) then continues: '... and in doing so have regard amongst other matters to ...', and then provides a list of other matters (paragraphs (a)–(f)) which includes the interests of the company's employees; the need to foster business relationships with suppliers, customers, and others; and the impact on the community and the environment.

Section 172 thus imposes only one duty—owed to the company—to promote the company's success for the benefit of its members. But in fulfilling that duty directors must have regard to the listed factors. This is a long way from directors owing a duty to any stakeholder or other interest appearing in the s. 172(1) list; the duty is still to the company alone. To that extent this follows the approach of the Companies Act 1985 which required directors to have regard to employees' interests (CA 1985, s. 309) but this duty was still owed to the company, not to the employees themselves.

The approach of **s. 172** was labelled 'enlightened shareholder value' (ESV) by the Company Law Review. It is fundamentally a 'shareholder primacy' approach in that companies should be run for the benefit of their members, rather than a 'stakeholder' or 'pluralist' approach (whereby companies should be run for the benefit of all those with a stake in the business). However, ESV acknowledges that taking other interests into account can enhance the success of the company which will benefit the shareholders. Under ESV these factors are relevant only in so far as they achieve that aim; they are not to be pursued for their own merits. It is a matter for the directors' business judgement how far those factors are relevant, if at all, in promoting the company's success for the members' benefit. If relevant factors are not taken into account, or are taken into account for reasons other than the success of the company, this would be a breach of the duty to the company and thus enforceable through the company; groups within the **s. 172(1)** list have no right of action. Furthermore, even if an action was brought in respect of a failure to take account of a **s. 172(1)** factor, it might be hard to establish any loss to the company as a result of this.

The position with regard to creditors is particularly interesting. Normally directors do not owe duties to creditors, whether individually or collectively (*Multinational Gas and Petrochemical Co v Multinational Gas and Petrochemical Services Ltd* [1983] Ch 258; *Kuwait Asia Bank EC v National Mutual Life Nominees Ltd* [1991] 1 AC 187). However, in *West Mercia Safetywear v Dodd* [1988] BCLC 250 the court adopted the statement in *Kinsela v Russell Kinsela Pty Ltd* [1986] 4 NSWR 722 that where a company is insolvent directors are obliged to have regard to creditors' interests. This does not mean that a duty is owed to creditors directly; instead the creditors' interests displace those of the members: 'It is in a practical sense their assets and not the shareholders' assets that, through the medium of the company, are under the management of the directors' (Street CJ in *Kinsela v Russell Kinsela Pty Ltd*). This applies also where the company is 'of doubtful solvency or on the verge of insolvency' (*Colin Gwyer and Associates Ltd v London Wharf (Limehouse) Ltd* [2003] 2 BCLC 153). Further, the **Insolvency Act 1986, s. 214** imposes liability on a director if he permits the company to continue to trade beyond the point when he knew or ought to have known there was no reasonable prospect of avoiding insolvent liquidation. Again this does not impose a duty owed to creditors individually; enforcement is through the liquidator and benefits unsecured creditors as a body, rather than those specific creditors who have suffered loss as a result of the breach of **s. 214**. The developing state of the law relating to creditors is reflected in **s. 172(3)** which provides that the **s. 172** duty has effect subject to 'any enactment or rule of law requiring directors, in certain circumstances, to consider or act in the interests of creditors of the company'.

Conclusion

It remains the case that a director owes his duties to the company alone, other than in the very limited circumstances where a direct duty arises in respect of an individual shareholder or shareholders. However, in exercising his overriding duty to act in good faith to promote the success of the company for the benefit of the members, the director must take into account all relevant matters which will include the interests of a whole range of stakeholders and other considerations. **Section 172** thus provides important guidance to directors, but does not give rise to a duty owed to anyone other than the company. Furthermore, since duties are enforceable by the company, any action taken in respect of any breach must be through the company, either through the directors or, more likely, the members in a derivative action under **ss. 260–4**. This means that even if **s. 172** is breached, action is unlikely, and even if a claim were brought successfully, any remedy would benefit the company rather than the aggrieved stakeholder.

The changes wrought by **s. 172** thus do not really change the law in terms of to whom the duties are owed but reflect a more general cultural change in recognizing wider interests and responsibilities as does the business review required under **s. 417** (other than for small companies) which requires analysis of the company's business and the principal risks and uncertainties facing the company and, for quoted companies, information on matters such as employees, community, and the environment. Encouragement of corporate responsibility more generally is a current political priority (see Department for Business, Innovation and Skills, 'Corporate responsibility: a call for views' (BIS/13/964), June 2013). Under the current law duties remain owed to the company while directors are made more aware of their wider responsibilities.

 Question 3

Datacon plc specializes in IT installations for the retail trade. Tariq, a director of Datacon plc, was approached in a private capacity as a well-known expert in the field and invited to join the board of Input Ltd, whose business mirrors to a certain extent Datacon plc's business. Tariq accepted an invitation to be a director while remaining on the board of Datacon plc, and acted as a consultant and adviser.

Having developed a rival system to Datacon plc, Input Ltd organized a public launch of the new product. For the launch, Tariq contacted a number of Datacon plc's clients. The launch led to the signing up of a number of major clients, including some clients of Datacon plc.

(a) **Advise the board of Datacon plc of any breaches of duty committed by Tariq, and any remedies available against him**

(b) **Would your answer be different if he had resigned his directorship of Datacon plc when he joined the board of Input Ltd?**

 Commentary

This problem question raises two related issues: whether a director of one company can become a director of a competing company; and the duty of confidentiality. These are related since early decisions on the issue of overlapping directorships accept the possibility, and only envisage a problem where the director breaches his duty of confidentiality in carrying information from one company into the other. Since the 1970s the problem of overlapping directorships has been frequently discussed but the matter is still not fully resolved.

Answer plan

- Identification of legal problems raised by the questions
- Discussion of legality of interlocking/overlapping directorships
- Breach of confidentiality during directorship and after leaving

Suggested answer

The legal issues raised by this question concern whether a person can hold directorships in competing companies and the issue of the duty of confidentiality in the situation of interlocking directorships.

The first issue to examine is whether by merely joining the board of Input Ltd, Tariq had acted in breach of his fiduciary duties to the company. The legal issue of overlapping directorships was raised initially in *London and Mashonaland Exploration Company Ltd v New Mashonaland Exploration Co Ltd* [1891] WN 165 *(Mashonaland)* where the plaintiff company sought to restrain its chairman and director from acting as director of a rival company. The judgment of Chitty J initially approached the issue by looking for any contractual restraint and concluded that there was nothing in the articles which required him to give any part of his time, much less the whole of his time, to the business of the company, or which prohibited him from acting as a director of another company. He then identified the problem as one of confidentiality stating that no case was made out that the chairman was about to disclose to the defendant company any confidential information gained from his position. This decision was cited with approval by Lord Blanesborough in *Bell v Lever Bros* [1932] AC 161.

The issue was raised again in the light of the decision in *Hivac Ltd v Park Royal Scientific Instruments Ltd* [1946] Ch 169 which held that employees could be restrained from working for a business competing with that of their employer. Following this decision, doubts were expressed as to whether *Bell v Lever Bros* still accurately reflected the law: per McDonald J in *Abbey Glen Property Corpn v Stumborg* (1975) 65 DLR (3d) 235.

The issue was dealt with in *Plus Group Ltd v Pyke* [2002] EWCA Civ 370, [2002] 2 BCLC 201 where the Court of Appeal approved the trial judge's statement that: 'it is not a breach of fiduciary duty for a director to work for a competing company in circumstances where he has been excluded effectively from the company of which he is a director'.

The court, however, seemed to indicate that, in general, the holding of competing directorships would require the approval of the companies in question; but that there was no rigid rule that a director could not be involved in the business of another company which was in competition with the company of which he was a director, and stressed that the situation was 'fact specific'. In this case the court referred to *Scottish Co-operative Wholesale Society Ltd v Meyer* [1959] AC 324 which, while not entirely relevant to the situation, shows the problems that can arise regarding owing fiduciary duties to more than one company, although the situation in that case concerned the problem of the nominee director. More recently the Scottish courts in *Commonwealth Oil & Gas Co Ltd v Baxter* [2009] CSIH 75 cast doubt on the judgment in *Mashonaland* and limited the case to its own facts.

The fiduciary and common law duties of directors have now been codified in **CA 2006** and **s. 175** (dealing with conflicts of interest) makes explicit that the duty applies equally to a conflict of duty and duty (**s. 175(7)**). A breach of **s. 175** can thus clearly arise because of duties owed to two different companies pulling in two different directions, reflecting the views of the later cases discussed above. The only way to avoid this would be to ensure that both companies are fully aware of the position and agree to it, although even with this protection it can be hard to avoid a breach of duty, as recognized outside the company sphere in *Bristol and West Building Society v Mothew* [1996] **4 All ER 698**. Accordingly, while *Mashonaland* suggests there would not appear to be a breach of duty by merely joining the board of another company, once Tariq acts in that position, in a competing company, it is hard to envisage how he could possibly avoid being in breach of **s. 175**.

In any event Tariq clearly acts in breach of his duty of confidentiality in publicizing the launch of Input Ltd's competing software to clients of Datacon plc, while remaining on the board of Datacon plc. In this case, Datacon plc would be entitled to claim damages against Tariq. This would clearly be a breach of the general duty to avoid situations in which a director has, or can have, a direct or indirect interest that conflicts, or possibly may conflict, with the interests of the company (**s. 175(1)**), which applies to exploitation of any property, information, or opportunity: **s. 175(2)**. In addition, the decision in *Item Software (UK) Ltd v Fassihi* [2004] EWCA Civ 1244 suggests that the director would also have a duty to disclose to the company his own wrongdoing as part of his duty to act in good faith in the interests of the company (**s. 172**), although this has met with some criticism.

The position would be different, however, had Tariq resigned from the board of Datacon plc as soon as he joined the board of Input Ltd. Once he had resigned from his directorship, and in the absence of any restraint of trade clause prohibiting him from contacting clients of Datacon plc during a reasonable period of time, Tariq would be able to escape claims of breach of confidentiality in contacting Datacon plc's clients.

The situation would be analogous to the decision in *Island Export Finance Ltd v Umunna* [1986] BCLC 460 where the plaintiff company was unsuccessful in an action regarding breach of confidentiality against the defendant, the ex-managing director of the company. The issue in this case concerned Umunna's knowledge of the Cameroon postal authorities' need for postal boxes, previously supplied by IEF Ltd. The court held that, once Umunna had resigned from the company, this knowledge ceased to be confidential and could be used by him in the absence of any restraint of trade clause to bring in business to the business that he had since established. The court applied the classification of confidential information that had been established in *Faccenda Chicken Ltd v Fowler* [1987] Ch 117. In this case, the court held that there were three types of confidential information and that knowledge of a former employer's client list was category 2 information which an employee (and by analogy a director) was able to use once leaving their employment or the board. However, Tariq would have to be careful to ensure that he did not use confidential information or take active steps in promoting a competing business prior to his departure or he could be found in breach of duty (see, eg *Colman Taymar Ltd v Oakes* [2001] 2 BCLC 749 and *Shepherds Investments Ltd v Walters* [2007] 2 BCLC 202). Furthermore, a former director remains subject to **s. 175** in relation to exploitation of information or an opportunity he became aware of while he was a director (**s. 170(2)(a)**) in circumstances where there is a conflict of interest; so Tariq could still be liable if he resigned in order to take up an opportunity or use confidential information (see *Foster Bryant Surveying Ltd v Bryant* [2007] 2 BCLC 239).

Thus, although by merely joining the board of a competing company Tariq may not in breach of any duty to Datacon plc, by acting as a director in a competing business and communicating confidential information belonging to Datacon plc to the board of Input Ltd he is in breach of his duty to avoid conflicts of interest: **s. 175**. Once he has resigned from the board of Datacon plc, however, he is free to use this information in his new position as director of Input Ltd, provided he did not leave in order to exploit the information obtained through his directorship with Datacon Ltd.

 Question 4

Analyse the development of the director's duty of care, skill, and diligence from the common law position of *Re City Equitable Fire Assurance Co Ltd* [1925] Ch 407 to the present day.

 Commentary

This essay question requires you to analyse the influences that have changed the law from the old laissez-faire attitude typified by the decision in *Re City Equitable Fire Assurance Co Ltd* into something more suited to the modern, regulated world of business. You will need to examine how the common law duty of care, skill, and diligence was influenced by **IA 1986** and **Company Directors Disqualification Act 1986 (CDDA 1986)** provisions, and how this has been recognized in the statutory duty to exercise reasonable care, skill, and diligence under **CA 2006, s. 174**.

 Answer plan

- The three propositions of *Re City Equitable Fire Assurance*
- Influence of **IA 1986, s. 214** and relevant decisions
- Influence of **CDDA 1986** and relevant decisions
- Evidence of change to the understanding of the duties of care, skill, and diligence of directors
- The current position in **CA 2006, s. 174**

Suggested answer

It was long felt that in respect of directors' duties of care, skill, and diligence, statements of the law in long-established cases reflected the nineteenth-century approach to the role of the director and were no longer compatible with current perceptions of the standards to which directors should aspire. The current law is now contained in **Companies Act 2006 (CA 2006), s. 174** as one of the 'general duties' of directors, and it will be argued that this reflects developments already seen in the case law prior to codification.

The classic authority in this area was the judgment of Romer J in *Re City Equitable Fire Assurance Co Ltd* [1925] Ch 407 which established, first 'A director need not exhibit in the performance of his duties a greater degree of skill than may reasonably be expected from a person of his knowledge and experience', secondly 'A director is not bound to give continuous attention to the affairs of his company. His duties are of an intermittent nature ...' and thirdly that 'In respect of all duties that ... may properly be left to some other official, a director is, in the absence of grounds for suspicion, justified in trusting that official to perform such duties honestly.'

These propositions reflected the contemporary values and culture exemplified in decisions like *Re Cardiff Savings Bank, Marquis of Bute's Case* [1892] 2 Ch 100 where the Marquis, who became chairman at the age of six months and attended only one board meeting in 38 years, was not in breach of duty, and *Re Brazilian Rubber Plantations and Estates Ltd* [1911] 1 Ch 425 where Neville J stated that: 'directors were not bound to bring any special qualifications to their business'; and could 'undertake the management of a rubber company in complete ignorance of anything connected with rubber'.

Even before the **CA 2006**, the law had evolved from this position. The initially subjective nature of the duty owed by directors was influenced by the dual objective/subjective test imposed in respect of wrongful trading under **Insolvency Act 1986 (IA 1986), s. 214(4)** which judged directors against: (a) the general knowledge, skill, and experience that may reasonably be expected of a person carrying out the same functions as are carried out by that director in relation to the company; and (b) the general knowledge, skill, and experience that that director has. In *Norman v Theodore Goddard (A Firm)* [1991] BCLC 1028, Hoffmann J was willing to assume that the test of the director's duty of care should be based on this and he restated this as a proposition of the law in *Re D'Jan of London Ltd* [1994] 1 BCLC 561 *(Re D'Jan)*.

Another major influence came from decisions relating to the disqualification of directors under the **Company Directors Disqualification Act 1986 (CDDA 1986)** on the ground that a director's 'conduct as a director of that company ... makes him unfit to be concerned in the management of a company': **CDDA 1986, ss. 6** and **8**. In determining whether the director is unfit, **s. 9** requires the court to have regard in particular to the matters in **Part I** of **Schedule 1** and where the company is insolvent (as will be the case in the majority of disqualification cases) **Part II** of **Schedule 1**, which includes: 'Any misfeasance or breach of any fiduciary or other duty by the director in relation to the company.'

The courts have explicitly acknowledged that the main purpose of disqualification under the **CDDA 1986** is to protect the public, and part of this protection is by raising standards of conduct among directors generally. Thus, in *Re Westmid Packing Services Ltd, Secretary of State for Trade and Industry v Griffiths* [1998] 2 All ER 124 Lord Woolf MR stated that the purpose of disqualification was not simply to keep 'bad' directors 'off the road' but to protect the public in a wider sense by encouraging other directors to behave well. The influence of this legislation can be seen in the statement by Hoffmann LJ in *Bishopsgate Investment Management Ltd v Maxwell (No. 2)* [1994] 1 All ER 261:

> 'In the older cases the duty of a director to participate in the management of a company is stated in very undemanding terms. The law may be evolving in response to changes in public attitudes to corporate governance as shown by the enactment of the provisions ... in the Company Directors Disqualification Act 1986.'

The second and third propositions that directors are not bound to give continuous attention to the company's affairs, and can delegate responsibility to others were also qualified by subsequent decisions. Thus, in *Re Barings plc (No 5)* [2000] 1 BCLC 523, in formulating the scope and extent of directors' duties of care, skill, and diligence Jonathan Parker J highlighted the 'inescapable, personal duties' of a director and established that:

(a) Directors have, both collectively and individually, a continuing duty to acquire and maintain a sufficient knowledge and understanding of the company's business to enable them properly to discharge their duties as directors.

(b) While directors are entitled to delegate particular functions to those below them and to trust their competence and integrity to a reasonable extent this does not absolve a director from the duty to supervise the discharge of delegated functions. (This is also recognized in *Re Westmid Packing Services Ltd, Secretary of State for Trade and Industry v Griffiths* [1998] 2 All ER 124: 'a proper degree of delegation is of course permissible, and often necessary, but total abrogating of responsibility is not ...').

The judge held that the extent of the duty and the question whether it has been discharged must depend on the facts of each particular case, including the director's role in the management of the company.

Judicial intolerance of inactivity can be seen in *Lexi Holdings (in administration) v Luqman and ors* [2009] EWCA Civ 117 where a fraud was committed by the first defendant and it was held that the failure of two other directors to perform their duties had prevented the misconduct from being discovered; as a result of their inactivity, the two defendants were held liable for the full amounts claimed against them. It was further held that directors who do nothing cannot rely on what is now **CA 2006, s. 1157** which allows the court to give relief where a director has acted 'honestly and reasonably' (although in *Re D'Jan* it was accepted that the relief provision can be invoked where a director has acted 'reasonably' albeit in breach of his duty of care and skill).

In *Re Landhurst Leasing plc* [1999] 1 BCLC 286, in disqualification proceedings, Hart J appeared to align the standard of the duty at common law and the standard for unfitness under the **CDDA 1986** with the *Re D'Jan* test based on **IA 1986, s. 214**. However, a breach of the duty of care and skill is not a pre-requisite for a finding of unfitness (in *Cohen v Selby* [2001] 1 BCLC 176 a director escaped personal liability for breach of duty through failure to insure the company's property since it was regarded as reasonable for him to trust the other director, his father, but he was nonetheless disqualified).

It can be seen then that, even without an express overruling of *Re City Equitable Fire Assurance* the law had already developed towards the recognition of an objective standard with an emphasis on monitoring and supervision. This was consolidated by **CA 2006, s. 174** which establishes that a director must exercise 'reasonable care, skill and diligence': that exercised by a 'reasonably diligent person' with both the general knowledge, skill, and experience reasonably expected of someone carrying out the functions of that individual in that company, and the general knowledge, skill, and experience that the individual has. Just as in **IA 1986, s. 214(4)**, **CA 2006, s. 174** thus provides an underlying objective standard (although a standard that can vary according to the nature of the company and the position of the director) and then a further subjective layer of expectation where a director has skills or experience above that which might be expected. This resolves any conflict between *Re City Equitable Fire Assurance* and *Re D'Jan* in favour of the latter, increasing the expectations on directors and improving the prospects of finding a director in breach of duty. This has been strengthened by *Weavering Capital (UK) Ltd v Dabhia and Platt* [2013] EWCA Civ 71 which held there is no need for a judge to set out what the particular knowledge, skills, and experience expected are in a case:

> '... provided a judge recognises the law's requirements as to the duties placed upon directors and, having reviewed the facts, considers that the relevant duty has been broken, it is not necessary to spell out any further what the duty is or the standard of care to be exercised by the particular director whose conduct is being called into question.' (McCombe LJ)

? Question 5

Paradise plc, a quoted company, produces fresh organic fruit. There are three executive directors, Adam, Eve, and Barry as well as three other non-executive directors. Three years ago, Utopia Ltd approached the board of Paradise plc and offered to sell the company a plot of land adjoining one of its principal market gardens.

Because of current uncertainties and a large debt burden, the board rejected the proposal. Subsequently, Adam and Barry, acting through AB Properties Ltd, of which they are the only shareholders and directors, acquired the land in the name of their company for the original asking price of £250,000.

Owing to a recent fall in interest rates and optimistic economic forecasts, the board of Paradise plc regretted its initial failure to acquire the property, which is back on the market at £350,000, and the board contracted on behalf of Paradise plc to acquire the property from AB Properties Ltd. The board was not informed about the identity of the controllers of AB Properties Ltd. Adam and Barry attended the board meeting at which the decision was taken.

Consider the liability of Adam and Barry.

Commentary

This problem question raises the following legal issues: the potential liability of Adam and Barry in taking up a corporate opportunity of Paradise plc and, in the resale of the asset to the company at a profit to a company controlled by them, of their statutory obligation to declare an interest in the transaction and, in view of the size of the transaction, the statutory obligation to obtain the approval by a resolution of the members of the company. This involves you in a discussion of a number of important common law decisions and the application of the statutory provisions of the **CA 2006**.

Answer plan

- Identification of the legal issues raised by the question
- Discussion of the potential conflict of interest of Adam and Barry in the acquisition of a corporate opportunity of Paradise plc
- Statutory controls regarding the resale of the asset owned by AB Ltd to Paradise plc

Suggested answer

This question involves the long-established fiduciary duties of 'no conflict' and 'no profit', that is that a director cannot (without the company's agreement) have an interest that conflicts (or may conflict) with the interests of the company, nor profit from his position. These duties have traditionally been strictly applied in order to ensure that a director is not tempted to further his own interests and position at the expense of the company (*Bray v Ford* [1896] AC 44). These duties were part of the codification of directors' duties in the **Companies Act 2006 (CA 2006)** and so this question requires consideration of the general duties of avoiding conflicts of interests (**s. 175**) and declaring any interest in a proposed transaction or arrangement with the company (**s. 177**). The case law preceding the **CA 2006** remains relevant in interpreting and applying the general duties of directors (**s. 170(3) and (4)**). In addition the question raises the need to obtain members' approval for substantial property transactions between the company and directors under **s. 190**.

Paradise plc's rejection of the offer of a plot of land adjoining one of its principal market gardens resulted in two of Paradise plc's directors, Adam and Barry, taking up the offer personally and purchasing the property in the name of their company, AB Properties Ltd. Subsequently, once Paradise plc reconsidered the matter, the property was sold to Paradise plc by AB Properties Ltd at a profit.

This raises two legal issues. In the first place, it is necessary to consider whether Adam and Barry were in breach of their duty to the company in taking up the offer personally.

Directors must avoid situations in which they have, or can have, a direct or indirect interest that conflicts, or possibly may conflict, with the interests of the company: **CA 2006, s. 175(1)**. This is stated to apply in particular to the exploitation of any property, information, or opportunity (and it is immaterial whether the company could take advantage of the property, information, or opportunity): **s. 175(2)**.

Applying the 'no conflict/no profit' rule established in *Regal (Hastings) Ltd v Gulliver* **[1942] 1 All ER 378** *(Regal Hastings)* Adam and Barry would appear to have acted in breach of the duty since they learned of the opportunity in their position as fiduciaries: in *Regal Hastings* the directors were held in breach of duty even though the directors acted in good faith and in circumstances where the company could not take up the opportunity itself. In *Bhullar v Bhullar* **[2003] 2 BCLC 241** directors were held to be in breach of duty in purchasing land adjacent to the company without telling the company of the opportunity, even though they had found out about the opportunity quite outside their directorship.

However, the issue is complicated by the fact that it would appear that the offer to Paradise plc was rejected bona fide by the company's board. In *Peso Silver Mines Ltd v Cropper* **[1966] SCR 673** the defendant, one of the directors of the claimant, was not liable to account when he formed a syndicate with others to take up an offer of mining claims that had bona fide been rejected by the company.

It is important to note that this decision is by a Canadian court and is probably influenced by the adoption in Canada of the more flexible 'corporate opportunity doctrine' (see also *Canadian Aero Service Ltd v O'Malley* **(1973) 40 DLR (3d) 371**) which moves away from the rigidity of *Regal Hastings*. The UK decision in *Boardman v Phipps* **[1966] 3 All ER 721**, while not a company law case, is nevertheless an example of the application of *Regal Hastings* and reveals a much stricter approach which is also reflected in recent cases such as *Bhullar v Bhullar* and *O'Donnell v Shanahan* **[2009] 2 BCLC 666**.

Adam and Barry could have protected themselves by seeking authorization under **s. 175(4)(b)** which prevents a breach of duty where authorized by the directors (excluding the votes of any interested directors), but it appears they have chosen to keep their intentions secret. On the current state of the authorities then it seems as if Adam and Barry are in breach of duty and could be liable to account for their profits from the subsequent sale.

A further problem arises in connection with the sale of the property by AB Properties Ltd to Paradise plc. Directors who are in any way, directly or indirectly, interested in a proposed transaction or arrangement with the company, must declare the nature and extent of that interest to the other directors: **CA 2006, s. 177(1)**. Although this would obviously be a conflict of interest, **s. 175** does not apply in this situation by virtue of **s. 175(3)**.

This declaration need not be made at a meeting of the directors and can be in writing or in the form of a general notice but it must be made before the company enters into the transaction: **s. 177(2) and (3)**. There are statutory exceptions to this duty to disclose. One does not require a declaration of an interest of which the director is not aware or where a director is not aware of the transaction or arrangement in question: **s. 177(5)**. Since, for this purpose, a director is treated as being aware of matters of which he ought reasonably to be aware, this defence is unavailable. The other cases where a director does not need to declare an interest relate to situations where the transaction cannot be regarded as likely to give rise to a conflict of interest, or to the extent that the other directors are aware of it: **s. 177(6)(a)** and **(b)**. Once again, these are not available for Adam and Barry. As a result of this failure to declare an interest, the company can avoid the contract as in ***Aberdeen Rly Co v Blaikie Bros*** (1854) 2 Eq Rep 1281 since the civil consequences of a breach of the statutory general duties are stated to be the same as if the corresponding equitable principle applied: **CA 2006, s. 178(1)**. In the alternative, the company could also claim damages against the pair. Furthermore, once the transaction is entered into by the company, **s. 182** imposes an obligation on Adam and Barry to declare any interest in it to the other directors as soon as reasonably practicable. Failure to comply with **s. 182** makes them liable to a fine.

Since the transaction is for the sum of £350,000, the transaction also falls within the statutory regulations relating to substantial property transactions. Under these regulations, a company may not enter into an arrangement under which a director of the company or of its holding company, or a person connected with such a director, acquires from the company a substantial non-cash asset, or the company acquires a substantial non-cash asset from such a director or person so connected unless the transaction is approved by a resolution of the members or is conditional on their approval: **s. 190(1)**. An asset is substantial if its value exceeds 10 per cent of the company's asset value and is more than £5,000, or exceeds £100,000: **s. 191(1)**. The civil consequences of a failure to comply with this requirement is that the contract is voidable: **s. 195(2)**. Adam and Barry would also be liable to account to the company for any gain and indemnify the company for any loss: **CA 2006, s. 195(3)**.

In conclusion, Barry and Adam will probably be in breach of their fiduciary duties in respect of the purchase by their company of the property offered to Paradise plc unless the court is prepared to follow the decision in ***Peso Silver Mines Ltd v Cropper***. They will also be in breach of their statutory obligations under **ss. 177, 182** and **190**. As a result, Paradise plc can avoid the contract. Should the company decide to continue with the purchase, Adam and Barry will be liable to account for the profits derived from the sale and indemnify the company for any loss. While Adam and Barry could seek relief from the court under **s. 1157**, it is highly unlikely that the court would find that they acted honestly, reasonably, and ought fairly to be excused, as required by this provision.

 Question 6

A director must use his powers only for proper purposes.
Discuss.

Commentary

For this question you need to analyse the duty now contained in **CA 2006, s. 171(b)**, that a director must 'only exercise powers for the purposes for which they are conferred'. The use of the phrase 'proper purposes' in the question harks back to the common law on which **s. 171(b)** is based; directors must exercise their powers for a proper purpose and not for any collateral purpose. While at common law the 'proper purpose' duty was combined with the duty to act bona fide in the interests of the company, codification in the **CA 2006** has split them into two, the latter being found in **s. 172**.

 Examiner's tip

Keep your focus on the 'proper purposes' duty but deepen your discussion by recognizing links between **s. 171(b)** and other areas of directors' duties.

 Answer plan

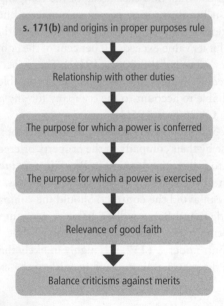

s. 171(b) and origins in proper purposes rule

↓

Relationship with other duties

↓

The purpose for which a power is conferred

↓

The purpose for which a power is exercised

↓

Relevance of good faith

↓

Balance criticisms against merits

 Suggested answer

The 'proper purposes' doctrine is an important part of the duties imposed by law on directors. The articles of association of companies invariably give directors the power to manage the company (eg Article 3 of the Model Articles for Private Companies (**Companies (Model Articles) Regulations 2008, Schedule 1**) and leave very few decisions in the hands of shareholders. To counter this extensive power, the law imposes duties on directors—these are now codified in statutory form as the 'general duties of directors' in **Companies Act 2006 (CA 2006), ss. 171–7.**

Section 171(b) requires a director to 'only exercise powers for the purposes for which they are conferred'. This is based on the long-established fiduciary duty on directors to act only for 'proper purposes' or not for any ulterior purpose (eg to benefit themselves). Accordingly, when exercising any power (cases have shown its application in areas as diverse as entering into agreements (*Lee Panavision Ltd v Lee Lighting Ltd* [1992] BCLC 22) and dealing with company assets (*Extrasure Travel Insurances Ltd v Scattergood* [2003] 1 BCLC 598)), a director must ensure he exercises it only for its proper purpose. If he fails to do so he will be in breach of duty and the exercise of the power will be invalid, although the company in general meeting can choose to affirm the exercise of power and/or ratify the director's breach (**s. 239**) if it chooses.

At common law the proper purpose duty was combined with the duty to act bona fide in the interests of the company. For example in *Re Smith and Fawcett Ltd* [1942] Ch 304 it was said that directors must act: 'bona fide in what they consider – not what a court may consider – is in the interests of the company, and not for any collateral purpose' (Lord Greene MR). However, codification in the CA 2006 has split them with the 'bona fide' duty, reformulated as the duty to promote the success of the company for the benefit of its members, found in **s. 172.** Despite the split, there are still clear links between the two as will be discussed later in this answer. The duty in **s. 171(b)** also overlaps with **s. 171(a)** as a director who fails to 'act in accordance with the company's constitution' may also, depending on the purpose for which he was exceeding his authority, be in breach of **s. 171(b).** A director may also be at risk of breaching **s. 171(b)** when considering other directors' duties, such as **s. 175** (conflict of interest) as 'more than one of the general duties may apply in any given case' (**s. 179**).

Howard Smith Ltd v Ampol Petroleum Ltd [1974] AC 821 *(Howard Smith)* made clear that in assessing this duty the first stage is to consider the power in question and ascertain 'on a fair view' the nature of the power and, 'in the light of modern conditions' the limits within which it may be exercised. The power may be specific (as in *Howard Smith*) or general (the general power of management: *CAS (Nominees) Ltd v Nottingham Forest FC plc* [2002] 1 BCLC 613) and the limits of the power will depend upon the breadth of the power itself. On this point the interrelation of **s. 171** and **s.172** may be relevant as if a director is to avoid breaching **s. 172** (the duty to promote the success of the company for the benefit of the members as a whole) then he must exercise his powers for the ultimate purpose of promoting the success of the company as well as any more specific, narrower purpose.

In *Howard Smith* it was clear that the limits to the exercise of a power are not necessarily drawn narrowly. In that case, dealing with the power to allot shares, the power could properly be exercised not just to raise capital for the company but also to foster business connections, ensure the requisite number of shareholders and to reach the best commercial agreement for the company. However, it could not be exercised in order to alter the majority shareholding, even though done without any intention of personal gain on the part of the directors.

In *Extrasure Travel Insurances Ltd v Scattergood* the court considered that in transferring company assets to another company within the group, the directors were exercising their power to deal with the assets of the company in the course of trading. The purpose for which such a power was conferred was to promote the company's commercial interests, and so exercising the power in order to enable the other company to meet its liabilities was not a proper exercise of that power.

A problem arises where a power is exercised for more than one purpose, one of which is 'proper' and one of which is not—when should this be regarded as exercising the power for the purpose for which it was conferred? In *Howard Smith* the House of Lords determined that once the power had been identified and its limits ascertained, it was necessary to establish the 'substantial purpose' for which it was exercised, and then address whether that substantial purpose was within the previously identified limits of the power. If so, then the power was exercised properly (even if there were other 'improper' purposes), if not the directors were in breach of duty (even if they had acted in good faith).

In assessing what the 'substantial purpose' is, *Howard Smith* made clear that the court should engage in an objective assessment of the situation. Accordingly, the evidence of the directors as to their motives can be challenged. By assessing objectively how 'critical or pressing' a particular issue might have been, the court can evaluate the assertions of directors as to the importance of this factor in their minds when exercising the power, although the directors' judgment on matters of management should be respected.

Accordingly, where directors are motivated by aims other than the purpose for which the power was conferred, they will be in breach of duty and the exercise of power will be invalid. This can be seen in several cases, eg *Hogg v Cramphorn Ltd* [1966] 3 All ER 420 where the directors' allotment of shares was invalidated when made primarily to retain control of the company for the directors and their supporters (and see also *Punt v Symons & Co Ltd* [1903] 2 Ch 506 and *Bamford v Bamford* [1970] Ch 212). In relation to the many cases on allotment of shares it should be noted that there are now additional statutory restrictions including, in most situations, rights of pre-emption for existing shareholders.

It is clear that the proper purpose duty is primarily an objective test; the fact that the directors have acted in good faith and in what they honestly believed to be the best interests of the company will not prevent a breach of **CA 2006, s. 171(b)**. This can be seen, for example, in *Lee Panavision Ltd v Lee Lighting Ltd* where directors were in breach of duty for committing the company to a management agreement, even though they thought it in the company's interests to do so.

While good faith does not prevent a breach of duty, it may still be relevant to a director in seeking relief from liability. If a director acted 'honestly, reasonably and ought fairly to be excused' then he may seek relief from the court under **s. 1157** in respect of any breach of duty and the court may relieve him in whole or in part.

In conclusion a director needs to ensure in any situation that they are exercising their powers for the purpose for which they have been conferred. This is so even if another duty applies as there is a degree of overlap. **Section 171(b)** provides an objective measure against which a director's actions can be measured. This is an important protection given the largely subjective nature of **s. 172** under which a director only needs to act in the way *he considers* in good faith will promote the success of the company for the benefit of the members.

The duty has received some criticism, notably by Professor Sealy (see, eg Sealy, L., 'Directors' duties revisited' (2001) 22 Co Law 79), on the ground that it allows courts to replace directors' business judgement with their own judgment. Furthermore, directors do not have clear boundaries as it has been declared 'impossible' to 'define in advance exact limits beyond which directors must not pass' (*Howard Smith*). However, it is submitted that the protection of **s. 171(b)** outweighs these problems, particularly as the courts are plainly aware of the danger of questioning directors' business judgements with the benefit of hindsight (as recognized in *Howard Smith*). The availability of relief through **s. 1157** or ratification by the company provides some additional leeway to a director honestly acting in what he believes to be the benefit of the company. Accordingly, it very much remains the case following the codification of the law on directors' duties that directors must exercise their powers only for 'proper purposes' and arguably this is as it should be.

Further reading

Aherne, D., 'Nominee directors' duty to promote the success of the company: commercial pragmatism and legal orthodoxy' (2011) 127 LQR 118

Aherne, D., 'Directors' duties, dry ink and the accessibility agenda' (2012) 128 LQR 114

Arden, M., 'Regulating the conduct of directors' (2010) 10 JCLS 1

Copp, S. F., 'S.172 of the Companies Act 2006 fails people and planet' (2010) 31 Co Law 406

Hemraj, M. B., 'Duty of loyalty: company directors' positive obligation to disclose their own misconduct' (2006) 27 Co Law 183

Keay, A., 'Directors taking into account creditors' interests' (2003) 24 Co Law 300

Keay, A., 'Section 172(1) of the Companies Act 2006: an interpretation and assessment' (2007) 28 Co Law 106

Keay, A., 'The duty of directors to exercise independent judgement' (2008) 29 Co Law 290

Keay, A., 'Good faith and directors' duty to promote the success of their company' (2011) 32 Co Law 138

Lim, E., 'Directors' fiduciary duties: a new analytical framework?' (2013) 129 LQR 242

Lynch, E., 'Section 172: a ground-breaking reform of directors' duties, or the Emperor's New Clothes?' (2012) 33 Co Law 196

Worthington, S., 'Reforming directors' duties' (2001) 64 MLR 439

Yap, J. L., 'De facto directorships and corporate directorships' [2012] JBL 579

9

Corporate governance in the UK

Introduction

Corporate governance in a wide sense covers everything from meetings and corporate decision making to shareholders' rights and directors' duties. However, it is often used in the narrow sense of the governance of public (particularly quoted) companies. The problem of good governance is particularly acute in large companies because of the way the corporate form separates 'ownership' (the shareholders) from 'control' (the directors), potentially allowing the directors to run the company for their own benefit rather than that of the shareholders. How then to ensure that directors act in the interests of the members? While statutory regulation would be an option, this is often inflexible, potentially imposing restrictions that unduly hamper a company's activities. The law on directors' duties and shareholder remedies (minority protection) may offer some protection from the worst behaviour, but this is of limited value to shareholders in public companies where shareholdings are diverse and shareholders often disengaged.

In the UK, the governance of listed companies since the early 1990s has been dominated by self-regulatory codes (currently the UK Corporate Governance Code). The Code operates through the London Stock Exchange's Listing Rules which require listed companies to comply with the Code or explain in their annual report why they have not done so. The Corporate Governance Codes have been created and developed as a result of a series of important reports, the first of which was the Cadbury Report (Report of the Committee on the Financial Aspects of Corporate Governance) in 1992. Further reports followed, the most important of which were the Greenbury Report (on directors' remuneration) in 1995, the Hampel Report in 1998 (which reviewed the impact of both Cadbury and Greenbury and made further proposals), the Higgs Report in 2003 (focusing on non-executive directors), the Walker Review (governance in the banking industry), and more recently the Davies Report in 2011 (considering gender issues on company boards), and the Kay Review of UK equity markets and long-term decision making in 2012.

In addition the EU has also shown an increasing interest in corporate governance issues, and the EU Commission Green Paper of April 2011 sought a debate over three main areas: (i) the composition and effectiveness of the board; (ii) shareholder engagement and encouraging long-term performance and (iii) the effectiveness of a 'comply or explain' system, with proposals being made in these areas over 2012–13. The EU has also been at the forefront of pursuing gender balance on boards.

Corporate governance is an increasingly popular subject, particularly in courses with a focus on public companies. It is always topical, as financial scandals and corporate failures periodically erupt into the public consciousness, and a wider interest in business and the economy more generally is an undoubted advantage when tackling this subject. Particularly important topics within corporate governance are the role of non-executive directors, the role of auditors, disclosure of information, executive remuneration, and shareholder engagement. As corporate governance covers such a potentially wide area, it can be linked with numerous topics including corporate management, directors' duties (including the stakeholder debate and corporate social responsibility) and shareholder remedies.

 Question 1

Critically assess the role of the Corporate Governance Code in encouraging and enforcing good corporate governance in the UK.

 Commentary

This question focuses on the UK Corporate Governance Code, which is the latest incarnation of the self-regulatory code of best practice in corporate governance applying to listed companies in the UK (formerly known as the Combined Code, and before that the Cadbury Code). In answering this question it is helpful to outline the origins of the Code in order to explain the context of corporate governance regulation in the UK, but you should avoid giving a purely historical account of the corporate governance regime. More importantly you need to consider the Code's main principles in order to evaluate 'good corporate governance': the most important areas being the balance between executive and non-executive directors, the separation of the roles of chairman and chief executive, and remuneration and appointment. You also need to discuss how these principles are applied and enforced. For this you will need to examine the self-regulatory nature of the Code, and discuss whether this is sufficient to encourage and enforce good corporate governance.

 Examiner's tip

Make sure you balance your arguments—for example don't just explain what self-regulation is; think about its benefits and problems.

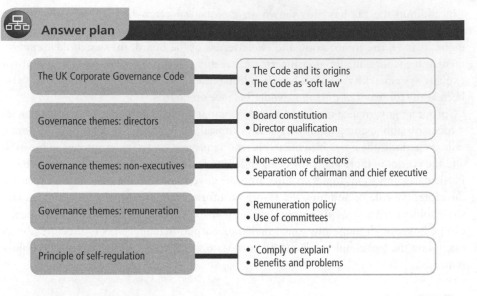

Answer plan

The UK Corporate Governance Code	• The Code and its origins • The Code as 'soft law'
Governance themes: directors	• Board constitution • Director qualification
Governance themes: non-executives	• Non-executive directors • Separation of chairman and chief executive
Governance themes: remuneration	• Remuneration policy • Use of committees
Principle of self-regulation	• 'Comply or explain' • Benefits and problems

Suggested answer

The UK Corporate Governance Code, published by the Financial Reporting Council (FRC) (the independent regulator for corporate reporting and governance), is a code of best practice in corporate governance and applies to public companies listed on the Stock Exchange. This essay will explain the Code's origins and examine the principles behind the Code and behind self-regulation in order to assess how far it promotes and enforces good corporate governance.

The Code started as the Code of Best Practice (or Cadbury Code) created following the Cadbury Report (Report of the Cadbury Committee on the Financial Aspects of Corporate Governance) in 1992. Cadbury focused on the need for a strong and balanced board, to ensure that managing directors/chief executives were not without challenge. This was to be achieved in particular through the use of independent non-executive directors, separating the roles of chairman and chief executive and using sub-committees on appointment, remuneration, and audit.

In 1995 the Cadbury Code was joined by the Greenbury Code (the Code of Best Practice for Directors' Remuneration) which emphasized the importance of the remuneration committee and improved disclosure of directors' remuneration. Subsequently (1998) the Hampel Committee reviewed the Codes of Best Practice and they, with some further recommendations, were consolidated into the 'Combined Code'. Further reports including the important review of Higgs in 2003 (focusing on non-executive directors) led to several revisions of the Code and following review by the FRC, the Combined Code was updated (taking account of the recommendations of the Walker Report on corporate governance in UK banks in 2009) and renamed as the

UK Corporate Governance Code in 2010. There have been further refinements to the Code since then, with notable reports by Davies (2011) on women on boards and Kay (2012) on equity markets and long-term decision making. The FRC has also initiated The Stewardship Code, which establishes good practice for investors, to encourage more active engagement by institutional investors.

The Code is an example of 'soft law'. It does not have the force of statute, working on a 'comply or explain' basis: listed companies are obliged (under the Stock Exchange Listing Rules) to make a compliance statement and explain to shareholders (in the annual report) if they are not compliant and why. However, as statute provides little on governance (the **Companies Act 2006 (CA 2006)** does have some provisions relating to meetings, resolutions, and service contracts) the Code is of utmost importance in the corporate governance of listed companies.

The UK Corporate Governance Code indicates best practice on corporate governance in a number of areas, most of which first appeared in essence in the initial Cadbury Code and have been revised and modified in later governance codes. The Code itself is split into five sections, each consisting of main and supporting principles; those sections are headed Leadership, Effectiveness, Accountability, Remuneration, and Relations with Shareholders.

In terms of board constitution, the Code does not specify any particular size but warns that it should not be too small or too large to operate effectively. Directors together should have 'appropriate expertise and experience' but there are no specific qualifications required. This is consistent with the underlying law: statute only imposes a minimum age qualification of 16 (**CA 2006, s. 157**) and while the Institute of Directors does offer a 'Chartered Director' qualification, this is entirely optional. The board should have a balance of skills, experience, independence, and knowledge of the company. Diversity on boards, and particularly gender balance, is a particularly topical issue following the Davies Report in 2011.

Independent non-executive directors are seen as key to good corporate governance, by providing an important check on the activities of the executive directors. The Code expects half of the board (or at least two directors in smaller companies) to consist of independent non-executive directors (NEDs), with NEDs being dominant on committees (and making up all the members of the remuneration committee). Independence (considering, eg family and current and former business relationships and also length of time on the board) is essential (although it should be noted that independence is something to be determined by the board itself). A senior independent director should be appointed so NEDs and shareholders can express any concerns through him/her.

The Code emphasizes that the roles of chairman and managing director should be held by different people to provide balance, with no individual having 'unfettered powers of decision'. Executive directors should not be appointed chairman on their retirement from executive office.

Director remuneration has been a concern of corporate governance for many decades. The Code requires that remuneration policy and pay levels are set (following a 'formal and transparent procedure') by a remuneration committee made up entirely of NEDs. Remuneration of NEDs is set by the board. Remuneration of each director must be stated in the company's annual report. Appointments to the board must be under a 'formal, rigorous and transparent procedure'. A nomination committee should make recommendations to the board and every director should be up for re-election annually (for FTSE 350 companies). Service contracts must be open to inspection by members (CA 2006, ss. 227–30) and are limited to two years' duration without prior authorization of members (ss. 188–9).

The Code also requires companies to enter into dialogue with shareholders. In order to encourage greater shareholder engagement with corporate governance, institutional investors are expected to comply with the FRC's Stewardship Code on a 'comply or explain' basis.

However admirable its principles, the Code is only of value if it actually encourages and enforces good corporate governance. As there are no penalties for failure to comply with its provisions the Code's ability to encourage and enforce good corporate governance might then be doubted. However, in practice the Code is largely followed. It seems the 'comply or explain' requirements of the Listing Rules impose just enough pressure, and directors are aware that if the Code were seen to be failing they should expect more rigid statutory regulation to take its place. Although the self-regulatory system cannot ensure full compliance with best practice, successive governments have chosen to leave governance as primarily self-regulatory in nature.

The self-regulatory system has the benefit of flexibility, both by allowing alterations to the Code to reflect changes in practice and by allowing businesses some freedom to operate within guidelines rather than rigid limits. By focusing on principles rather than strict rules the Code encourages compliance with the spirit of the rules rather than just a thoughtless box-ticking exercise. Further, involving experts in drawing up the Code ensures provisions better reflect real practices so that self-regulation is generally accepted by those it regulates in a way that statutory regulation could never expect. However, there are obvious concerns where those making the rules are the people who will benefit most from a relaxed system.

The current system of self-regulation is clearly not without its critics. It has not prevented a series of corporate failures and significant public disquiet with corporate activities. Does it follow that the Code is 'broken'? Certainly its limits have been exposed—not least the inability of the system to impose any sensible restriction on corporate pay—but it is not clear that the problems would be avoided even if the Code had legally binding force. It is interesting that despite the limits of the Code in preventing corporate failure and promoting public confidence, the government has not seen fit to take regulation of corporate governance entirely into the statutory sphere (and the 'comply and explain' system is one adopted in very many other jurisdictions), although some further boundaries have been added in the **Enterprise and Regulatory Reform Act 2013 (ERRA 2013)**. This suggests that while the Code might need tightening, it is not without merit, or possibly that governments simply do not have the stomach for the fight with the City that such a change would entail (it is telling that the provisions of the **ERRA 2013** are significantly weaker than initially proposed by the government).

To conclude, good corporate governance is essential if investors are to have confidence in UK companies and so needs to be encouraged and enforced. The Corporate

Governance Code is obviously an important part of this, and the self-regulatory system can be seen as an important guide in developing good practice. However, the Code and the system have their failings, as corporate failures and continuing debates over excessive director remuneration have shown. It remains a matter of debate whether the Code simply needs strengthening, or the system itself is inadequate—while corporate governance has undoubtedly improved since 1992, there is still room for improvement.

A weakness of the Code in promoting good corporate governance is its application only to listed companies—the vast majority of companies are not listed. Outside listed companies, there is little encouragement to apply good corporate governance practice proactively (as the Code does for listed companies) although failures of governance can be used as a post-failure stick against directors (through, for example, director disqualification). If the Corporate Governance Code were truly to promote good corporate governance, perhaps its principles should be applied over a wider range of companies, and its enforcement mechanisms strengthened to further encourage observance.

Question 2

Evaluate the roles of shareholders and auditors in achieving good corporate governance in listed companies.

Commentary

This question touches on two important elements of the corporate governance system—shareholders and auditors. The shareholder primacy approach continues to dominate in modern company law in the UK—companies are run in the interests of the shareholders—although the argument for a wider stakeholder approach continues to be made. Accordingly, it is shareholders who have most to gain from good corporate governance—and have every reason to hold directors accountable. However, the extent to which shareholders play an active part in corporate governance is limited. Listed companies tend to have very diverse shareholdings which mean shareholders often lack both the ability and inclination to engage with the company in any meaningful way. In addition, a large proportion of shares are held by institutional rather than individual shareholders. The auditor provides an independent mechanism for ensuring financial propriety as a protection for shareholders, and providing the information that should allow shareholders to hold directors to account. Issues can arise in ensuring that auditors are sufficiently robust and independent to act as an effective check on managerial misbehaviour or incompetence.

In this question you need to assess the role of shareholders and the problems of encouraging active engagement with corporate governance. You should consider both shareholders generally and the particular issue of institutional investors, looking at steps taken to encourage shareholder activism. The role of the auditor must also be examined, including the limitations on that role in corporate governance.

Examiner's tip

As well as explaining the role that shareholders and auditors should play in corporate governance, think about the factors that might inhibit the proper fulfilment of those roles.

 Answer plan

Introduction
- Explanation of corporate governance
- Different roles in corporate governance

Role of shareholders
- Dismissal of directors
- Engaging shareholders
- Proxy votes and apathy
- Information availability

Role of auditor
- The audit requirement
- Audit committee
- Independence

Institutional investors
- Active engagement
- Stewardship Code

 Suggested answer

Good corporate governance (corporate governance being, according to the Cadbury Report (1992) 'the system by which companies are directed and controlled') should prevent directors from operating the company for their own benefit rather than that of the company's members. This potential problem arises from the long-recognized (see Berle and Means, 1932) separation of ownership (the members) and control (the directors) in large companies. For listed companies, the UK Corporate Governance Code provides principles of best practice for corporate governance with the Listing Rules requiring companies to 'comply or explain' as a condition of listing. Of great importance in ensuring good corporate governance are non-executive directors, shareholders, the company secretary, and the auditor. This essay will examine the roles of shareholders and auditor.

Shareholders

The company's constitution invariably gives the board of directors the power to manage the company on a day-to-day basis (Article 3 of the Model Articles for Private Companies: **Companies (Model Articles) Regulations 2008, Schedule 1**) and members have no power to instruct the directors how to act or overrule their decisions (see

Automatic Self-Cleansing Filter Syndicate Co Ltd v Cuninghame [1906] 2 Ch 34).
Statute reserves some limited matters to shareholders, including changes to the company's constitution (**Companies Act 2006 (CA 2006), s. 21**), but clearly shareholders
have a very minor role in the running of the company. However, it would be wrong to
suggest that shareholders have no role to play in corporate governance. While shareholders' powers are limited, and there are significant barriers to using what powers
they have, shareholders are the ultimate beneficiaries of good corporate governance
and accordingly need to accept responsibility in enforcing it.

It might be said that shareholders' power lies in their ability to dismiss directors by
ordinary resolution (**CA 2006, s. 168**), which can be exercised notwithstanding any
provisions in a director's service contract and can take effect before expiry of a term
of office. It is highly unlikely that mechanisms such as that successfully used in ***Bushell
v Faith*** [1970] AC 1099 to entrench a director's position by weighting votes would be
permitted by the Stock Exchange for a listed company, so directors in listed companies are always at risk of dismissal without need to show cause. However, in practice
shareholders would have to be very determined to go through the special notice process
of **ss. 168–9**. Furthermore, if a director is removed before the expiration of his term of
office, there is likely to be generous compensation payable under his service contract
(or damages for breach of contract), and this may be a substantial disincentive for
shareholders wishing to remove a director (as well as removing any real incentive for
a director to keep the shareholders happy, as the pain of any removal is heavily cush-
ioned). Furthermore, even a sizeable portion of unhappy shareholders will struggle to
get sufficient votes to pass even an ordinary resolution—particularly when faced with
the problem of disengaged shareholders and the use of proxy votes.

The role of shareholders in good corporate governance is limited through lack of engagement. Most shareholders in listed companies hold their shares as an investment,
whether for capital gain or dividend income, and often have little interest in the company itself or its governance, provided returns keep coming. If individual shareholders
choose to vote at all, they will often do so by giving proxy votes to the chairman of the
meeting—something that further entrenches the power of the board. It is highly unlikely that individual shareholders (other than activists who have taken shares for this
purpose and will be a tiny minority of total shareholders) will take the trouble (and expense) to attend meetings and question the board. While the introduction of additional
provisions for electronic voting may be a step in the right direction in encouraging individual shareholder votes, it is unlikely to make a significant difference.

The general lack of engagement of an individual shareholder is unsurprising as such
a shareholder will typically hold only a tiny proportion of the shares. Since a shareholder's vote would be unlikely to make a difference, shareholders are disinclined to
participate in governance, trusting to other shareholders to resolve any issues (the 'free
rider' problem), or simply trusting to the executive to keep making profits. Even if a
shareholder is inclined to take an active role he faces the problem of asymmetric provision of information—directors have all the information about the company while
shareholders have very little. While disclosure and transparency are important elements
of statute and the Code, its use to a non-expert individual shareholder is often limited.

The problems faced by individual shareholders mean that if shareholder engagement is to be effective, much then rests on those shareholders with more expertise and proportionately larger stakes in the company—institutional investors such as pension funds and unit trusts.

Institutional investors have traditionally been seen as taking too passive a role, rarely challenging the actions of the board and with a tendency to 'rubber stamp' the board's resolutions. The Myners Report of 2001 recommended more active and constructive involvement in corporate governance. Similarly, the Walker Report of 2009 sought greater engagement on the part of institutional shareholders and fund managers, and the UK Corporate Governance Code encourages dialogue between companies and investors and expects investors 'to make considered use of their votes'. In an important development, the UK Stewardship Code 'aims to enhance the quality of engagement between institutional investors and companies'. The Stewardship Code was produced by the FRC in 2010 following recommendations in the Walker Report and operates on a 'comply or explain' basis. It requires institutional investors to disclose their policy on stewardship (including when they will intervene to protect shareholder value) and monitor companies in which they have investments. Investors are reminded that they should not automatically support the board and should disclose their voting records.

More recently, shareholders have been seen exercising a bit more muscle in challenging board decisions. However, the role of institutional investors is more often 'behind the scenes' than open, preferring to exercise their influence in direct communication with the board rather than in public debate. This, while potentially more effective, does not provide the visible lead that might encourage other small investors to engage.

Auditor

Company accounts must be audited (unless the company is exempt by virtue of being a small private company or a dormant company): **CA 2006, s. 475**. This audit is effectively a certification of the validity of the accounts—an independent check on the company finances. Accordingly the role of the auditor is crucial for the financial accountability of the board and for corporate governance more generally.

Auditors must make a report on the annual accounts to the members under **s. 495** stating whether the annual accounts have been properly prepared and give a 'true and fair view'. They also state whether the directors' report is consistent with the accounts. Although this is an important protection for shareholders, it must be emphasized that auditors cannot provide a guarantee of accuracy. Furthermore, auditors' duties are owed only to the company and the shareholders, not to creditors (*Moore Stephens v Stone & Rolls Ltd* [2009] 2 BCLC 563).

Overseeing the audit process is the audit committee, which should have a majority of independent non-executive directors. The audit committee reduces the amount of influence that the management might otherwise have over the audit process, and minimizes the risk of auditors being pressured to present information in a favourable light. The audit committee monitors both the company's internal audit function and the external audit process, and makes recommendations on the appointment of external auditors. In FTSE 350 companies, the auditor position must be put up for tender every ten years.

Concerns about the auditor's role largely relate to independence and the stranglehold that the large accountancy firms have over accountancy and audit work in listed companies. There are fears that a 'cosy' relationship can exist between audit firms and directors, with audit firms being so reliant on work from large companies that they could be tempted not to highlight unfavourable information, or might be more willing to accept an executive's explanation. To counter this, where the auditor also provides non-audit services, the Code requires the annual report to explain how auditor 'objectivity and independence' is assured.

In conclusion it can be seen that the roles of both shareholders (particularly institutional investors) and auditors are critical to the proper functioning of corporate governance, but that there are very real limits on the extent to which those roles are fulfilled in practice. This inevitably means that the checks and balances on the activities of directors are not as effective as they could be, and further emphasizes the importance of other governance requirements such as independent non-executive directors.

 Question 3

Consider the effectiveness of controls on executive remuneration in the UK, considering in particular the role of the non-executive director in this area.

 Commentary

Both executive remuneration and the role of the non-executive director are important topics in corporate governance. In this question you need to look at the underlying legal position on remuneration and then focus on the Corporate Governance Code and the role of non-executive directors. The question gives you the opportunity to engage in discussion as to the problems of remuneration and the difficulties in controlling this, bringing in consideration of the **Enterprise and Regulatory Reform Act 2013** which aims to enhance shareholder oversight on director remuneration policy.

 Examiner's tip

Bring in both legal discussion and an awareness of topical issues in order to demonstrate your full understanding of the area.

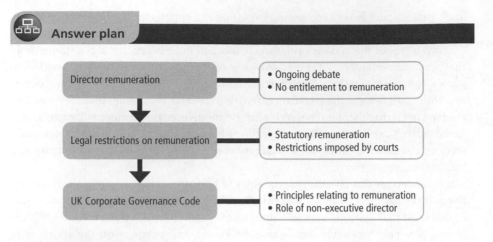

Answer plan

| Director remuneration | • Ongoing debate |
| | • No entitlement to remuneration |

| Legal restrictions on remuneration | • Statutory remuneration |
| | • Restrictions imposed by courts |

| UK Corporate Governance Code | • Principles relating to remuneration |
| | • Role of non-executive director |

Suggested answer

Director remuneration is a frequent topic of debate amongst politicians, business people, and the public. The high, indeed sometimes lavish, pay of some directors has been the subject of public disquiet, particularly in the case of former publicly-owned utilities (such as British Gas/Centrica) and companies that have needed substantial taxpayer assistance (such as Royal Bank of Scotland). But how effective are the existing controls on director remuneration?

Directors have no outright entitlement to remuneration (*Hutton v West Cork Railway Co* (1883) 23 Ch D 654), and are accordingly reliant on the articles making proper provision for payment of directors. This became very clear in *Guinness plc v Saunders* [1990] 2 AC 663 where the House of Lords held that payment to a director was void when agreed to by a committee of the board rather than the full board as required by the company's articles. Usually, however, companies will comply with the provisions of their articles in paying remuneration (articles usually giving the power to the board) and so this will not be an issue. Statute could impose restrictions on director pay but governments are understandably reluctant to interfere too much in internal corporate matters and so there are few legal restraints. For listed companies additional regulation of remuneration is provided through the UK Corporate Governance Code which puts non-executive directors at the heart of this control.

There are few statutory restrictions on executive remuneration. One important exception is **Companies Act 2006 (CA 2006), ss. 188–9** which limits contracts to two years unless approved by the members and is designed to stop companies granting long contracts which effectively entrench directors' positions by making it prohibitively expensive to dismiss them. Payments on loss of office other than pursuant to a contractual obligation must also be approved by members (**ss. 215–22**). Furthermore, the **Enterprise and Regulatory Reform Act 2013 (ERRA 2013)** amends the **CA 2006** (**s. 422A**) (due to take effect October 2013) to require shareholder approval (in quoted companies) of director remuneration policy, although voting on how it has been implemented will be advisory only. The **CA 2006** also makes provision for disclosure of remuneration information. Under **s. 412** companies must disclose in the annual accounts aggregate directors' remuneration, while quoted companies must produce a remuneration report (**s. 420**), including individual directors' pay. **Sections 227–30** require directors' service contracts to be available for inspection by members.

Even where shareholders do have corporate governance powers (eg the ability to dismiss a director under **CA 2006, s. 168**), a lack of engagement by shareholders in larger companies means that these powers are little used. If shareholders do not vote, or always vote in line with the board's wishes, there is little to be gained by giving more power to the general meeting. Even if shareholders were given binding votes on the implementation of remuneration policies or individual pay packages, the reality of the general meeting is that decisions of the board are often 'rubber stamped'. In this regard the new binding vote on remuneration policy introduced by the **ERRA 2013** may have limited impact.

The courts have made occasional forays into director remuneration. In *Re Halt Garage (1964) Ltd* [1982] 3 All ER 1016, the court rejected payments made to a director after she had ceased working for the company (although she remained registered as a director) labelling them a gratuitous distribution out of capital rather than genuine remuneration. Director disqualification may also operate as a restriction on director remuneration, at least for companies in financial difficulty. While it is not in itself 'unfit' (under **s. 6** and **s. 8** of the **Company Directors Disqualification Act 1986**) to pay directors even while the company is insolvent, payment of generous remuneration to directors while creditors are going unpaid is evidence of unfitness, and in setting director pay directors must consider what the company can afford and not just the 'going rate' (*Secretary of State for Trade and Industry v Van Hengel* [1995] 1 BCLC 545). While this is unlikely to make much of an impact in setting director remuneration, it could, provided directors are aware of the disqualification risk, operate to reduce remuneration when a company is struggling.

For listed companies the UK Corporate Governance Code sets out best practice for corporate governance including provisions relating to remuneration of directors (Section D of the Code). The Code does not have the force of law, taking effect through the Listing Rules which require companies to 'comply or explain'. The Code requires that company remuneration levels should be sufficient to 'attract, retain and motivate' quality directors but that the company should 'avoid paying more than is necessary for this purpose'. In ensuring good governance of director remuneration, the role of the non-executive director (NED) is very important, as indeed it is in other areas of corporate governance.

The importance of the NED generally was recognized in the Cadbury Report of 1992, and the NED's role has increased through subsequent reports and changes to the Corporate Governance Code. Independent NEDs provide a company with complementary expertise and experience that should inform corporate decision making and improve strategy and profitability. As they are not involved full-time in running the company they are able to provide independent judgement and a check on the executive directors. The Corporate Governance Code expects listed companies to have a remuneration committee to set remuneration policy and pay, and this remuneration committee should be filled entirely by independent NEDs (as a whole the board of larger companies should consist of at least half independent NEDs). The remuneration committee offers a more transparent and less obviously conflicted process than the former situation where executives decided each other's pay (with an obvious incentive to ensure that pay scales were high).

The question remains whether NEDs are sufficiently independent to exercise real control over remuneration. The Code sets out requirements for 'independence'—including an absence of family and business links and a limit on the length of time a NED can be within a company and still be viewed as independent (currently nine years). While independence in this sense is obviously important, it should be remembered that NEDs are often drawn from the same talent pool as executive directors and often sit as executive directors in other companies (or are retired executive directors). There can thus be a commonality of interest and outlook that may limit the extent to which decisions of the managing director might be challenged and this can be exacerbated by gender imbalance on corporate boards. While independent NEDs may avoid direct conflicts of interest, there remain indirect conflicts—is a NED truly independent in setting remuneration at Company A, knowing that this will impact on pay awards generally, including at Company B where he is an executive director? Similarly NEDs may overvalue business skills and experience, since it is only human nature to put a high price on one's own skills and experience. Since it is the NED's experience that makes him/her of value to a company, it is difficult to formulate a solution to this particular problem, although there are moves to encourage candidates from other walks of life including charities and the public sector.

Another issue is the time a NED has to spend in his/her role in any individual company. These positions are part-time and it is thus not possible for a NED to be fully attuned to the business and operation of a company. In some ways this ensures his independence, but it undoubtedly also reduces his ability to question and challenge decisions of the executive. The time spent by NEDs was a particular concern of the Walker Report (2009) which recommended a significant increase in the number of days NEDs should devote to their role.

The Code, like the **CA 2006**, seeks to control director remuneration through transparency. Unfortunately increased transparency (introduced initially by Cadbury) was not wholly positive—as well as informing shareholders, it meant that directors were able to compare their own pay with that of other directors and this had the effect of increasing pay awards. In addition, although transparency is a worthwhile aim, disclosure has little impact if shareholders are unable or unwilling to take action when pay is seen to be excessive. Since members have no power to reject pay packages they would be left with the ultimate sanctions of selling shares or triggering a vote for director removal (**CA 2006, s. 168**), which of course are only effective if sufficient shareholders act. There are rare cases where directors have retreated from generous remuneration awards or payoffs, but this has largely come about through political or media pressure, rather than shareholder action. It remains to be seen whether the new binding vote on remuneration policy in quoted companies introduced by the **ERRA 2013** will encourage shareholders to take a more active role in challenging excessive director remuneration.

Further reading

Adeyeye, A., 'The limitations of corporate governance in the CSR agenda' (2010) 31 Co Law 172

Arora, A., 'The corporate governance failings in financial institutions and directors' legal liability' (2011) 32 Co Law 3

Bartlett, S., and Chandler, R., 'The private shareholder, corporate governance, and the role of the annual report' [1999] JBL 415

Cheffins, B. R., and Thomas, R. S., 'Should shareholders have a greater say over executive pay? Learning from the US experience' (2001) 1 JCLS 277

Dignam, A., 'A principled approach to self-regulation? The report of the Hampel Committee on Corporate Governance' (1998) 19 Co Law 140

Du Plessis, J. J., 'Corporate law and corporate governance lessons from the past: ebbs and flows, but far from "the end of history…": Parts 1 and 2' (2009) 30 Co Law 43 and 81

Gutierrez, M., and Saez, M., 'Deconstructing independent directors' (2013) 13 JCLS 63

Hemraj, M. B., 'Good corporate governance: the recipe for corporate survival' (2005) 26 Co Law 122

Ho, J. K. S., 'Is s. 172 of the Companies Act 2006 the guidance for CSR?' (2010) 31 Co Law 207

Keay, A., 'Company directors behaving poorly: disciplinary options for shareholders' [2007] JBL 204

Pedamon, C., 'Corporate social responsibility: a new approach to promoting integrity and responsibility' (2010) 31 Co Law 172

Roach, L., 'The UK Stewardship Code' (2011) 11 JCLS 463

Sweeney-Baird, M., 'The role of the non-executive director in modern corporate governance' (2006) 27 Co Law 67

Villiers, C., 'Controlling executive pay: institutional investors or distributive justice?' (2010) 10 JCLS 309

Wheeler, S., 'Non-executive directors and corporate governance' (2009) 60 NILQ 51

Young, A., 'Frameworks in regulating company directors: rethinking the philosophical foundations to enhance accountability' (2009) 30 Co Law 355

10

Minority protection

Introduction

The rule in *Foss v Harbottle* (1843) 2 Hare 461 (combining both the majority rule principle and the 'proper claimant' principle) underpins the topic of minority shareholder protection. Accordingly, the usual position is that where a wrong is done to the company an individual shareholder has no right to bring a claim and majority rule prevails. While this makes sound sense, it also has obvious potential for injustice when those harming the company are those who control it, or where the majority set out to oppress the minority in some way. Accordingly, the law provides some limited protection or avenues of redress for a minority shareholder with grievances concerning the actions of the company, directors, or majority shareholders.

The first of these is the derivative claim—initially developed by the courts where there was a 'fraud on the minority'—now in statutory form in **Companies Act 2006 (CA 2006), ss. 260–4**. This permits a shareholder, in certain limited circumstances, to bring a claim on behalf of the company. Some attempts have been made to avoid the rule in *Foss v Harbottle* without having to establish a derivative claim by formulating a member's claim as a personal (rather than corporate) loss. These have not been met favourably by the courts, where claims for 'reflective losses' have been rejected in the vast majority of cases.

As well as the derivative claim, statute provides two other potential routes for a minority shareholder. By far the most important of these is **CA 2006, s. 994** (formerly **Companies Act 1985, s. 459**): the 'unfair prejudice' remedy. The other is a petition to wind up the company on the ground that it is 'just and equitable' to do so, under **Insolvency Act 1986 (IA 1986), s. 122(1)(g)**. These two provisions have some similarities in their application, but they remain distinct remedies.

The availability of 'shareholder remedies' in practice should not be over-emphasized; even though a minority shareholder may be effectively 'trapped' in a company with no power to influence decisions and no ready market for their shares (as will be the case in the majority of unquoted companies), the law does not recognize any general right of redress or exit route for disenchanted shareholders. A minority shareholder would be well advised to protect himself with a separate contractual agreement or appropriate buy-out clause in the articles of association; where this has not been done (or such provisions are being ignored by the majority) the shareholder may find himself needing to fall back on the (limited) assistance of the law on minority protection.

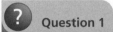

? Question 1

To what extent does the statutory right of members to bring a derivative claim in respect of a company mirror the derivative claim evolved at common law as an exception to the rule in *Foss v Harbottle*?

💬 Commentary

This question requires you to show your familiarity with the law relating to the old common law derivative claim and to compare and contrast this with the new statutory derivative claim introduced in the **CA 2006**. It is important to be aware of the old law since the situations when the new statutory right apply will, to a certain extent, mirror the situations that gave rise to a derivative claim previously. Obviously, the new provisions have widened the scope of the claim and the circumstances relating to the court giving permission for an action to continue are now statutorily defined and thus render the law more definite and predictable.

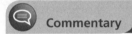

🗗 Answer plan

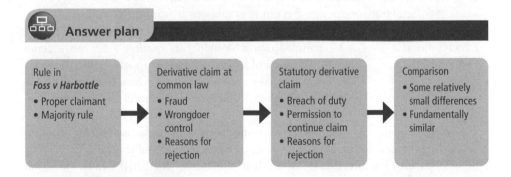

Rule in *Foss v Harbottle*	Derivative claim at common law	Statutory derivative claim	Comparison
• Proper claimant • Majority rule	• Fraud • Wrongdoer control • Reasons for rejection	• Breach of duty • Permission to continue claim • Reasons for rejection	• Some relatively small differences • Fundamentally similar

⇨ Suggested answer

The basic principle of majority control and the restriction of actions by minorities was established in *Foss v Harbottle* (1843) 2 Hare 461 and restated in *Edwards v Halliwell* [1950] 2 All ER 1064 in two propositions: (a) the proper claimant in an action in respect of a wrong to a company is prima facie the company; and (b) where the alleged wrong may be made binding on the company by a simple majority of the members, no individual member is allowed to maintain an action in respect of it.

To bring a derivative claim—where a shareholder brings a claim in respect of a wrong to the company—the minority had to establish prima facie that: (a) the company was the victim of a 'fraud', defined as an abuse of power as director or shareholder (*Estmanco (Kilner House) Ltd v GLC* [1982] 1 All ER 437); and (b) the wrongdoers were in control of the company and preventing it from bringing an action itself. The claim was equitable and discretionary.

The term 'fraud' covered most breaches of duty but did not cover 'mere negligence', *Pavlides v Jensen* [1956] 2 All ER 518, unless the alleged negligent action resulted in profit to a director, *Daniels v Daniels* [1978] Ch 406.

To establish that the wrongdoers were 'in control', the claimant had to establish actual voting control not mere *de facto* control through dominance of shareholding and management position: *Prudential Assurance Co Ltd v Newman Industries Ltd (No. 2)* [1982] Ch 204.

The court could order the company to indemnify minority shareholders where it was reasonable and prudent to bring an action and where it was brought in good faith: *Wallersteiner v Moir* (No. 2) [1975] 1 QB 373. In *Smith v Croft (Nos. 2 and 3)* [1987] BCLC 206 and [1987] BCLC 355, however, an indemnity was rejected as the derivative claim was in contradiction of an independent report and against the wishes of the independent majority shareholder.

Derivative claims would also be rejected for many reasons, including if the shareholder had a right to a personal action, or was not acting in good faith, or any impartial members were against the claim being brought.

Members now have a statutory right to bring derivative claims in respect of a cause of action vested in the company, and seeking relief on behalf of the company: CA 2006, s. 260(1). The statutory derivative claim thus takes over from the common law proceedings, although in *Universal Project Management Ltd v Fort Gilkicker Ltd* [2013] EWHC 348 (Ch) Briggs J concluded that a 'double' (or 'multiple') derivative claim (where the claimant is not a direct shareholder in the company to which the complaint relates, but is a shareholder in the company's parent company which is under the same 'wrongdoer control') can still be brought at common law (such a claim not being possible under s. 260).

A derivative claim may be brought in respect of a cause of action arising from an actual or proposed act or omission involving negligence, default, breach of duty, or breach of trust by a director: s. 260(3). It is immaterial whether the cause of action arose before or after the person seeking to bring or continue the derivative claim became a member of the company: s. 260(4). Wrongdoer control is no longer 'an absolute condition' for a statutory derivative claim (although if the company could itself commence proceedings this is an important element in the court's decision whether to allow the claim to continue): *Bamford v Harvey* [2012] EWHC 2858 (Ch).

Members bringing a derivative claim must apply to the court for permission to continue it (s. 261(1)), and if the application and evidence filed do not disclose a prima facie case for permission, the court must dismiss the application: s. 261(2). In *Iesini v*

Westrip Holdings Ltd [2009] EWHC 2526 (Ch) the court held that in this respect it was wrong to engage in a mini-trial of any action but the court had to form a provisional view on the strength of the claim. If the application is not dismissed, the court may give directions as to the evidence to be produced by the company and adjourn the proceedings to enable evidence to be obtained: s. 261(3).

Permission must be refused if the court is satisfied that a person acting in accordance with **CA 2006, s. 172** (duty to promote the company's success) would not seek to continue the claim: **s. 263(2)(a)**. In *Iesini v Westrip Holdings Ltd* the court held that the section only applied where the court was satisfied that no director acting in accordance with **s. 172** would seek to continue the claim. If some would and others would not then it is simply a factor to be considered in the exercise of discretion under **s. 263(3) (b)**. This test of the 'hypothetical director' has been considered in a number of cases. In *Mission Capital plc v Sinclair* [2008] EWHC 1339 (Ch), the court refused permission. Although the court 'could not be satisfied that the notional section 172 director would not continue the claim', it considered that the notional director 'would not attach great weight to it'. In this case, and in *Franbar Holdings Ltd v Patel* [2008] EWHC 1534 (Ch), the court was also influenced by the fact that the applicants could achieve all they could possibly want through a petition under **CA 2006, s. 994**. This was also endorsed in *Stimpson and ors v Southern Landlords Association and ors* [2009] EWHC 2072 (Ch). On the other hand, in *Kiani v Cooper* [2010] EWHC 577 (Ch) the court held that the existence of an alternative remedy under **s. 994** was only one factor to consider and a derivative claim was allowed to proceed notwithstanding the existence of a **s. 994** claim in *Phillips v Fryer* [2012] EWHC 1611 (Ch). In addition, the court must refuse permission where the action arises from a prospective act or omission that has been authorized by the company or where it arises from an existing act or omission that was previously authorized by the company or subsequently ratified: **s. 263(2)**.

If the claim is not rejected under **s. 263(2)**, the court considers whether to give permission, taking into account in particular: whether the member is acting in good faith in seeking to continue the claim; whether authorization or ratification is likely; whether the company has decided not to pursue the claim; and whether the act or omission gives rise to a personal cause of action for the member: **s. 263(3)**. The factors in **s. 263(3)** are not exhaustive and the courts have shown willing to consider many other matters thought to be relevant in a particular case including, in *Kleanthous v Paphitis* [2011] EWHC 2287, the fact that any recoveries from the directors would largely be returned to them as majority shareholders.

Where permission is granted to continue a derivative claim, the court will also grant a right of indemnity to the claimant for his reasonable costs subject to limits: *Stainer v Lee* [2010] EWHC 1539 (Ch) and *Kiani v Cooper* [2010] EWHC 577 (Ch).

Clearly the statutory remedy is wider in that it encompasses negligence and wrongdoer control is not a precondition. However, it remains the case that most of the statutory derivative claim requirements echo the common law derivative claim. The fact that claims can also be brought in respect of wrongs committed prior to a person becoming a shareholder merely reiterates the common law position. The need for permission to continue the claim also reflects the common law, as do the circumstances when permission must be refused as well as the criteria to be taken into account in giving permission. The requirement that the claimant acts in good faith reflects the equitable nature of the common law derivative claim and earlier case law such as *Barrett v Duckett* [1995] 1 BCLC 243. The provisions relating to adopting claims commenced by the company or another member are also merely clearly spelled out as opposed to radically new. The emphasis on whether the act or omission has been, is likely to be, or can be ratified, reflects the principle of majority control that gave birth to the rule in *Foss v Harbottle*.

One area of helpful change is in respect of the court ordering the company to produce evidence and adjourning the proceedings while the evidence is acquired: CA 2006, s. 261(3). This is an improvement on the common law where obtaining evidence of wrongdoing was always a problem for the claimant.

On balance it can be seen that the statutory derivative claim mirrors the common law claim to a significant extent, and principles applied under the statute largely echo the previous case law. It is telling that the statutory derivative claim has not resulted in the flood of cases feared by some when the provision came into force. However, there are some differences and there remain issues that are still being worked out by the courts.

 Question 2

Brenda, Charles, and Diana set up a catering business called Just Desserts Ltd. They each held one-third of the shares and were directors of the company.

Charles became involved in a new venture and neglected his duties. Brenda and Diana decided to remove Charles from the company. The articles provide that 'in the event of a resolution to remove a person from the board, the shares held by that director shall on a poll have three votes per share instead of the usual one'. It is known that Charles has overreached himself financially due to his involvement in the new venture.

Advise Brenda and Diana how they might go about removing Charles from the board and whether Charles might have a claim under CA 2006, s. 994 or IA 1986, s. 122(1)(g).

 Commentary

This problem question requires you to recognize the steps that Brenda and Diana would have to take in order to remove Charles from the board and also to recognize that taking such steps in the context of a quasi-partnership company could give Charles statutory rights of action against Brenda and Diana. You need to advise Brenda and Diana as to whether Charles would be able to succeed in a petition for unfair prejudice under **CA 2006, s. 994** and, if so, of the remedies available to him under **s. 996**. Because of his own behaviour he may not succeed in his petition and so you should advise on the alternative possibility of a petition for the just and equitable winding up of the company under **IA 1986, s. 122(1)(g)**.

Answer plan

- Need for Brenda and Diana to alter the company's articles by special resolution to remove the weighted voting provision
- Need to make a rights issue to enable them to acquire necessary voting control for a special resolution
- Recognition that this scheme could be regarded as a ground for a petition for unfair prejudice by Charles and discussion of possible remedies
- Problems of Charles succeeding in his petition because of his behaviour
- Alternative petition for just and equitable winding up of the company

 Suggested answer

Just Desserts Ltd appears to be a quasi-partnership company as Brenda, Charles, and Diana started the company together, hold equal shareholdings, and are all involved in the management of the company (see *Ebrahimi v Westbourne Galleries Ltd* [1973] AC 360).

Brenda and Diana have become discontented with Charles because of his neglect of the company's business but having decided to remove Charles from the board, they are faced with the problem that the articles contain a weighted voting provision as in *Bushell v Faith* [1970] AC 1099. It is possible for the articles to be altered to remove this weighted voting procedure as articles can be altered by special resolution: **Companies Act 2006 (CA 2006), s. 21** (unless a provision is entrenched as permitted by **s. 22**). Brenda and Diana thus need 75 per cent of the votes at the general meeting but at present they only have between them two-thirds of the issued shares.

A possible course of action open to Brenda and Diana is to increase the share capital of the company. Since it is a private company with one class of shares, the directors can allot shares: **CA 2006, s. 550**. Since it would be an allotment of ordinary shares, there would have to be a rights issue whereby existing shareholders have a right of pre-emption in respect of the new issue in proportion to their current shareholding: **s. 561**. (Although this right can be disapplied (**s. 569**) that would require such a power to be given by the articles or a special resolution.) Since, however, it is known that Charles is currently financially embarrassed, he will be unable to take up his entitlement, with the result that his shareholding will be reduced to below 25 per cent, making it impossible for him to block special resolutions. Brenda and Diana should be aware, however, that if the allotment is made primarily for the purpose of removing Charles this could be viewed as a breach of their duty to exercise powers only for the purposes for which they are conferred (**s. 171(b)**).

If shares are allotted and taken up by Brenda and Diana but not Charles, Brenda and Diana would be able to proceed with the removal of the weighted voting provision and ultimately propose an ordinary resolution with special notice to remove Charles as a director: **s. 168**. Charles would have a right to be heard at the meeting under **s. 169**, but this would not prevent his removal.

However, at any stage in the implementation of the scheme, Charles could petition the court under **CA 2006, s. 994**. This requires that the conduct of the company's affairs (construed widely: *Gross v Rackind* **[2004] 4 All ER 735**) is both prejudicial to his interests as a member (construed widely, and including exclusion from management: *O'Neill v Phillips* **[1999] 1 WLR 1092**) and unfair, see *Re Saul D Harrison and Sons plc* **[1995] 1 BCLC 14**. Clearly Brenda and Diana's actions are prejudicial to Charles' interests; the question is one of unfairness.

In *O'Neill v Phillips* Lord Hoffmann stated that unfairness would lie either in a breach of the terms on which the member agreed the affairs of the company would be conducted (such as a breach of the law, the articles, or a shareholder agreement) or some use of the rules in a manner which equity would regard as contrary to good faith. Here Brenda and Diana have acted at all times within their legal powers (with the proviso that their allotment of shares could be regarded as a breach of their duty under **s. 171(b)**), so the issue is whether equitable considerations render their otherwise lawful actions unfair in the context of **s. 994**. As the company is a quasi-partnership company the courts will be prepared to accept that acting contrary to the understanding of the parties (even if acting within the law) can be unfair.

In *Re Cumana Ltd* **[1986] BCLC 430** it was held that a rights issue in the knowledge that the minority could not afford to take it up constituted unfair prejudice. In respect of the alteration of the articles, whereas previously Charles might have based a claim on the grounds that the proposed alteration was not in good faith for the benefit of the company as a whole (*Allen v Gold Reefs of West Africa Ltd* **[1900] 1 Ch 656**), it would now be possible to petition under **CA 2006, s. 994** and ask for an order requiring the company not to make any, or any specified, alterations in its articles without leave of the court: **s. 996(2)(d)**. In many cases concerning quasi-partnership companies where there is an understanding that members shall be entitled to participate in the management of the company, removal from the board has been recognized as unfair prejudice, eg *Brownlow v G H Marshall Ltd* **[2000] 2 BCLC 655** and *Re OC (Transport) Services Ltd* **[1984] BCLC 251**.

In the event of Charles petitioning on the grounds of unfair prejudice, he would be likely to seek an order that Brenda and/or Diana and/or the company should purchase his shares at a value to be determined by the court under **s. 996(2)(e)**. In this case, his shareholding would normally be valued pro rata according to the value of the business as a whole (*Re Bird Precision Bellows Ltd* **[1984] Ch 419**) without a discount to reflect the minority holding.

However, for Charles the problem with a petition under **s. 994** is that Brenda and Diana could argue they are justified in commencing proceedings to remove him from the board, since his removal is due to his neglect of his duties as a director: in other words their actions are prejudicial but not unfair. In *Re RA Noble & Sons (Clothing) Ltd* **[1983] BCLC 273** the court held that because the director had neglected his duties as a director, his exclusion, although prejudicial, was not unfair. Thus, where the petitioner's behaviour totally justifies the action complained of as prejudicial, the petitioner will not succeed in a petition under **s. 994**: *Kelly v Hussain* **[2008] EWHC 1117 (Ch)**. In *Re London School of Electronics Ltd* **[1986] Ch 211**, however, the court held that the petitioner's misconduct (trying to attract students away from the school) did not prevent his petition as his misconduct was a reaction to the other shareholder's actions in trying to attract students away to another establishment.

If, as a result of his behaviour, Charles fails in his petition for unfair prejudice under **CA 2006, s. 994** he could, nevertheless, petition for the just and equitable winding up of the company under **Insolvency Act 1986 (IA 1986), s. 122(1)(g)**. The decision in *Ebrahimi v Westbourne Galleries Ltd* [1973] AC 360 established that the removal of a director of a quasi-partnership company from the board constituted grounds to petition for the just and equitable winding up of the company. *Re RA Noble & Sons (Clothing) Ltd* [1983] BCLC 273 and *Jesner Ltd v Jarrad Properties Ltd* [1993] BCLC 1032 have shown that, even if a person cannot petition successfully under **s. 994** against his removal from the management of the company of a quasi-partnership company, that person could succeed in a petition under **IA 1986, s. 122(1)(g)**—although a petitioner's misconduct (a lack of 'clean hands') may result in the petition being rejected (*Ebrahimi v Westbourne Galleries Ltd*). The Court of Appeal in *Hawkes v Cuddy* [2009] 2 BCLC 427 has confirmed (rejecting the contrary view in *Re Guidezone Ltd* [2000] 2 BCLC 321) that **IA 1986, s. 122(1)(g)** continues to exist as a separate jurisdiction from **CA 2006, s. 994**. Accordingly, Charles could bring a petition to wind up the company on the just and equitable ground, although he should be warned that the courts strongly discourage the bringing of claims in the alternative under **CA 2006, s. 994** and **IA 1986, s. 122(1)(g)**. Under **IA 1986, s. 125(2)** a court can reject a petition under **s. 122(1)(g)** if the petitioner has an alternative remedy and he is acting unreasonably in seeking to wind up the company rather than pursuing this alternative. The most common alternative remedy in such a situation would be **CA 2006, s. 994**, but the ability to sell one's shares may also be an alternative remedy, depending on the terms (*Virdi v Abbey Leisure Ltd* [1990] BCLC 342). Accordingly, if Brenda and Diana made an offer to Charles to purchase his shares at a fair value (guidance on this is provided in *O'Neill v Phillips*), the court is likely to conclude that this is an appropriate alternative remedy and reject Charles' petition. While having to purchase Charles' shares is not the outcome that Brenda and Diana might choose, not least as it would secure Charles the very remedy he would probably fail to achieve under **CA 2006, s. 994**, it might be preferable to the risk of the company being wound up under **IA 1986, s. 122(1)(g)**.

 Question 3

Mark became a shareholder in Landsite plc, a commercial property company, in January 2011. He subsequently learnt that during 2010 the board sold a major site scheduled for development. The property was sold for £20m but it is now valued at £50m in documents issued by New World Properties plc in connection with their flotation on the Alternative Investment Market (AIM).

Mark raised the issue at the AGM of Landsite plc but the managing director claimed that the property was sold at its market value on the basis of an independent valuation. He stated that the value had been affected by the need to decontaminate the site.

No reports to this effect were produced and the meeting became quite rowdy with angry share-holders demanding an inquiry.

The share price of Landsite plc fell by 10 per cent when it was reported in the financial press that the managing director of Landsite plc had a significant, financial stake in New World Properties plc.

Faced with inactivity by the company, advise Mark as to any action he could take.

 Commentary

In this question you need to consider the law relating to the statutory derivative claim to exam-ine whether Mark could bring a claim on behalf of the company and the grounds on which the court will refuse or grant permission for the bringing of the derivative claim. You should also con-sider whether Mark has the alternative of a right to bring a personal action in place of a derivative claim which involves a discussion of the concept of reflective loss.

 Answer plan

- Legal justification for the bringing of a derivative claim by Mark
- Need to establish prima facie case and role of court in organizing the production of evidence
- Grounds on which the court must either refuse or may grant permission to continue the action
- Discussion of Mark's right to bring a personal action
- Concluding advice as to the likely success of the claim

 Suggested answer

Following the sale of the company's property at an apparent undervalue, it is pos-sible for the company to bring an action against the controllers for damages for the loss suffered by the company through the potential breaches of duty by the directors. These breaches could consist, for example, of a breach of the duty of care, skill, and diligence (**Companies Act 2006 (CA 2006), s. 174**) or the duty to act in good faith to promote the success of the company (**s. 172**) if it is established that the price at which the property was sold was significantly below its market value. There is also the potential for a breach of **s. 177** (duty to declare an interest in a transaction with a company) because of the managing director's interest in New World Properties plc.

It has been held that the failure of the director to declare his own wrongdoing would also constitute a breach of his duty to act in the best interests of the company (*Item Software (UK) Ltd v Fassihi* **[2004] EWCA Civ 1244**) although this development has met with some criticism.

Faced with a refusal by the company to take action, Mark could commence an action on the company's behalf by way of a derivative claim under **CA 2006, s. 260(1)**. Unlike the common law derivative claim, it is no longer necessary to establish a 'fraud' against the company. Neither is there a need to establish that the wrongdoers are in control of the company (*Bamford v Harvey* [2012] EWHC 2858 (Ch)). The statutory derivative claim can be brought in respect of a cause of action arising from an actual or proposed act or omission involving negligence, default, breach of duty or breach of trust by a director of the company: **s. 260(3)**. The term 'director' extends to former and shadow directors: **s. 260(5)**.

Mark is able to bring the derivative claim even though the cause of action arose before he became a member of the company: **s. 260(4)**. The claim would be brought by Mark on behalf of Landsite plc seeking relief on its behalf (**s. 260(1)**) against the board of directors. Landsite plc would be joined as a defendant to ensure the company is party to the proceedings.

Mark would be required to apply to the court for permission to continue this claim (**s. 261(1)**) and the court must dismiss the claim if the application and the evidence filed in support of it do not disclose a prima facie case for giving permission: **s. 261(2)**.

This could be a potential problem for Mark since he can only point to documents establishing the price at which the property was sold in 2008 and its current valuation in the documents lodged by New World Properties plc. Although the managing director of Landsite plc referred to an independent valuation prior to the sale and indicated that the value of the site was affected by the need for it to be decontaminated, there are no documents to that effect apart from the fact that the statement that such an independent valuation existed is in the public domain through the minutes of the AGM and the reports in the financial press.

In this case, Mark would have to request the court to give directions requiring Landsite plc to produce the documents in question and the court could adjourn the proceedings to allow the evidence to be obtained: **s. 261(3)**. Once this documentary evidence had been produced the court could then, at a reconvened hearing, give permission to continue the claim on such terms as it thinks fit if the evidence produced supports Mark's claim: **s. 261(4)**. The 'prima facie' stage is intended to remove unmeritorious cases at an early stage rather than conduct a 'mini-trial'. If the company is unable to produce the documents that it claims to have, this would be likely to be sufficient to enable the court to give permission to continue the claim.

In deciding whether to refuse or give permission, the court must have regard to the provisions of **s. 263**. If the court holds that a person acting to promote the interest of the company in accordance with **CA 2006, s. 172** (duty to promote the success of the company) would not seek to continue the claim (**s. 263(2)(a)**), or that the sale was authorized or has since been ratified by the company, it must refuse permission: **s. 263(2) (b) and (c)**. Neither of these grounds appear to apply here. The court must then exercise its discretion as to whether or not to give permission, and in so doing must in particular take into consideration whether Mark is acting in good faith in seeking to bring his claim (**s. 263(3)(a)**) and the importance that a person acting in accordance with **s. 172** would attach to continuing it: **s. 263(3)(b)**. It must also consider whether authorization or ratification is likely (**s. 263(3)(c) and (d)**); whether the company has decided not to pursue the claim (**s. 263(3)(e)**); and whether the act gives rise to a cause of action that the member could pursue in his own right as a personal action rather than on behalf of the company: **s. 263(3)(f)**. The court must have particular regard to the views of members of the company who have no personal interest in the matter (**s. 263(4)**), although it may prove difficult to establish the views of such members in large companies as Landsite plc appears to be.

The reference in **s. 263(2)(a)** and **s. 263(3)(b)** to the person acting in accordance with **s. 172**, is a reference to the hypothetical or notional director of the company. In deciding whether to refuse permission to continue the action, this has been an important consideration and the court has been loath to grant permission, particularly when the applicant has an adequate remedy in respect of a petition for unfair prejudice under CA 2006, s. 994 where the applicant has brought an action under both heads: *Franbar Holdings Ltd v Patel* [2008] EWHC 1534 (Ch), although the availability of a s. 994 claim is certainly not an absolute bar to proceedings, as seen in *Phillips v Fryer* [2012] EWHC 1611 (Ch). In any event this would not appear to be an issue in this case as there is no suggestion that Mark wishes to bring a petition under **s. 994** and it is notoriously difficult to succeed in unfair prejudice claims in relation to public companies (see, eg *Re Astec (BSR) plc* [1998] 2 BCLC 556). The other matters required to be considered under s. 263(3) do not appear to be a problem: the sale has clearly not been ratified by the company in general meeting and the company has not decided not to pursue the claim, it has merely failed to act.

As regards the possibility that Mark could pursue the action personally, he has clearly suffered a loss due to the collapse in the value of the shares which might suggest that he could sue personally. In *Prudential Assurance Co Ltd v Newman Industries Ltd (No. 2)* [1982] Ch 204, however, it was held that a shareholder could not bring a personal action in respect of a fall in the value of his shares caused by the wrongdoing of the company controllers who had disposed of a corporate asset at an undervalue. This approach was confirmed in *Johnson v Gore Wood and Co* [2002] 2 AC 1—a member cannot claim personally for a loss that is merely a reflection of the loss suffered by the company. Although *Giles v Rhind* [2003] 1 BCLC 1 provides a limited ability to claim for reflective losses where the company's inability to pursue the claim is caused by the wrongdoing itself, this does not assist Mark. As a result, Mark will not be able to bring a personal action in respect of the loss in value of his shares.

Since there is no possibility of Mark bringing a personal action against the directors of Landsite plc, it is probable that the court would grant permission to continue the claim. Of course permission is only the first stage; Mark will still need to proceed to trial and prove the case against the directors, and he should be aware that if he is successful any relief ordered will benefit the company rather than Mark directly. Mark also runs the risk of costs orders against him as the claimant, although *Wallersteiner v Moir (No. 2)* [1975] 1 All ER 849 demonstrates that a minority shareholder acting in good faith and on reasonable grounds is likely to succeed in securing a costs indemnity order from the company.

Question 4

Analyse the significance of the House of Lords' decision in *O'Neill v Phillips* [1999] 1 WLR 1092 in relation to the unfair prejudice remedy under **Section 994** of the **Companies Act 2006**.

Commentary

This question requires a good understanding of the unfair prejudice remedy so that you can properly assess the decision in *O'Neill v Phillips*. You need to be able to explain the way in which Lord Hoffmann formulated the remedy in the case and its relation to other important cases. In addition you should be aware of the guidance provided by the case on the effect of an offer to purchase a petitioner's shares which aims to reduce the number of shareholder disputes coming to court.

Minority protection through the unfair prejudice remedy is one of the most important areas of company law, and *O'Neill v Phillips* is a very important case in this topic—accordingly a good understanding of the case and its influence on unfair prejudice will provide a strong basis for any discussion or problem in this area.

☆ Examiner's tip

To assess the significance of the case fully you need both to analyse the judgment and consider how it has impacted on the remedy by considering subsequent cases.

Answer plan

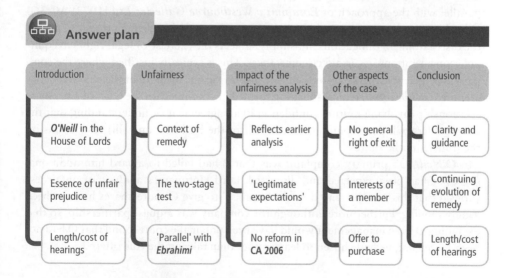

Introduction	Unfairness	Impact of the unfairness analysis	Other aspects of the case	Conclusion
O'Neill in the House of Lords	Context of remedy	Reflects earlier analysis	No general right of exit	Clarity and guidance
Essence of unfair prejudice	The two-stage test	'Legitimate expectations'	Interests of a member	Continuing evolution of remedy
Length/cost of hearings	'Parallel' with *Ebrahimi*	No reform in CA 2006	Offer to purchase	Length/cost of hearings

Suggested answer

O'Neill v Phillips [1999] 1 WLR 1092 (*O'Neill*) gave the House of Lords its first opportunity to consider the important shareholder remedy of 'unfair prejudice'. This originated as a remedy against 'oppression' in **Companies Act 1948, s. 210** but this was restrictively interpreted. It was redrafted in **Companies Act 1980, s. 75** allowing a member to petition where the company's affairs have been conducted in a manner unfairly prejudicial to their interests, and this became **Companies Act 1985, s. 459** and is now **Companies Act 2006 (CA 2006), s. 994**. This formulation proved much more successful but this led to concerns about the number, length, and cost of proceedings.

This essay will assess the significance of *O'Neill* by considering the impact of the court's analysis of 'unfairness' and other elements of the remedy, including the effect of an offer to purchase shares.

Lord Hoffmann, giving the only speech in *O'Neill*, identified the key element of the remedy as 'unfairness': a concept chosen 'to free the court from technical considerations of legal right and to confer a wide power to do what appeared just and equitable'. However, the concept of fairness had to be applied judicially with the content based upon rational principles which depended on the context. The context here was found in two elements—first the commercial nature of a company as a legal association for an economic purpose, and secondly the way company law developed from the law of partnership, so incorporating equitable concepts of good faith. This created a dual notion of unfairness: first 'a member of a company will not ordinarily be entitled to complain of unfairness unless there has been some breach of the terms on which he agreed that the affairs of the company should be conducted', but secondly 'there will be cases in which equitable considerations make it unfair for those conducting the affairs of the company to rely upon their strict legal powers'. The judge drew a parallel with the approach of *Ebrahimi v Westbourne Galleries Ltd* [1973] AC 360 (*Ebrahimi*) for just and equitable winding up—the equitable element does not permit the disregarding of obligations but simply subjects the exercise of legal rights to equitable considerations in certain circumstances. This is typically justified where the company is a 'quasi-partnership company', ie displaying one or more of the characteristics identified in *Ebrahimi*: i) an association formed or continued on the basis of a personal relationship involving mutual confidence; ii) an agreement or understanding that the shareholders will participate in the conduct of the business; and (iii) restrictions on the transfer of the shares.

In *O'Neill*, O's primary complaint was that P had failed to award him additional shares as had been expected and discussed. Lord Hoffmann's analysis of unfairness showed that this was not unfair as the 'promise' to give O more shares had not been legally binding. Furthermore, although the company was a quasi-partnership, so that excluding O from management would have been unfair, the court found that O had not been forced out; he had chosen to leave rather than take on the role offered.

How significant was this interpretation of unfairness? Clearly the formulation of 'unfairness' in *O'Neill* was not new, it mirrored the analysis (of Hoffmann LJ) in *Re Saul D Harrison & Sons plc* [1995] 1 BCLC 14. The significance of *O'Neill* lies more in the explicit rejection of the concept of 'legitimate expectations', a notion introduced in *Re Saul D Harrison & Sons plc*, but recognized as 'probably a mistake' in *O'Neill*. Lord Hoffmann explained 'legitimate expectations' was a 'label' for the equitable restraint and 'should not be allowed to lead a life of its own'. It was this focus on legitimate expectations that had led the Court of Appeal to find in favour of O, and generally loosen the boundaries of unfair prejudice.

Accordingly, while *O'Neill* did not break new ground it tightened the remedy somewhat. Following the decision, the Law Commission thought that the remedy would be less readily available while the Company Law Review Steering Group (see 'Modern Company Law for a Competitive Economy: Final Report' (June 2001)) believed it remained substantially unchanged but agreed with the analysis of *O'Neill*. There was perceived to be no need for reform, contrary to the views of the Law Commission prior to *O'Neill*.

Later cases have accepted *O'Neill* as providing the necessary guidance for unfair prejudice (*Oak Investment Partners XII v Boughtwood* [2010] 2 BCLC 459), while *Re Tobian Properties Ltd* [2012] EWCA Civ 998 reflects its essence in describing the remedy as 'elastic but not unbounded'. The *O'Neill* analysis has shown that for the majority of companies, where the relationship is purely commercial, unfairness will lie only in a breach of the terms of association—the articles, company law, or binding shareholder agreements. Commonly such complaints lie in respect of breach of directors' duties, or a failure of the majority to abide by the constitution. Only where equitable constraints can be justified, as in quasi-partnership companies, can the petitioner rely on a wider notion of 'unfairness', but even here the petitioner will have to establish a clear understanding on which the association is based or continued and cannot simply rely on a failure to meet his 'legitimate expectations'.

Prior to *O'Neill*, the Law Commission had considered the possibility of providing a more general exit route for aggrieved shareholders. *O'Neill* made clear that the unfair prejudice remedy does not provide 'no fault divorce' allowing a petitioner to be bought out wherever trust and confidence has broken down; unfairness has to be established. This was followed in *Re Phoenix Office Supplies Ltd* [2003] 1 BCLC 76—a shareholder wanting to leave cannot oblige other shareholders to purchase his shares. Even deadlock between the shareholders is not enough in itself to trigger s. 994: *Hawkes v Cuddy* [2009] 2 BCLC 427. These limits show how important it is to place dispute resolution mechanisms and exit provisions in the articles or shareholder agreements from the start.

While tightening the concept of 'unfairness', *O'Neill* did accept that the 'interests of a member' for the purposes of the provision should be interpreted widely ('the requirement ... should not be too narrowly or technically construed'). This has been followed in later cases, eg *Gamlestaden Fastigheter AB v Baltic Partners Ltd* [2007] 4 All ER 164.

Another significant element of *O'Neill* is guidance on the effect of an offer to purchase the petitioner's shares—advice given expressly to encourage parties to avoid litigation. It was well established that an appropriate offer could lead to the dismissal of the petition—the petitioner having received the full relief that might eventually be awarded; Lord Hoffmann asserted that such an offer prevents conduct from being unfair as the minority is no longer trapped. *O'Neill* set out the principles to be expected of a 'fair' offer—normally a pro-rata valuation without a minority discount to be determined by a competent expert with both parties having equal access to information and the opportunity to make submissions to the expert. The judge also recognized that an offer should usually include legal costs incurred, although a respondent should be given 'a reasonable opportunity to make an offer' before any obligation for costs arose. This guidance has been followed in later cases in evaluating an offer (eg *North Holdings Ltd v Southern Tropics Ltd* [1999] 2 BCLC 625) but *Harborne Road Nominees Ltd v Karvaski* [2011] EWHC 2214 made the point that an offer within the *O'Neill* guidance will not inevitably lead to the striking out of a petition.

In conclusion, the significance of the House of Lords' decision in *O'Neill* lies in the way it has aided clarity and increased the opportunities for resolving disputes out of court, while not unduly restricting this important and flexible remedy. **Section 994** of the **CA 2006** continues to be praised for its 'adaptability' (Arden LJ in *Re Tobian*, who also recognized it as a tool for encouraging good corporate behaviour) and its 'wide and flexible' nature (*Re Coroin Ltd*; *McKillen v Misland (Cyprus) Investments Ltd* [2013] EWCA Civ 781), and courts have not been deterred from developing the jurisdiction in appropriate cases, albeit within the constraints of *O'Neill*. For example in *Gross v Rackind* [2004] 4 All ER 735 it was held that the conduct of a holding company towards its subsidiary company could be the subject of a complaint by the shareholder of the subsidiary, while in *Oak Investment Partners XII Ltd Partnership v Boughtwood* the court stated that there was no reason in principle why the conduct of a senior manager should not be relevant. Although *Hawkes v Cuddy* [2009] 2 BCLC 427 has confirmed that **Insolvency Act 1986, s. 122(1)(g)** remains available as a potential remedy in shareholder disputes, **CA 2006, s. 994** continues to be the favoured option in most cases. Unfortunately, *O'Neill* has not entirely resolved the problems of long and complex proceedings in such cases, as seen in *Re Coroin Ltd* where Arden LJ commented upon 'heavy' and 'resource intensive' **s. 994** cases and the need to reduce hearing times for such cases.

Further reading

Almadani, M., 'Derivative action: does the Companies Act 2006 offer a way forward?' (2009) 30 Co Law 131

Arsalidou, D., 'Litigation culture and the new statutory derivative claim' (2009) 30 Co Law 205

Boyle, A. J., 'Unfair prejudice in the House of Lords' (2000) 21 Co Law 253

Cheung, R., 'Corporate wrongs litigated in the context of unfair prejudice claims: reforming the unfair prejudice remedy for the redress of corporate wrongs' (2008) 29 Co Law 98

Gibbs, D., 'Has the statutory derivative claim fulfilled its objectives? Parts 1 and F 2' (2011) 32 Co Law 41 and 76

Goddard, R., 'Taming the unfair prejudice remedy: sections 459-461 of the Companies Act 1985 in the House of Lords' (1999) 58 CLJ 461

Gray, A. M., 'The statutory derivative claim: an outmoded superfluousness?' (2012) 33 Co Law 295

Hemraj, M. B., 'Maximising shareholders' wealth: legitimate expectation and minority oppression' (2006) 27 Co Law 125

Paterson, P., 'A criticism of the contractual approach to unfair prejudice' (2006) 27 Co Law 204

Payne, J., and Prentice, D., 'Section 459 of the Companies Act 1985 – the House of Lords' view' (1999) 115 LQR 587

11

Corporate insolvency

Introduction

Corporate insolvency is a large and important subject in its own right but aspects of the subject are often included within company law courses. Topics often included (although rarely all of these) are: forms of corporate rescue, particularly administration and company voluntary arrangements; compulsory and creditors' voluntary winding up; the assets available to creditors in a winding up; the distribution of assets to creditors; transactions that are vulnerable on winding up. In addition many courses include remedies against directors on winding up (particularly wrongful trading) and disqualification of directors under the **Company Directors Disqualification Act 1986**, whether as part of insolvency or as an adjunct to directors and their duties.

An important aspect of corporate insolvency is corporate rescue, primarily administration and Company Voluntary Arrangements (CVA). In administration an administrator is appointed over the company with a view either to rescuing the company or securing a better realization of assets than would be achieved on winding up, or to realizing assets for the benefit of a secured creditor. A CVA provides a mechanism whereby a company can enter into a binding agreement with its creditors with a view to saving the company. Other 'corporate rescue' options exist including a scheme of arrangement under **Companies Act 2006 (CA 2006), ss. 895–901** (a more complex, but for some companies more suitable, alternative to a CVA), and administrative receivership (an alternative to administration but only available to floating chargeholders whose charge predates 15 September 2003). Administration is now the dominant rescue procedure.

An insolvent company may be wound up voluntarily or compulsorily. In a creditors' voluntary winding up (a members' voluntary winding up is only available to solvent companies) the members must pass a resolution to wind up the company, and then the company must call a creditors' meeting. If the members and the creditors nominate a different person to be liquidator then the creditors' choice prevails. In a compulsory winding up a petitioner presents a petition for the winding up of the company to the court.

While there are different categories of petitioner and different grounds for petition (see Chapter 10 of this volume in relation to **IA 1986 s. 122(1)(g)**), in an insolvent company the usual petition will be by a creditor on the ground that the company is unable to pay its debts (**IA 1986, s. 122(1)(f)**). On the making of a winding up order by the court the Official Receiver becomes liquidator, unless and until another person is appointed.

A liquidator or administrator may take action to recover assets or overturn transactions for the benefit of the creditors. The most important of these provisions are **IA 1986, ss. 238–45**. In addition a liquidator may bring proceedings against a director for misfeasance (**s. 212**), fraudulent trading (**s. 213**), or wrongful trading (**s. 214**). The liquidator must then ensure that assets of the company are distributed correctly to various groups of creditors in accordance with the statutory scheme.

Insolvency overlaps with many topics within company law, not least because many problems only come to light once a company has declined into insolvency (because it is only at this point that there is not enough money to go around). Particularly important connections are: corporate personality and lifting the veil, directors and directors' duties, and loan capital.

Question 1

Explain and assess the circumstances in which a creditor can bring a petition to wind up a company and whether there are any grounds on which the petition might be rejected.

Commentary

This question looks at petitions to wind up a company (ie compulsory winding up), requiring you to address both the grounds on which a petition can be brought and the reasons why a petition might not succeed. The first issue looks at the ways in which creditors can establish that a company is unable to pay its debts for the purpose of a winding up petition, while the second looks at situations such as where the debt is disputed by the company or the company has a cross-claim.

Answer plan

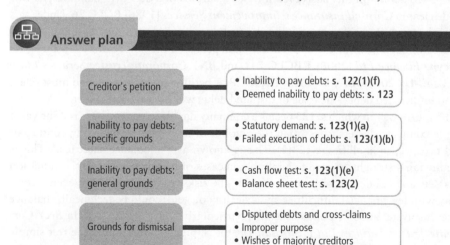

Creditor's petition	• Inability to pay debts: **s. 122(1)(f)** • Deemed inability to pay debts: **s. 123**
Inability to pay debts: specific grounds	• Statutory demand: **s. 123(1)(a)** • Failed execution of debt: **s. 123(1)(b)**
Inability to pay debts: general grounds	• Cash flow test: **s. 123(1)(e)** • Balance sheet test: **s. 123(2)**
Grounds for dismissal	• Disputed debts and cross-claims • Improper purpose • Wishes of majority creditors

Suggested answer

Creditors may petition for the compulsory winding up of a company on the ground that it is unable to pay its debts: **Insolvency Act 1986 (IA 1986), s. 122(1)(f)** and the company's inability to pay its debts must be established by the petitioner. A company is deemed to be unable to pay its debts in four circumstances set out in **IA 1986, s. 123**. In summary these are: (i) a failure to pay a statutory demand for £750 or more (**s. 123(1)(a)**); (ii) a failed execution of judgment (**s. 123(1)(b)**); (iii) the inability to pay debts as they fall due (**s. 123(1)(e)**) and (iv) where the company's assets are less than its liabilities (**s. 123(2)**).

Turning to the first of these, the statutory demand under **s. 123(1)(a)**, requires a creditor to serve a written demand for payment (for a due debt that is currently payable: *JSF Finance v Akma Solutions* [2001] 2 BCLC 307) at the company's registered office. If after three weeks the company has failed to pay the debt or to secure or compound for it to the creditor's satisfaction, it is presumed unable to pay its debts. The debt must be for at least the statutory minimum of £750. The problem with this procedure is the element of delay.

The second option, under **IA 1986, s. 123(1)(b)** is where a creditor has a judgment or court order against the company, has tried to enforce this through the court but has not been paid. This obviously requires the petitioner to have gone through the process of obtaining judgment and attempting execution and so is unattractive to most creditors.

As a result, many creditors prefer to use the third option under **s. 123(1)(e)**—that a company is unable to pay its debts as they fall due—known as 'the cash flow test'. The fact that a company has not paid a debt is evidence that a company cannot pay its debts as they fall due so the creditor presents a petition declaring that the company owes them an amount exceeding the statutory minimum (£750); that the debtor has not disputed its liability in respect of the debt; and that the company is, therefore, unable to pay its debts and should be wound up. This approach was endorsed by the Court of Appeal in *Taylor's Industrial Flooring Ltd v M & H Plant Hire (Manchester) Ltd* [1990] BCLC 216 where it rejected a claim that the process was abusive. A company can be wound up on this basis even if it has a surplus of assets over liabilities, as was made clear in *Cornhill Insurance v Improvement Services* [1986] BCLC 26. Under this head the court is entitled to consider debts that will fall due in the 'reasonably near' future although how far the court will look depends on the nature of the business: *Re Cheyne Finance Ltd* [2008] 1 BCLC 741 and *BNY Corporate Trustee Services Ltd v Eurosail-UK 2007-3BL plc* [2013] UKSC 28. A petition under this ground must relate to an undisputed debt—the issue of disputed debts will be considered later.

The fourth way in which **s. 123** deems a company unable to pay its debts is if the value of the company's assets is less than the amount of its liabilities, including contingent and prospective liabilities: **s.123(2)**. This is known as 'the balance sheet test'. This is usually fairly straightforward to apply, but in cases of marginal solvency the valuation of assets and liabilities can become critical. The risk with this test is that even a company with few financial difficulties and a healthy outlook could be technically 'balance sheet insolvent' at some points in its life, particularly when it starts out. In *BNY Corporate Trustee Services Ltd v Eurosail-UK* the Supreme Court stated the test simply required the court to make a judgment as to whether the company cannot reasonably be expected to meet its liabilities, bearing in mind that the more distant those liabilities, the harder it will be to establish this. The Supreme Court rejected the view of Lord Neuberger in the Court of Appeal that it required a demonstration that a company had reached the point of no return (or 'the end of the road'); this is not necessary.

In order for a creditor to petition, the debt relied on (under **IA 1986, s. 123(1)(e)**) must be undisputed. The two main reasons for this are first that a petitioner whose debt is justifiably disputed is not in a position to present a petition for a winding up order as he is not established as a creditor (*Mann v Goldstein* [1968] 1 WLR 1091) and secondly that the winding up jurisdiction is not intended for the resolution of disputes between the parties (*Re Selectmove Ltd* [1995] 1 WLR 474).

In order to secure the dismissal of a winding up petition by a creditor whose claim is disputed it is necessary for the company to establish that there is a genuine and bona fide dispute, that the company honestly believes this to be the case and there are reasonable or substantial grounds for this belief. The court should not conduct a lengthy or elaborate hearing on this matter (*Tallington Lakes Ltd v Ancasta International Boat Sales Ltd* [2012] EWCA Civ 1712). If this is established it has been stated that the dismissal of the petition is not discretionary but compulsory: *Re Bayoil SA* [1999] 1 WLR 147. There are, however, cases where the court has allowed a petition to proceed even where there is a bona fide dispute as to the exact amount of the debt if the company clearly owes money to the petitioner in excess of the statutory minimum: *Re Tweeds Garages Ltd* [1962] 1 Ch 406. In *Re GBI Investments* [2010] 2 BCLC 624 it was suggested that a petition might also, exceptionally, be allowed to proceed notwithstanding a dispute as to the debt if injustice would otherwise result.

Even where a debt is due and not disputed, a petition may be dismissed where the company has a 'genuine and serious' (*Re Bayoil SA*) cross-claim against the petitioner that exceeds the company's debt to the petitioner. This allows the court to dismiss the petition (it remains a matter for the court's discretion) even if the company had been in a position to litigate their claim but had chosen not to (*Montgomery v Wanda Modes Ltd* [2002] 1 BCLC 289, doubting *Re Bayoil SA* on this point).

Of course if the debt that is the subject of the petition has been paid by the time of the hearing then the petition will also be dismissed—although the court has the ability to substitute another creditor to the petition in certain circumstances.

The other principal reason for rejecting a petition is where it is brought for an improper purpose. The courts have held that a petitioner must not act in order to obtain some private advantage or for some ulterior motive. For example in *Re Leigh Estates Ltd* [1994] BCC 292 the court rejected a petition brought against a company in administration where the petitioner brought the petition to put themselves in a stronger position—winding up is a collective remedy and petitions should be brought for the benefit of creditors generally. That said, *Mann v Goldstein* made clear that the mere fact that a petitioner has acted with 'personal hostility' or the hope of some indirect advantage is not in itself an abuse of process.

Finally the court may reject a petition where the creditors disagree as to whether the company should be wound up. For example in *Re ABC Coupler & Engineering Ltd* [1961] 1

WLR 243 a petition was rejected where other creditors opposed the making of a winding up order and the court found they were reasonable in wanting the company to continue as there were good prospects of payment in due course. While the views of the majority of creditors will be highly influential, the court may still choose to make a winding up order (*Re P & J MacRae Ltd* [1961] 1 WLR 229); it remains a matter for the court's discretion.

 Question 2

On the liquidation of a company, all of the assets belonging to the company at the commencement of the liquidation are available for the creditors.

Discuss.

 Commentary

This question requires you to distinguish between assets belonging to the company in liquidation which are available to the creditors and those which are unavailable through mechanisms such as security and trusts. In addition, you should discuss the liquidator's right to disclaim onerous assets. You should also consider the liquidator's ability in compulsory winding up to reclaim assets of the company disposed of between the petition being presented and the making of the winding up order under **IA 1986, s. 127**. You must also show familiarity with the statutory provisions allowing liquidators (and administrators) to set aside transactions at an undervalue and preferences (**ss. 238–9**). The avoidance of floating charges (**s. 245**), the setting aside of extortionate credit transactions (**s. 244**), and transactions with intent to defraud creditors (**s. 423**) should also be referred to as these can all affect the company's assets.

These are important topics with which you need to be familiar. Any or all of these topics can easily appear in a wide variety of problem and essay questions.

 Answer plan

Assets not available to liquidator
- Trust property
- Security
- Reservation of title
- Set off
- Disclaimer of onerous property

Swelling the assets by the liquidator
- Void dispositions: **s. 127**
- Transactions at undervalue: **s. 238**
- Preferences: **s. 239**
- Invalid floating charges: **s. 245**
- Extortionate credit transactions: **s. 244**
- Transactions defrauding creditors: **s. 423**

Suggested answer

The commencement of a voluntary winding up is the date of the passing of the resolution to wind up (**Insolvency Act 1986 (IA 1986), s. 86**), and for a compulsory winding up, the date of the presentation of the petition (**s. 129(2)**) except where the company is already in voluntary winding up: **s. 129(1)**. In effect, not all of the property apparently belonging to the company at the commencement of the winding up passes to the liquidators but, on the other hand, liquidators may be able to recover property previously disposed of. The effective back-dating of the liquidation in compulsory winding up can be particularly important in identifying assets that the liquidator may be able to add to the company's assets for distribution to the creditors.

Assets that do not pass to the liquidator include property held as agent, trustee, or bailee for another. In *Re Kayford Ltd* [1975] 1 All ER 604, customer deposits paid into a special account pending delivery of the goods ordered were held on trust and so had to be returned to the customers. It must also be remembered that assets subject to a valid fixed charge can be realized by the chargeholder to meet their own debt without involvement of the liquidator.

In addition, property in the company's possession under a contract containing a valid reservation of title clause (also known as a '*Romalpa* clause' after *Aluminium Industrie Vaassen v Romalpa Aluminium* [1976] 1 WLR 676) does not pass if the goods remain identifiable and removable (*Hendy Lennox v Grahame Puttick* [1984] 1 WLR 485). The contract may also validly include an 'all-monies' clause, reserving title until all outstanding debts between the parties have been met (*Clough Mill v Martin* [1985] BCLC 64).

Not all money owing to the company is recoverable by the liquidator. If an individual both owes money to the company and is owed money by the company, these sums must be set off (**Insolvency Rules 1986, r. 4.90**) and only the balance can be claimed by the liquidator (or proved in the liquidation).

Liquidators may wish to reject onerous property belonging to the company under their right of disclaimer in respect of unprofitable contracts, property that is unsaleable or not readily saleable, or property giving rise to liability to pay money or perform any other onerous act: **s. 178**. Disclaimer terminates the rights, interests, and liabilities of the company and victims of disclaimer must prove as creditors.

It has thus been seen that not all assets apparently belonging to the company are available to the liquidator. However, there are several statutory provisions allowing the liquidator to recover previously disposed of property.

First 'any disposition of the company's property ... after the commencement of the winding up is void unless the court otherwise orders': (**IA 1986, s. 127**). Accordingly the liquidator can recover any property disposed of after the presentation of a petition to wind up the company unless the disposition is validated by the court. The court will normally approve bona fide payments in the ordinary course of business where the parties were unaware of the petition and the payment does not seek to prefer the creditor: *Re Gray's Inn Construction Ltd* [1980] 1 WLR 711. Problems in relation to the company's bank honouring cheques drawn payable to creditors were largely resolved (in the banks' favour) by *Bank of Ireland v Hollicourt (Contracts) Ltd* [2001] 1 All ER 289.

Liquidators may also avoid transactions at an undervalue within a relevant time: s. 238. This is within two years prior to the onset of insolvency and the company must at the time have been unable to pay its debts for the purposes of s. 123, but this is presumed for transactions with connected persons: s. 240(2).

A company enters into a transaction at an undervalue if: (a) it makes a gift to a person, or enters into a transaction on terms whereby it receives no consideration; or (b) where the consideration is significantly less than the value of the consideration supplied by the company: (IA 1986, s. 238(4)). Under (b) this requires the balancing of consideration received and given and it is usually for the liquidator to establish the value of any consideration (*Phillips v Brewin Dolphin* [2001] 1 WLR 143). The creation of a charge is not a transaction at an undervalue (*Re MC Bacon Ltd* [1990] BCLC 324). An order to avoid the transaction will not be made if the company entered into the transaction in good faith and where there were reasonable grounds for believing that it would benefit the company: s. 238(5), but this defence must be established by the person relying on it (*Re Barton Manufacturing Ltd* [1999] 1 BCLC 740).

Liquidators can also challenge preferences under IA 1986, s. 239—where the company does something within the relevant time prior to the onset of insolvency that puts creditors (or guarantors or sureties) into a better position in the event of the company's insolvent liquidation than they would otherwise have been. The relevant time is two years for connected persons and six months for outsiders (s. 240(1)(a) and (b)), and the company must have been unable to pay its debts within the meaning of s. 123. Preferences are only voidable where the company was motivated by a desire to confer a benefit on the person preferred, which requires a positive wish to improve the position of the individual. Accordingly in *Re MC Bacon Ltd* there was no preference where the company gave its bank the benefit of security, but did so because the bank was otherwise threatening to withdraw the company's bank account. For connected persons, defined in s. 249, a desire to prefer the person is presumed: s. 239(6).

In respect of transactions at an undervalue and voidable preferences, the court may order retransfer of property, release or discharge of security, repayments to administrator or liquidator, revival of guarantees, and so on: s. 241. Third parties who are bona fide purchasers for value are protected: s. 241(2) and (2A). Proceeds of a successful claim are held for the unsecured creditors: *Re Yagerphone Ltd* [1935] 1 Ch 392.

A liquidator should also be aware that floating charges created other than in relation to money paid, goods or services supplied or discharge or reduction of the company's debts at the same time or after the creation of the charge will be invalidated by s. 245 if created at a relevant time. This is one year for non-connected persons provided the company was unable to pay its debts at that time or became so as a consequence: s. 245(4). For connected persons, the period is extended to two years and is not conditional upon the company being unable to pay its debts. In *Re Shoe Lace Ltd; Power v Sharp Investments Ltd* [1994] 1 BCLC 111, the court decided that, on the basis of the ordinary meaning of the words used, loans made between April and early July in consideration of the proposed creation of a debenture secured by a floating charge were not made at the same time as the creation of a debenture executed on 24 July 1990. The floating charge was, therefore, invalid. There are advantages for banks and suppliers under a current account due to the operation of the rule in *Clayton's Case* (1816) 1 **Mer 572,** which provides that credits to a current account discharge debts in the order in which they were incurred in the absence of specific appropriation. In *Re Yeovil Glove Co Ltd* [1965] **Ch 148,** the bank honoured cheques totalling some £110,000 after the creation of a debenture. This was held to be a new advance made after the creation of the charge, even though the charge was created in respect of an existing debt and the overdraft remained virtually unchanged.

Liquidators may also apply to set aside extortionate credit transactions within the three years prior to the commencement of the liquidation: **s. 244.** Transactions are presumed to be extortionate, and the court has a range of possible orders including the setting aside or varying of the transaction, and requiring any person to refund sums paid by the company or surrender of any security.

Liquidators (and victims) can also challenge transactions at an undervalue made at any time provided the transaction is made with the aim of putting assets beyond the reach of someone who is or may make a claim against the company or otherwise prejudicing the interests of such a person or to prejudice their interests: **s. 423(3).** Possible court orders are similar to those in **s. 241: s. 425.**

From this, it can be seen that liquidators have enormous scope for increasing the available assets of companies in liquidation for the benefit of creditors, although the use of these provisions is limited by the expense of proceedings and the risk of failure (which would reduce the assets available to creditors). The liquidator may also be able to claim contributions from company directors using misfeasance proceedings (**s. 212**) or fraudulent or wrongful trading (**ss. 213–14**).

? Question 3

A winding up order was made on 30 April 2013 against Hebejebe Ltd, following a creditor's petition which was presented to the court on 8 April 2013. Lara has been appointed liquidator. The creditors of Hebejebe Ltd include:

i. Wizzerd Bank, which is owed £250,000 and has a fixed charge (duly registered) over Hebejebe Ltd's freehold premises. Hebejebe Ltd's premises have been valued at £200,000

ii. Pocus Finance plc which provided an initial £10,000 loan to Hebejebe Ltd on 2 April 2012, and then a further loan of £5,000 on 20 April 2012. Hebejebe Ltd granted Pocus Finance plc a floating charge (which was duly registered) to secure the full £15,000 on 20 April 2012

iii. Hebejebe Ltd's senior employees who received no pay during the company's last three months of trading

iv. HM Revenue and Customs which is owed £30,000 in respect of unpaid PAYE and national insurance payments

v. Abracadabra, a trade creditor, who is owed £2,000. Abracadabra had been owed £3,000 but Hebejebe Ltd paid off £1,000 of this debt on 12 April 2013 as Abracadabra refused to continue to supply essential raw materials until the debt was reduced. Hebejebe Ltd would have had to cease trading immediately had these materials not been supplied

Advise Lara on how the company's assets should be distributed to the creditors in light of the information above. Lara has incurred costs and expenses of £10,000.

 Commentary

The order of distribution of assets on liquidation is a common topic in corporate insolvency. When dealing with a question on this topic you will need to be confident in formulating the creditor priority list and understand where different claimants fit within this. To answer the question you then need to be able to identify all the claimants and the nature of their claim (and any surrounding issues as it is easy for questions to add in any number of other insolvency topics) and slot them into place.

 Examiner's tip

Keep an eye on any dates in insolvency questions—they can be crucial to whether particular provisions (namely **IA 1986, s. 127** and **ss. 238–45**) apply or not.

Answer plan

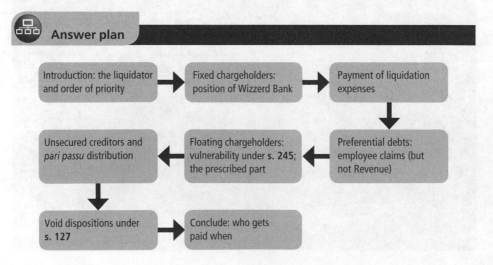

Suggested answer

As liquidator, Lara's function is 'to secure that the assets are got in, realised and distributed to the company's creditors and, if there is a surplus, to the persons entitled to it' (**Insolvency Act 1986 (IA 1986), s. 143(1)**). Accordingly, having gathered in all the assets belonging to the company (which may be swelled by claims in respect of, eg preferences (**s. 239**), transactions at an undervalue (**s. 239**) or wrongful trading (**s. 214**)), she must distribute the assets according to a strict order of priority. Creditors must submit a proof of debt in order to claim in the liquidation.

The basic order for priority of payment is as follows, although the situation is more complex than the list suggests:

- Secured creditors with a fixed charge
- Expenses of liquidation
- Preferential creditors
- Secured creditors with a floating charge
- Unsecured/ordinary creditors
- Deferred creditors
- Members

Secured creditors with the benefit of a fixed charge, such as Wizzerd Bank, are in a strong position, and if their security is sufficient to satisfy their debt in full they need not prove in the liquidation at all. Wizzerd Bank could choose to surrender the security to the liquidator and prove as an unsecured creditor, but as an unsecured creditor Wizzerd Bank would rank *pari passu* with other unsecured creditors and would probably only recover a small part of the debt. Wizzerd Bank should realize the security, which in this case will cover £200,000 of the debt and then prove in the liquidation for the remaining £50,000, in respect of which it will be an unsecured creditor.

The expenses of the liquidation (including Lara's costs and remuneration) are paid in priority to all other payments. Furthermore, if the company's free assets are insufficient to meet the liquidation expenses then assets subject to a floating charge can be used by virtue of **IA 1986, s. 176ZA** (reversing *Re Leyland Daf Ltd* [2004] UKHL 9). If there are insufficient assets to meet all liquidation expenses they are paid according to the order set out in **Insolvency Rules 1986, r. 4.218**.

Preferential debts are those debts that statute provides are paid in priority to other debts, other than the expenses of winding up (**IA 1986, s. 175**) and are found in **IA 1986, Schedule 6**. The main preferential debts are unpaid employee remuneration relating to the four months prior to the liquidation (to a maximum of £800 per employee), accrued holiday pay, and loans used specifically for paying employee remuneration. Accordingly the unpaid senior employees can claim as preferential creditors but only for £800 each—if they are owed more they will need to claim for this as unsecured creditors. Unpaid PAYE and national insurance are no longer preferential debts after the **Enterprise Act 2002** which reduced the category of preferential debts in order to benefit unsecured creditors. HM Revenue and Customs will, therefore, not be a preferential creditor. If the company's free assets are insufficient to pay the preferential debts, then property subject to a floating charge can be used (**s. 175(2)**). Should there be insufficient assets to meet all the preferential debts in full, then preferential creditors are paid rateably (or '*pari passu*').

Pocus Finance claims to have a floating charge securing £15,000. However, a floating charge created at a relevant time is only valid to the extent it is created in consideration for money paid or goods or services supplied 'at the same time as, or after, the creation of the charge' (**IA 1986, s. 245**). Here the first £10,000 of the debt was provided before the creation of the charge and so would be invalid (*Re Shoe Lace Ltd; Power v Sharp* [1994] 1 BCLC 111). The relevant time for a person who is not connected with the company (**s. 249** and **s. 435**) is 12 months ending with the onset of insolvency (**s. 245(3)**), provided the company is unable to pay its debts within the meaning of **s. 123**. In a compulsory liquidation the 'onset of insolvency' is the date of presentation of the petition, so this charge has been created just within the 12 month period, but Lara would need to check whether the company was unable to pay its debts at that time. If so then the floating charge is likely to be valid only in relation to the £5,000, leaving Pocus Finance to claim as an unsecured creditor for the remaining £10,000. If Hebejebe Ltd was able to pay its debts as at 20 April 2012 then it would not be a relevant time and the floating charge will be valid for the full £15,000. Although providing security for an existing debt (as here) can also amount to a preference under **s. 239**, Lara cannot use **s. 239** as the charge was created outside the relevant time of six months.

As has been seen, even where Pocus Finance has the benefit of a floating charge, it may lose some of the benefit of that security if the company's free assets are insufficient to meet the liquidation expenses and preferential debts. In addition, following the **Enterprise Act 2002**, a 'prescribed part' of the realizations of assets subject to a floating charge is reserved for unsecured creditors unless disapplied (in exceptional circumstances) by the liquidator or the court (**IA 1986, s. 176A**). The prescribed part is 50 per cent of net property under £10,000 and 20 per cent over this, to a maximum of £600,000.

Unsecured creditors share *pari passu* in the remaining assets of the company and the prescribed part although secured creditors with a shortfall (here Wizzerd Bank and Pocus Finance) cannot share in the prescribed part (*Re Airbase Ltd* [2008] EWHC 124). Abracadabra is also an unsecured creditor, but her position is complicated by the company's payment of £1,000 after presentation of the petition. Dispositions of the company's property after the commencement of the winding up (ie the presentation of the petition: **s. 129**) are void under **s. 127** unless validated by the court. Disposition is defined widely, *Re J. Leslie Engineering* [1976] 1 WLR 292, and so prima facie Lara can recover the £1,000 from Abracadabra and Abracadabra would have to prove as an unsecured creditor for the full £3,000. However, the court is likely to be willing to validate the payment retrospectively. In *Re Gray's Inn Construction* [1980] 1 WLR 711 the court indicated that a payment made in good faith in the ordinary course of business, where the parties were unaware of the petition and there was no intention to prefer the creditor, is likely to be validated. These factors seem to apply to Abracadabra and this conclusion is supported by ***Denney v John Hudson*** [1992] BCLC 901 where a good faith payment of a debt to a fuel supplier in order to ensure continued trading was validated.

To conclude it appears that Wizzerd Bank can realize its security to recover £20,000 but will need to claim the outstanding £50,000 as an unsecured creditor. Lara's costs and expenses including her remuneration will be paid first out of the free assets of the company, and out of the floating charge realisations if necessary. Next come the preferential creditors, including the senior employees to a maximum of £800 each but not including HM Revenue and Customs. Pocus Finance's floating charge could be entirely valid (if the company was able to pay its debts as at the date of the charge) or may be valid only for the 'new debt' of £5,000. To the extent that the debt is not secured by the charge, Pocus Finance will have to claim as an unsecured creditor. So far as the charge is valid, property subject to it will have the prescribed part set aside for distribution amongst the unsecured creditors (other than Wizzerd Bank and Pocus Finance). Abracadabra faces having to return the £1,000 to Lara as a void disposition, but could apply to the court for validation and has quite a strong case. Depending on the outcome of that validation application, Abracadabra will claim either £2,000 or £3,000 as an unsecured creditor. Having paid the expenses of the liquidation, the preferential debts and the claim of any valid floating chargeholder, Lara must distribute the remaining assets of the company *pari passu* amongst the unsecured creditors. If there were any assets remaining (which is improbable in an insolvent liquidation), she should then pay any deferred debts (which include interest on proved debts: **s. 189**) and pay any surplus to members. Once the winding up is complete Lara should apply to have Hebejebe Ltd dissolved (**IA 1986, s. 205**).

? Question 4

Pineapple Press plc is a successful publisher with a string of bestselling authors. Due, however, to major problems not of their making in India and China, where their books are produced, the company lost its whole autumn production for the Christmas market. Unable to find alternative printers, the company found it difficult to continue meeting its salary bills and the rental for its warehouse in the UK.

The company had created a floating charge over the undertaking several years previously to Croesus Bank, and with the collapse in income is now unable to pay the interest payments on the loan. Once the immediate production problems are over, the business should return to its normal profitable state.

Advise Pineapple Press plc and Croesus Bank of the legal possibilities to resolve the problems.

Commentary

This question requires you to consider the alternative solutions to liquidation bearing in mind that a return to profitability is likely once the immediate crisis is over. This involves looking at non-terminal insolvency and the possibility of the company entering into a company voluntary arrangement (CVA) or an administration. You should consider the advantages offered by entering a CVA by way of administration.

It is unlikely that your course will require you to have detailed knowledge of the legal processes and procedures relating to CVAs and administrations. It is more usual to expect outline knowledge of the procedures and an appreciation of the different options and their merits and drawbacks as an alternative to liquidation.

Answer plan

- The notion of corporate rescue and the role of CVA and administration in this respect
- CVA—basic procedure; advantages and disadvantages
- Administration—basic procedure; advantages and disadvantages
- Options for Pineapple Press and Croesus Bank

Suggested answer

The Report of the Insolvency Law Review Committee, 'Insolvency Law and Practice' (Cmnd 8558) 1982—the 'Cork Report'—proposed moving towards a 'rescue culture' to save sick businesses. To this end, it recommended the introduction of the CVA and administration.

The CVA provides a mechanism to allow companies to enter into binding arrangements with their creditors, offering the possibility of rescuing the company itself. The CVA may be a scheme of arrangement (delaying or changing the terms of debt repayment) or a composition of the company's debts (where creditors agree to accept a smaller sum in total settlement of the debt, eg 75 pence in the pound), and is administered by a supervisor.

Administration was inspired by the perceived success of administrative receivership. Unlike an administrative receiver, however, the administrator acts on behalf of all creditors (and not just the appointing chargeholder). In administration an administrator is appointed (either by the court or out of court) over the company, for the purpose of (a) rescuing the company as a going concern, or (b) achieving a better result for the company's creditors than on winding up or, if neither of those objectives are possible, (c) realizing the company's property in order to make a distribution to one or more secured or preferential creditors. Administration may save the company itself but in practice this is unusual. The second objective is more commonly obtained with the business saved by the administrator selling off the business (or the viable parts of it) to a purchaser but the company itself being wound up. Where the sale is arranged before the company enters into administration the administration is known as a 'pre-pack administration'.

The facts of the question suggest that Pineapple Press plc's business is fundamentally sound, and so a CVA may be attractive in order to save the company itself. As the company is a public company, only a CVA without a moratorium under **Insolvency Act 1986 (IA 1986), Part 1** is available. A moratorium prevents creditors from taking action against the company or petitioning for winding up during its existence. While a CVA with a moratorium is possible under **IA 1986, Schedule A1** these are only available to small private companies, and in any event have not proved popular because of cumbersome requirements.

To enter into a CVA the directors of Pineapple Press plc must make a proposal (if the company were already in administration or winding up, the proposal is by the administrator or liquidator), providing for a 'nominee' (a qualified insolvency practitioner who will become the supervisor) and explaining why a CVA is desirable. The nominee submits a report to the court on whether the proposal should be put to meetings of the company and creditors and then calls those meetings as notified. The lack of moratorium means creditors can still take action during this period, reducing the chances of a CVA being successfully approved.

If both meetings accept the CVA proposals (by a 75 per cent majority for the creditors' meeting and a simple majority for the members' meeting) the proposals bind all notified creditors and the company without need for formal court approval (**IA 1986, s. 4**). Proposals affecting the rights of secured or preferential creditors can only be approved with their consent: **s. 4**. On approval, the CVA binds all creditors with notice of and entitled to vote at the meeting, even those who dissented (**s. 5**). However, the approval of the CVA can be challenged under **s. 6** on the grounds that the CVA unfairly prejudices the interests of a creditor, member, or contributory (eg *Mourant Trustees v Sixty UK Ltd* [2011] BCLC 383); or there is some material irregularity in relation to either meeting (eg *HMRC v Portsmouth FC* [2010] EWHC 2013 (Ch)).

Once the CVA is approved, the court can stay all winding up proceedings, discharge any administration and give directions to facilitate the composition or scheme: **s. 7**. On completion of the CVA, the supervisor notifies all creditors and members of its full implementation, together with a financial report, with copies to the registrar of companies and the court.

If Pineapple Press plc wanted to pursue a CVA but was worried about the lack of moratorium during the proposal period, the company could obtain the benefit of a moratorium by entering into administration and pursuing the CVA within the administration (using administration as a 'wrapper' for the CVA). This would increase the chances of the CVA being approved but would increase the costs of the rescue process.

The administration procedure was completely revised by the **Enterprise Act 2002** and is now regulated by **IA 1986, Schedule B1**. Administrators act in the interests of all the company's creditors, are officers of the court, and must be licensed insolvency practitioners. They can be appointed by the court, by the holder of a qualifying floating charge, or by the company or its directors. In this case then, the most sensible option would be an out-of-court appointment by either Pineapple Press plc's directors or by Croesus Bank as the holder of a qualifying floating charge (a charge over the whole or substantially the whole of the company's property: **para. 14**). Either the directors or the bank can appoint an administrator by filing notice of intention to appoint with the court, followed by notice of appointment—an application to the court for an administration order is not necessary. An interim moratorium applies from the time notice of intention is filed with the court until the appointment of the administrator takes effect (or until a specified period of time has elapsed without an administrator having been appointed). Once administration commences, there is a permanent moratorium against legal proceedings for the duration of the administration.

Once appointed the administrator sets out proposals for achieving the purpose of the administration. This could include a proposal for a CVA or alternatively the administrator may conclude that the best option is a sale of the business (and it is not unusual for the sale of the business of a company in administration to be to persons already involved with the business, for example the company's directors). The **IA 1986** provides detailed requirements for the sending of the administration proposals to the registrar of companies and creditors and the holding of a creditors' meetings, although there are circumstances in which this does not have to be done, and in a 'pre-pack administration' this process will not be followed as the assets will have been sold in advance of the creditors' meeting (the validity of this was upheld in *Re Transbus International* [2004] 1 WLR 2654).

On their appointment, administrators take custody or control of all the company's property and manage the company's affairs, business, and property in accordance with the approved proposals. Their appointment terminates after one year subject to extension by the court or by consent of the creditors.

The administrator can apply to the court to end the administration (a) if its purpose cannot be achieved; (b) if the company should not have entered administration; or (c) where a creditors' meeting requires him to make an application. Administrators appointed by floating chargeholders and the company or directors may notify the court and the registrar of companies that the administration's purpose has been sufficiently achieved and the appointment will then automatically cease: **para. 80**.

To conclude, while the directors of Pineapple Press plc can propose a CVA, there is a risk that creditors could take action to enforce their rights or petition for the winding up of the company prior to approval of the CVA. To prevent this, the directors or Croesus Bank could exercise their right to appoint an administrator without the need for any application to the court, which will provide the benefit of an interim moratorium on any actions against the company (which will become permanent once the administration commences). The administrator could propose a CVA as a solution to the company's immediate crisis and, once the crisis is over, the company could resume normal trading. The success of the CVA is of course dependent on 75 per cent or more of the creditors agreeing.

Alternatively the company could enter into administration and the administrator could seek to sell off the viable parts of the company's business (following the second objective of administration). The administrator would then distribute the proceeds of sale to Pineapple Press plc's creditors and the company would proceed to winding up and dissolution. The business would continue under the hands of its new owners, hopefully able to survive without its current problems. The directors of Pineapple Press plc may wish to discuss the financial situation in detail with Croesus Bank and an appropriate insolvency practitioner in order to work through their options—if a sale of the business is the preferred option then a pre-pack administration could be arranged in order to reduce the damage to the business that could be caused by a lengthier administration.

Question 5

Joe, and his wife Chelsey, are the shareholders and directors of Stamford Vista Ltd, a company that owns and manages several health spas. The day-to-day running of the business is undertaken by Joe, and although Chelsey undertakes clerical and administrative tasks, she leaves management decisions to Joe and simply signs documents as and when directed by him to do so. The company pays them each an annual salary of £45,000.

Stamford Vista Ltd was incorporated in 2006 and was profitable initially, but was hit heavily by the economic downturn and began making losses from early 2009. Although the losses were apparent from the company's financial documents, Joe continued to believe that the problems were temporary and Chelsey was happy to believe him. In 2011 one of the company's spas was forced to close and no buyer could be found for the property, although Joe continued to include the property at full value in the company's accounts. Pressure from unpaid creditors continued through 2011 and 2012, but Joe continually assured Chelsey that the problem was simply a short-term cash flow issue that would be resolved as the economy improved, which Joe believed would be very soon. In the meantime Joe only paid those creditors who actively demanded payment, while creditors who did not demand payment were left unpaid. The business continued to decline and in March 2013 a winding up order was made against Stamford Vista Ltd.

Luigi has been appointed liquidator.

Advise Luigi in relation to possible wrongful trading and/or disqualification proceedings against Joe and Chelsey.

Commentary

This is a not unusual scenario in corporate failures, and one in which the directors are at serious risk of wrongful trading proceedings (if the liquidator considers it cost effective to pursue these) and disqualification. While the former has an immediate financial consequence for the directors, the latter can have a serious impact on the future activities of directors which is particularly important for individuals whose career is based on business management. Most disqualification cases are now dealt with by means of an undertaking by the directors concerned, rather than going through court proceedings. You need to assess the requirements for wrongful trading and apply this to the individuals, and then go on to consider how the facts might relate to disqualification.

Examiner's tip

Make sure you explain the law and then apply each element to the facts of the question. Don't be tempted simply to recite the problem facts—show explicitly how they are relevant.

 Answer plan

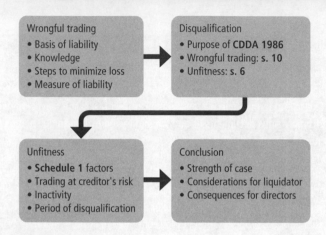

Wrongful trading
- Basis of liability
- Knowledge
- Steps to minimize loss
- Measure of liability

Disqualification
- Purpose of **CDDA 1986**
- Wrongful trading: **s. 10**
- Unfitness: **s. 6**

Unfitness
- **Schedule 1** factors
- Trading at creditor's risk
- Inactivity
- Period of disqualification

Conclusion
- Strength of case
- Considerations for liquidator
- Consequences for directors

 Suggested answer

Luigi seeks advice regarding possible wrongful trading proceedings (**Insolvency Act 1986 (IA 1986), s. 214**) and disqualification (**Company Directors Disqualification Act 1986 (CDDA 1986)**). This answer will accordingly address each in turn but will not address other potential areas of liability such as misfeasance (**IA 1986, s. 212**) or fraudulent trading (**s. 213**).

Wrongful trading

Proceedings under **IA 1986, s. 214** are brought by the liquidator (although Luigi will need the sanction of the liquidation committee or the court). A director of a company in insolvent liquidation is liable for wrongful trading if, prior to the commencement of winding up, he knew or should have realized that there was no reasonable prospect of the company avoiding insolvent liquidation (**s. 214(2)**) unless he took every step to minimise loss to creditors (**s. 214(3)**). Stamford Vista Ltd is in insolvent liquidation and Joe and Chelsey are (*de jure*) directors of the company so both directors are potentially liable.

The issue is thus whether Joe and/or Chelsey knew or ought to have known, before liquidation commenced, that the company could not reasonably avoid insolvent liquidation. The facts a director knew, or should have known, and the conclusions he should have reached are those known or reached by a 'reasonably diligent person' with (a) the general knowledge, skill, and experience of someone carrying out the functions of that director (including the functions that should have been carried out but weren't: s. 214(5)) and (b) the general knowledge, skill, and experience that the director has (s. 214(4)). Thus, part (a) imposes a minimum objective standard (*Re DKG Contractors Ltd* [1990] BCC 903) varying according to the type of company and the director's role, while (b) is subjective, imposing additional expectations on someone with greater skills than expected of someone in that position. Joe and Chelsey do not appear to have any particular skills, etc so their knowledge will be assessed on the basis of the minimum objective standard to be expected of directors in their roles in a company of the size and type of Stamford Vista Ltd. In *Re Produce Marketing Consortium Ltd* [1989] BCLC 520 the court took account of information the directors should have had, even though they did not actually have that information because of their own failures to draw up accounts. So reliance on inaccurate accounts will not protect Joe and Chelsey, nor will Joe's continuing belief that problems were temporary. In *Re Rod Gunner Organisation Ltd* [2004] 2 BCLC 110 the directors hung on to hopes of refinancing, but these hopes were unrealistic—similarly Joe's hopes do not seem to be based on facts. Chelsey, as a director, should have been aware of the financial position and not simply accepted Joe's reassurances.

Although the company started making losses in 2009, making losses does not of itself mean insolvent liquidation was inevitable—even knowledge of insolvency is not sufficient in itself (*Re Hawkes Hill Publishing Ltd* [2007] BCC 937)—but by 2011 as losses continued, the property could not be sold and creditor pressure mounted, the directors should have realized liquidation was inevitable. In *Re Brian D Pierson Ltd* [1999] BCC 26, a husband and wife were both liable where they refused to face the facts and made only superficial judgements as to the company's financial position—this is similar to the position of Joe and Chelsey.

Directors can avoid liability if they took 'every step' they ought to have taken to minimize loss to creditors (**IA 1986, s. 214(3)**), assessed using the s. 214(4) dual objective/subjective standard. In *Re Brian D Pierson Ltd* the court suggested directors should show specific steps to preserve or realize assets for creditors—Joe and Chelsey have taken no such steps. Chelsey might allege that in relying on Joe she acted 'honestly and reasonably and ought fairly to be excused' and so should be relieved from liability under the **Companies Act 2006 (CA 2006), s. 1127** but even if a court were convinced her behaviour was reasonable, *Re Produce Marketing Consortium Ltd* concluded that s. 1127 does not apply to wrongful trading.

If Joe and Chelsey were found liable for wrongful trading the court can order the directors to make such contribution to the company's assets as it thinks proper (**s. 214(1)**). The measure of liability is compensatory—'the amount by which the company's assets can be discerned to have been depleted by the director's conduct which caused the discretion ... to arise' (*Re Produce Marketing Consortium Ltd*)—ie the losses incurred after Joe and Chelsey should have realized the company was unlikely to avoid insolvent liquidation. Accordingly, provided Joe and Chelsey have sufficient private resources to meet the claim Luigi should seriously consider bringing proceedings against them.

Disqualification

The primary purpose of the **CDDA 1986** is to protect the public from those who are unfit to be directors (*Re Sevenoaks Stationers (Retail) Ltd* [1991] Ch 164 (*Re Sevenoaks*)). A disqualification order against a director prohibits that person, for a period of time, from being a director, receiver, or taking part in the promotion, formation, or management of a company or acting as an insolvent practitioner.

If Luigi successfully brings wrongful trading proceedings against Joe and Chelsey, the court can disqualify the directors under **CDDA 1986, s. 10**. However, the more common ground for disqualification is 'unfitness' where a company has gone into insolvent liquidation (**s. 6**). Proceedings under **s. 6** would be brought by the Secretary of State, but as liquidator Luigi has an obligation under **s. 7(3)** to report suspected cases of unfitness to the Disqualification Unit of the Department of Business, Innovation, and Skills.

In assessing unfitness **CDDA 1986, s. 9** directs the court to **Schedule 1**, which sets out a non-exhaustive (*Re Amaron Ltd* [1998] BCC 264) list of relevant factors including breach of duty, failure to keep accounting records, responsibility for the causes of insolvency, and failure to co-operate with the liquidator. Unfitness does not require deliberate wrongdoing or dishonesty; negligence (or even marked incompetence) can amount to unfitness (*Re Sevenoaks*).

A common ground for disqualification is trading at creditors' risk, which is similar to wrongful trading, although it is not necessary to establish a breach of **IA 1986, s. 214**. By continuing to trade and building up further debts when there is little prospect of creditors being paid, a director is unfit, see, eg *Re Living Images Ltd* [1996] 1 BCLC 348. A policy of paying only pressing creditors, as in this case, is clear evidence of unfitness (*Re Sevenoaks*). While paying directors' salaries is not in itself unfitness, this may be unfit if it is more than the company can afford (eg *Secretary of State v Van Hengel* [1995] 1 BCLC 545).

Chelsey's failings lie in inactivity which can amount to unfitness. Directors can delegate but cannot abrogate their responsibilities or allow themselves to be dominated by a board member (*Re Westmid Packing Services Ltd* [1998] 2 All ER 124). *Re Barings plc (No. 5)* [2000] 1 BCLC 523 makes clear that each individual director has inescapable minimum obligations and Chelsey seems to have failed to meet these.

If unfitness under **s. 6** is established—there seems to be evidence of unfitness for both—the court must make a disqualification order of at least two years (with a maximum of 15 years). *Re Sevenoaks* established three brackets: 2–5 years for relatively not very serious cases, 6–10 years for serious cases not meriting the top bracket, and 11–15 years for particularly serious cases. Here Chelsey's behaviour would put her in the lower end of the bottom bracket, while Joe's behaviour warrants a higher tariff, although still not a particularly serious case. While the period may be reduced by mitigating factors (including the age and health of the director and his/her general conduct before and after the liquidation), there are no particular mitigating factors mentioned in this case.

Conclusion

Luigi seems to have a good case against Joe and Chelsey for wrongful trading in continuing to trade for over a year after they should have realized there was no reasonable prospect of the company avoiding insolvent liquidation, and if successful the creditors will benefit from the recovery of losses made after that point. If wrongful trading proceedings are successful then the directors could be disqualified under **CDDA 1986, s. 10**. In any event Luigi must make a report to the Disqualification Unit with regard to unfit conduct and the case under **s. 6** against Joe and Chelsey appears strong. The directors may wish to offer a 'disqualification undertaking' (**CDDA 1986, s. 1A; s. 7(2A)**) to avoid the cost of proceedings; the undertaking operates just like a disqualification order. While unfitness does not attract a financial penalty (although this has been the subject of recent consultation: Department for Business, Innovation, and Skills, 'Transparency and trust: discussion paper' (BIS/13/959), July 2013) if Joe or Chelsey were to act as directors of another company while disqualified they would incur personal liability for debts incurred by that company during their breach (**CDDA 1986, s. 15**) as well as criminal liability (**s. 13**).

Further reading

Finch, V., 'Corporate rescue: who is interested?' [2012] JBL 190

Frieze, S., 'The company in financial difficulties: the alternatives' (2008) 21 Insolv Int 124

Hicks, A., 'Director disqualification: can it deliver?' [2001] JBL 433

Kastrinou, A., 'An analysis of the pre-pack technique and recent developments in the area' (2008) 29 Co Law 259

Keay, A., 'Disputing debts relied on by petitioning creditors seeking winding up orders' (2001) 22 Co Law 40

McCormack, G., 'Swelling corporate assets: changing what is on the menu?' (2006) 6 JCLS 39

Milman, D., 'Personal liability and disqualification of company directors' (1992) 43 NILQ 1

Moore, M. T., 'Directors' pay as a creditor concern: the lesson from MG Rover' (2006) 27 Co Law 237

Oditah, F., 'Wrongful trading' [1990] LMCLQ 205

Prentice, D., 'Preferences and defective floating charges' (1993) 109 LQR 371

Walton, P., '*Re Kayley Vending Ltd*: pre-pack administration—is its Achilles' heel showing?' (2010) 31 Co Law 85

Wilkes, A., 'Setting aside vulnerable transactions: an update' (2011) 4 CRI 189

Williams, R., 'Disqualifying directors: a remedy worse than the disease' (2007) 7 J Corp Law Studies 213

Xie, B., 'Regulating pre-pack administrations' [2010] JBL 513